Presence, Kindness, and Freedom

Aaron's Teachings on Living from an Open Heart

As told through Barbara Brodsky

ISBN 0-9745552-0-7

Published by:
Deep Spring Press
3455 Charing Cross Rd
Ann Arbor, MI 48108-1911

Contents

Beginnings

People often ask me what I teach. The essence is presence, kindness, and freedom.

From the perspective of your human understanding, you are going home, to that sweetness and brilliant light that you once knew so well and now only dimly remember. From the perspective of Spirit, you are going nowhere.

Whenever you have a doubt about what to believe in, return to this heart of all truths—God is love and you are expressions of God. Either you believe and act in harmony with that love or in a manner discordant to love.

The ego itself is not bad, anymore than the physical body or mental body is bad. These are all just expressions of being, part of the human experience.

Frequent Questions

Looking Within

The Deepening Path of Practice

Appendices

Introductions from Barbara and Aaron

Barbara

Many of you have asked me how I met Aaron. I'd like briefly to share the story.

I lost my hearing in 1972, soon after my first child was born. I coped well with the loss, on the surface. I continued with my sculpture and teaching at the university and had two more children. Through those years I was aware that although I did what I needed to do for my self and my family, I was very bitter about the isolation my deafness seemed to impose.

This anger didn't negate the fact that my life was full. I had a loving and beautiful family, work I loved, and caring friends. I honor how well I was able to cope with the difficult body changes and emotions. But in striving to cope, I didn't allow myself to feel the pain of my isolation, which was real. Afraid that pain would overwhelm me, I denied it and turned my anger to outward things. I was angry at people who talked near me when I couldn't understand them. I couldn't see that it was the anger, not the deafness, which deepened my sense of separation. In my anger at God, I lost all sense of a spiritual aspect to my life.

I became aware that I had to look at what was happening. It had been years since I had attended Quaker Meeting, my primary adult religious affiliation; I began to go and to look forward to that weekly hour of silent communion with spirit. In time, I began to meditate again as a daily practice, although with no clear sense of direction. I also wrote daily in a journal, a tool that put me into deeper touch with my subconscious mind. I felt drawn to read from spiritual works, especially teachings from Eastern religions concerning reincarnation and karma. As I opened to myself and became more caring and forgiving, I found an increasing inner peace.

Despite all that I was learning, I felt stuck. I was still bitter, cut off from normal human communication, and blaming outward things for my situation. I began to pray for help, understanding that I just couldn't go any farther on my own.

As the weeks passed, I began to notice that in the question-answer format I often used in my journal, the "answer" part was beginning to speak from a new perspective, pushing me to open myself to new ideas and ways of thinking.

Soon after that, I met Aaron. One day during meditation, I was aware of a figure standing just off to one side. I asked him who he was. Very simply he told me he was Aaron, and he was my guide.

I'm not going to suggest that I took this casually. The idea of a spirit guide was new and startling to me; I went into the kitchen to get a cup of tea. When I returned, he was still there. I wondered briefly if I was hallucinating. But every time I looked, Aaron was there, just patiently waiting for me to be ready to move ahead. It was important to the process of trust that I never felt any pressure to accept him. He made it clear from the beginning that we had all the time I needed to be ready for any learning that he offered. I wasn't frightened because I felt so much love from him, and a gentleness and connection dimly remembered from some unknown past.

At first my rational mind asked, "Who is Aaron?" Slowly I realized it didn't matter. I began to listen with my heart, and not play mind games. I understood that it was irrelevant whether Aaron was simply a deeper part of my subconscious or was external. I was getting information that I needed for growth and to which I lacked previous access. As I began to trust that information and my own ability to hear it, I became clearly aware of Aaron's existence as a separate entity.

Aaron tells me he is a being who has evolved beyond the need to return to the physical plane. He is from "beyond the causal plane." He defines himself as a "being of light," which he says we all are. I've come to know him as a being of infinite love, compassion, and wisdom. He also has a wonderful warmth and sense of humor. He is a wise teacher.

As my trust deepened, Aaron led me on a beautiful journey into myself; into past lives to unearth the sources of some of the pains of this life and into examining the questions of isolation and separation on which my deafness forced me to focus. Together we healed the suffering of that deafness and went on to investigate the origins of these issues of separation and isolation. The journey has been painful and joyous, frightening and beautiful. Always, Aaron's love has been there to help me through the rough places.

Yes, my deafness is still painful. I doubt that I'll ever be completely used to this silence. But I also embrace it. Thirty one years of silence is a profound teacher, and I thank it for the ways it's led me to deepen in understanding. I no longer fight with it. I no longer feel this silence as *my* pain. It is *our* pain, the aloneness of us all, and its arising serves as a reminder for connection and compassion.

Constantly, I see Aaron's wisdom and compassion touching others' lives as it has touched mine. As I learned to be a clear channel for Aaron, many others came to love him and trust his guidance: first my friends, then their friends, and on in an expanding circle around the globe. It humbles me to see myself as part of this chain of sharing, to be permitted this part in it, to learn and to watch others learning. It brings me much joy. I am in awe of the process.

Channeling is a simple process. I'm not in a deep trance, but deep enough to feel Aaron's energy and "hear" his thoughts. I receive a whole thought and then find words for it. If he's not content with my articulation, he'll say, "please rephrase that." I get one portion of a complex idea at a time; I don't know what will come next. It is an act of faith that the final statement will make sense, and it does!

This book is a collection of Aaron's replies to frequently asked questions through the past fourteen years. Most of the talks included here were first offered to groups. Almost everything in this book is worded as it was transcribed from tape and as Aaron spoke it. One edits a discarnate entity with great care and respect. Where there are additions, Aaron has made them to clarify a thought. Any editing is of a grammatical nature and has been approved by him.

With great love and gratitude, I offer you Aaron, *Barbara*

Aaron

Greetings and love to you all. I am Aaron. What and who am I? What and who are you? What is the difference between us, or is there none?

I have taught that we are all beings of light. What does that mean? Some of you may be familiar with the meditative experience of the dissolution of ego and body. Those who have experienced that have ascertained that what remains is light. That's all; just light, energy and awareness. There is no ego in that space. There is no sense of self or other. There is no permanence of form, no individual thought, no selfish will, no personal consciousness.

Beyond all the attributes of separate self there is pure awareness, pure heart-mind. Essence expresses as radiant light, pure sound, awareness, intelligence, and energy. These are direct expressions of That which Is. This is what you are. This is what I am.

As we each evolve, we materialize in whatever form is best suited to our growth and to our present learning needs, as directed by karma. This earth is a schoolroom. You are here in material form because it is here that you will find the next lessons that you need. I have evolved beyond the need for material form, and so I have none. Nevertheless I am still learning and am in the form best suited to those lessons I now seek to learn.

I do have a different perspective than the human one. I can call on the knowledge and wisdom of all of my past lives, as well as the wisdom I've gained in these 450 of your earth years since I passed from your plane. On my plane we have passed beyond any illusion of the separate, small ego self. We communicate telepathically, one spirit with another or with many others. As there is no ego, there is no need to protect the self from embarrassment or to cover up unskillful choices. Thus our sharing is complete and honest. Wisdom accrues rapidly, for each spirit shares its own understandings and experiences completely, and I can learn from another's experiences just as well as from my own. I also learn deeper compassion, and it is partially for this learning that I choose to teach. You remind me of the pains of being human; remind me not to judge another, but to keep my heart open in love. A great teacher has said, "Never put anyone out of your heart," but it is so easy to fall into that judgment on any plane. My contact with you reminds me that what I work toward is unconditional love.

I have the advantage of the perspective of many lifetimes. My final lifetime on your human plane was as a Theravadin Buddhist monk in Thailand, a meditation master. The wisdom and understandings of many lifetimes came together then, enabling me to find freedom for myself and also to help many beings to discover that path. Yet I do not teach you only as that Thai master. I have been a monk in many lifetimes. I have wandered forests, dwelled in caves, and lived in magnificent temples.

Through many lives I've practiced most forms of Buddhism. That is only a small part of it. I have been a Christian monk in just as many lifetimes, a priest, and in positions that are higher in the hierarchy of that church. I have been Muslim, Jew, Sufi, Taoist, and so many more. I have lived in all colors of skin, in male and female form, in many and diverse cultures. I have prayed in hovels and palaces. I have starved, and I have lived in luxury while those around me starved. I have been a nobleman and a murderer. I have loved and hated, killed and cherished, in short, I have done just about everything in the realm of human experience. So have all of you.

What does it mean to have compassion for another? Can you see that the potential for negativity exists in you also? Can you move from judgment of the tyrant to compassion for his pain and situation? This does not mean condoning his acts. It means having compassion, acceptance, and unconditional love.

Remember that this learning is a process. If you had already arrived at that space of unconditional love and perfect compassion and acceptance, you would not need to be here learning in a human body.

Let me return to my present perspective. I teach you as all of those beings that I was, the murderer and his learning so painfully gained, as well as the beloved meditation master and his. Beyond that, I teach from my present perspective that knows the illusion of all form, that sees clearly that all any of us are is light and energy, slowly evolving to a brilliance and clarity as all self and ego are dissolved.

As such I do not teach Buddhism or any "ism" separate from the Truth. I know of only two truths with a capital "T", God and love. All formal religions are merely paths to the understanding of these two truths, which are in fact one.

Much of what I teach falls under the label "Buddhism." I had my greatest understandings as a Buddhist. I am not attached to this form but do find it a useful tradition to use as a teaching tool. No pride is implied when I state that I was a wise teacher in that lifetime, and my understanding of the tools of meditation helped many beings find their way. So it is natural that I again draw on that wisdom as I teach.

But I am not a Buddhist. I have a great love for that being who was known as the Buddha, also for him who was known as the Christ, and for many other great saints and teachers. I do not label myself here.

I do emphasize the use of vipassana meditation,[1] not as an end in itself, but as a learning tool. The practice of this form of meditation will lead you to a clear understanding of impermanence, of the conditioning that leads to suffering, and of the interdependence of all things. Understanding these concepts intellectually will not lead to freedom. You are not here just to understand these three truths but to learn from your insights and to grow in love and faith, in compassion and wisdom.

The Buddha taught that there is no self that continues, and yet here I am, and I seem to continue. What am I? What is it that continues? You have many

---

[1] Insight meditation; see Appendix B on Meditation Instructions.

aspects. One of these is the personal that you now experience. This aspect has form, thought, and so on, but of course it is impermanent. It is the conscious self. Then there is what might be termed the higher self or superconscious mind. This combined mental and spirit body retains the memories of all the forms in which you have manifested and the wisdom attained by all those forms. Within the same memory pattern, misunderstandings may also be retained until they are resolved. Notice that I have called this aspect *higher self.* It is still a self.

Beyond that self is what I term the *pure spirit body.* This aspect is pure light and energy. Some of you have had glimpses of this aspect of Being through meditative experience. Thus, you can come to know that this is your true nature. There is no self here, and no possibility of such delusion. There is only energy, manifested as light, Pure Being. This is pure awareness that looks at the rest—the form, the thoughts—with kindness but without self-identification. Thus we are all, in essence, beings of light. This is what I am, but I retain the use of the mental body to teach. There is no self-identification with the mental body or with memories, only the use of them when necessary.

This is our true being. We begin as sparks of that perfect light, and experience material form as a way of evolution. As it evolves, that first spark increases in its brilliance and clarity, losing all shadow, until it shines as a small sun. If you were to take my essence at this phase of my evolution, and place it in front of that perfect light, you would see the barest edges of form and a gray shadow cast against that brilliance. If you were to take the essence of a perfectly evolved being such as the Buddha or the Christ and put it in front of that perfect light, it would be invisible. That is what each of you is evolving to: perfect invisibility, immaculate emptiness, oneness with God.

Your meditation practice is the way to come to know your true nature by experience. It takes you past the delusion of a separate self. It leads you toward compassion and away from judgment. I cannot overemphasize the importance of these paths of learning. From my many lifetimes of experience I've found that the most valuable forms of meditation for those beings that are in a place of readiness for greater responsibility on their path are a mixture of vipassana and devotional meditation. Vipassana is hard work and requires courage and faith. Devotional meditation inspires you, reminds you of the reason for this work and of the path of your evolution to unity with that perfect light that may be called God. Please remember that devotion takes many forms. For example, service is an aspect of devotion.

What I teach you must be filtered through your own processes. I can only guide you. The real learning must come from your own experiences. If what I say is of help and provides guidance, that is fine. Use it. If it doesn't help, put it aside and follow your own inner wisdom.

I thank you for this opportunity to speak with you. I hope I have left you with more questions than answers. Perhaps one day we will meet and I can speak to some of those questions, but please remember that the answers are all already there, within your own hearts. Practice well and find them for yourselves.

Go with my love, *Aaron*

A Note on language from Aaron

As we begin to talk together, I wish to make some statements about my use of specific words so we can better understand each other. Words are symbols. If I say, "circle," you will form an image of a circle. If the circular form has positive meaning for you, for example, as a religious symbol or if sitting in circles has been a positive experience for you, then you will lay a positive emotional energy on my word. If you were forced as a schoolchild to sit in sharing circles and found the experience to be difficult and embarrassing, then the word *circle* would have a negative overlay.

When we speak about spiritual matters there are two confusing words that are bound to arise, *God* and *soul.*

When I use the word *God,* some of you who were raised in a Judeo-Christian culture will envision that proverbial old man with a beard sitting on a cloud, directing the show, so to speak. At the least, the word *God* may represent a distorted concept, often of a masculine energy, and with a placement outside one's direct experience. Different religions use different names: Allah, Ram, God, Goddess, Infinite, and many more. They all can carry the same weighted perspective, of something beyond us. This, then, is a difficult word because that image is not what I mean when I say "God."

We must understand that the divine is not outside of the self, is not some separate thing, but is All that Is or the Ground of Being. It is not outside or inside; it simply is. To be God is to be everything and nothing, to be everywhere and nowhere. There is no single word in your language to convey this essence.

In Buddhist terminology, the words from the Udana scripture, "unborn, undying, unchanging, uncreated," are helpful, for they tell us what this essence is not. Buddhism also offers the term *Unconditioned,*[2] but an inaccurate image is still possible, separating the Unconditioned from the structures of the conditioned, relative world. The Unconditioned and the conditioned are nondual.[3] The conditioned is an expression of the Unconditioned. They cannot be separated.

The term *Ground of Being* comes closest for me as a clear expression of what I mean by God, but it is a long phrase to repeat. In this book, I will sometimes use the word *Being* as a short cut to Ground of Being and a term such as *Essence* or *All that Is* to articulate that which is sometimes called God. As we read through the original talks in preparation for this edition, I often chose to retain the word *God.* I trust you will now better understand my use of that word.

You have four bodies: spirit, mental, emotional, and physical. This concept is from traditional metaphysics. These bodies have been referred to in many cultures for well over two thousand years. The word *soul* in the English language most often refers to the combination of the mental and spirit bodies. The mental body still partakes of the personal self. It is conditioned and impermanent.

Buddhist teaching suggests that there is no permanent soul, yet there is this "unborn, undying, unchanging, uncreated," and we all partake of that, not only in the spirit body but in all the bodies. The spirit body is the clearest expression of it. Within this spirit body there is no "self," meaning the small ego or personal self. There is only Being. Here is the drop of water that is part of the sea and cannot be separated from the sea. In each of the other, heavier bodies, there is increasing distortion, lower vibrational frequency, and more illusion of self.

I propose the following terms. The *self* refers to the personal, egoistic self, including the physical, emotional, mental and spirit bodies. Sometimes I may use the phrase *small ego self.* This is not offered as a derogatory statement, but as a means of distinction. This aspect of the self has a purpose. The *higher self* is the combined mental and spirit body, free of the heavier two bodies but still partaking in the conditioned expression of mental body. In most cases I will avoid the use of the ambiguous word *soul.* The *spirit* is the pure spirit body. No separate self is experienced.

I thank you for your consideration of this language.

---

[2] Unconditioned: that which exists free of any conditions. Conditioned: that which arises from conditions and ceases when the conditions cease. A flower is dependent on the conditions of seed, soil, sun, and water. When those conditions are lacking, the flower will cease. These concepts will be expanded upon throughout the book.

[3] Nondual: not separate. Please see the chapter "Nonduality" for more information.

Deep Bows of Thanks

No work of this size can come from just one, or even a few people. Aaron and I would especially like to thank those people whose energy, time, material resources, and love have made this sharing of his work possible.

There are too many such friends to mention you all, but loving gratitude is sent to the late Karen Weber for countless hours of transcribing the early tapes and to Karen Agne, David Brown, and Janice Keller, who continued the transcribing work after Karen's passing. So many others have helped. Hugs go to the Wednesday Night Study Group participants, some of whom have joined us regularly for over a decade. John Orr and Michael Forster Rothbart spent many hours opening their hearts and thoughts to Aaron and inspiring his sharing. And a bow of gratitude to all of you around the world who have joined us for evenings and workshops, lending your energy, enthusiasm, curiosity, and inspiration. You'll find many of your questions and Aaron's responses here. Finally, a thank you to my family—Hal, Peter, Davy, and Mike—who put up with an abundance of reheated leftovers and order-out pizza and hours and weekends of losing me to a computer or to meditation.

This book exists because of the persistence of my husband, Hal Rothbart, whose vision brought it forth. Kate Leshock spent countless hours with Aaron and me, transcribing while Aaron worked out small details and whole pages. Michele Matossian provided the beautiful lotus photograph for the cover. Jim Jarvis designed the cover, created the internal graphics and did the layout along with Pam Chastain. Vicki Lawrence and Jacqueline Kracker were our primary editors. Aaron and I appreciate both of their persistent requests for consistency in phrasings and word choices, and their willingness to challenge us when text felt unclear. The eagle-eyed final editing of Roann Altman, Dianne Austin, Delyth Balmer, Alice Britt, Jacqueline Kracker and Kate Leshock brought us closer to perfection. Nicholas de Paul helped in countless ways. I feel grateful for the technical expertise of all these people, but even more, for their loving energy and support through the two years in which this book developed.

I offer a bow to my loving parents and brother, from whom I first learned love and kindness in this incarnation. They are the ones who awoke in me the desire to serve others and the curiosity and courage to walk this path.

And grateful thanks to the dear dharma friends who travel this path with me and offer their ongoing support. You know who you are.

Forehead to the floor and heart bursting with love, my most heartfelt gratitude and devotion to my guru, Neem Karoli Baba, without whose grace none of this work with Aaron could have happened. And especially, to Aaron, my dearest forever friend, I offer grateful appreciation for your loving and patient teaching.

Beginnings

Q: Sometimes I feel a push to work on spiritual things; other times I feel lazy. Does it matter?

You are always working on "spiritual things." Each moment of your life, each thought, feeling, or event, is part of your path and able to teach you. You have free will, and you decide whether or not you will utilize these opportunities to learn what you came to learn.

There is no time schedule here; you have all the time you need. But you must recognize that each moment is precious. There is only one "now." Learn what you can in this moment, and you will be a wiser and more compassionate person in the next now.

I am Aaron

My blessings and love to you. I am Aaron.

I often begin my talks with these words, so that you will know me and will feel my love present with you.

I rejoice in this opportunity to share my thoughts. As I speak, I realize that those who will read these words have diverse backgrounds. Some of you have just started a conscious spiritual path, and much of what I say is new to you. Others of you will find much here that is familiar. I envision this book as a river; near to shore the clear, still water invites those who have not yet waded in to remove their shoes and wet their feet. Farther out, the water deepens but remains still. It is a safe environment for the novice swimmer to strengthen his stroke. Still farther out, the current runs fast and deep and will carry the experienced swimmer toward new mysteries and delights. Please wade in gently or leap off the rocks into the swift current as best suits your need.

Just as a river flows, from its early start as a small stream into a wide, rushing waterway, so I have intended this book to flow. It does have an order to it, yet I invite the reader to plunge in anywhere along the river that draws attention. I hope you will browse through the contents in the same manner that the hiker walks the river shoreline, until you see just the pool that catches your eye and invites your entry.

People often ask me what I teach. The essence is presence, kindness, and freedom. So many of you have difficulty clearly seeing your own issues and choices. You become lost in self-criticism, judgment, and fear. You create complexities where none exist. I bring you a new perspective, of love and of faith in that higher awareness that is your true self. I help you see beyond the bounds of the physical, mental being which is just the skin you wear, to the true Being that is your essence and your birthright. You are not a human being having a spiritual experience but a spiritual being having a human experience.

From that perspective the world looks different, and many of your situations and choices may seem less difficult. You are not working to end thought and emotion. You can never be entirely free of thought or emotion for a sustained period while in human form. Rather, you are working toward what we would call equanimity with emotions, where the rising of an emotion no longer leads to reactivity and contraction. Your lives do not need to be painful. Each being is whole and perfect in its essence. You can learn to take the obstructions you have manifested in your lives and understand them as instruction for the spiritual being that you truly are.

As I help you to see things from a new perspective, I will not make your choices for you. Part of growing to a mature expression of divinity is learning to make your own choices. Whether they be skillful or not, they are part of your path and are your tools for learning. Your journey is your own. Another being can only serve as a signpost on your path.

With love, I offer you my guidance to help you find your way.

Q: Are you real?

I am as real as you are. And no, I am not "dead," thank you! I simply exist on a different plane. You are made of light and substance; I am made only of light. When you move beyond the substance of your human form, then you also will be only light, until your next human incarnation. You call this death. I call it just a step in the process of our evolution to maturity.

The Journey

Q: We often hear the phrase "our journey" or "our path."
Can you talk about this journey? Where are we coming from
and where are we going?

From the perspective of your human understanding, you are going home, to that sweetness and brilliant light that you once knew so well and now only dimly remember. From the perspective of spirit, you are going nowhere.

The whole journey is an illusion. How can you have ever left God, when God is within you and you within God? Do you really imagine you could leave that heart of perfect love and light and be alone and separate in the world?

You are as children, camped in your parents' back yard, learning the skills and independence that lead to maturity. The illusion tells you that you are away from home. Do you see the necessity of that illusion? But your parents keep a watchful eye from the window and the back light shines brightly. You are never truly alone.

You began as a spark of God. Developing self-awareness, you chose the human path to maturity, accepting this illusion of separateness from divinity. The illusion has been necessary to your growth, to becoming mature and responsible beings, so that you might be ready to return to That-which-Is, no longer just a spark but a pure and shining light.

You have agreed, with each birth, to live with this veil of forgetfulness and to have only dim memories of your origins and your home. The forgetting has been necessary to bring forth the illusion and has been part of your human learning experience. Your past lives are the infancy and childhood of the journey. Now many of you are adolescents and even approach mature adulthood. Slowly the veil lifts, and you begin to remember who you truly are. You have reached a time for remembering.

What is this journey? It is the slow unfolding of that which you must learn to return to God as mature and compatible co-creators in the dance of life.

It is the blossoming of your beautiful self, from an ember into brilliance.

It is time to move beyond your fears, to acknowledge your true being and the oneness of all creation. It is the time to penetrate the illusion.

You have never been anywhere, and the illusion has served its purpose. Now shed the illusion. Learn to acknowledge your perfection, your unlimited nature, your oneness with God and all things, the wonderful beauty of you.

Understand that fear is all that keeps you from knowing who you are. Let your fear go, and feel the love that is your birthright. Love is the only truth. With love, fear crumbles.

You ask, "Are we all on the same place on this journey? Are we all ready to let go of the illusion?" No. You are each in your own place, and just where you should be. Only those who are ready will hear and understand this message. For others, who are not yet so far along, the message will be there when they are ready to hear it, perhaps in this life, perhaps in another.

There is no rush. You each move as you need to. Be assured that every being will find its way home and in time will understand the illusion of the journey. Each will find that sweetness of its nonseparation with the perfect light and know the harmony of the universe.

Truly you are all home. You have only to discover this and know that it is so.

What Should I Believe In?

Aaron's answer to a thirteen-year-old boy.

You have asked an extremely difficult question. What to believe in? I cannot wrap up the answer for you and deliver it in a package. You must look into your own heart. The world lies before you. So many things seem to conflict. You look for truth with a capital "T" but truth cannot be narrowed down for you. This life is your adventure. It is your chance to grow and learn. What learning would there be for you on this physical plane if all the answers were written out in a book? You would have no more need to experience and none of the joy learning brings. Yes, I have said joy. There is always the choice to make your learning joyful, to love this earth you are given and this physical experience. For your pain is balanced with happiness.

The only two truths I know with a capital "T" are God and love. All those things that seem to be truth are part of God and of love, for God is love. Remember this if you will, and let it guide you. Whenever you have a doubt about what to believe in, return to this heart of all truths—God is love and you are all expressions of God.

Either you believe and act in harmony with that love or in a manner discordant with love. All your actions are one or the other. The more you move in harmony with love, the more peace and joy you find for yourself and bring to others.

When you find yourself acting in a disharmonious manner from what you perceive to be the flow of love, it does not mean in any sense that you are evil or have done anything for which you should severely criticize yourself. When you condemn yourself because of your mistakes, then learning becomes difficult. You become caught in a net of blaming and anger toward yourself, and that anger moves outward to others. Be gentle to yourself, compassionate and forgiving.

When you have erred, accept responsibility for the mistake. Notice it and try to grow from it. That is how you learn. If you were already perfect you would have no need to be learning on this physical plane. Your mistakes are part of the plan. They are part of your lessons. Allow them to teach you.

Accept your humanness, but learn to believe in the perfection of your own, and of every spirit. Listen with your heart and you will hear spirit's voice speak to you. At first it may be just a whisper. You will have to learn to listen well. Always it will speak of God and of love. The more you allow these truths to light your way, the less you will need to ask what to believe in. The answer will shine out from within, and you will know with certainty that you are part of God and God is love.

Ego

Q: Please explain what you mean by ego. Often it seems that ego is something distorted that we need to get rid of, but then you say there is nothing to get rid of. Can you explain?

First we must note that the word ego is used in different ways. Traditional psychology uses the word ego to describe a vital part of the being, that which we might say is in the driver's seat of the vehicle of consciousness. The word ego is also used in a somewhat derogatory way to describe a person with an over-inflated sense of self. Let us leave this second use aside and come back to the conventional, psychological terminology.

In the everyday world, something must direct consciousness. Psychology says that is the role of ego. I find this role is best played by a mix of what I call the personality self and pure awareness.[4] Let me define each of these terms—ego, pure awareness, and personality self—in the ways that I use them.

The ego is a voice of those levels of consciousness that still hold on to the illusion of a separate self. Psychology agrees that it is ego's job to maintain that sense of self and keep it strong. The ego creates stories that solidify a person's sense of being a discrete individual, separate from the rest of creation. These stories may be pleasant, even useful stories, but they inflate the sense of a separate self. Ego speaks from a fear-based aspect of self that wants to be safe, to know that personal needs are met, to feel in control. These are common desires for the sentient being, and they are not bad. To aspire to be safe and that all beings be safe is a statement of kindness and clarity. Such aspiration does not depend on ego. But to obsess about safety and create stories—fantasies really—deepens fear.

---

[4] See the chapter on Nonduality for an in-depth explanation of pure awareness.

Pure awareness is the perspective of the open heart, which perceives the world from a place free of fear and old conditioning. Pure awareness comes with the awakened mind. Resting in pure awareness, in the deepest truth of Being, you cannot feel other than safe. You know your power, not individual power but power grounded in nonduality.

The ego is a tool, not the essence of self but, like the physical and mental bodies, a vital tool of the incarnation. Personality comes from the ego. The personality expresses opinions, needs, and preferences. There are two faces of personality. One may be stuck in the ego mode, a more self-centered personality that often relates to the world from a fear-based perspective. I sometimes call this the small self or "small personality self." When I use the term personality self, I am usually referring to this expression of being. The other face of personality is that which is centered in awareness but still takes delight in the individuation of what we call self. It knows that self to be unlimited and interconnected with All that Is. This is a balanced place, aware of the divine essence and rejoicing in each expression of that essence. However, it does not take itself overly seriously. I call this aspect of personality "enlightened personality self."

Spiritual practitioners are often taught that they must transcend the ego. This leads to a belief that the ego is bad in some way. It is true that the ego often speaks in a fearful voice, which can be painful, but the ego itself is not bad, any more than the physical body or mental body is bad. These are all just expressions of being, part of the human experience. To experience the ego, physical body, or mind is not a problem. To take any of those experiences as ultimate truth creates pain.

In meditation we watch how mind gives rise to thought. Sometimes it is a loving thought, sometimes it is an angry thought. The thought arises with conditions and ceases when conditions cease. That which is aware of the thought is not caught up in the story of the thought. This is what I have named above as awareness. A second possibility is that what we call the small ego self grabs the thought and identifies with it. Then there is pain if things don't work out in the expected way. The ego gets caught in the stories of views, expectations, praise, and blame.

By caught in the story I mean that mind obsesses about what has arisen, perhaps asking why it happened, how to fix it, or who to blame. Mind becomes hard and closed, and there is often much pain. The pain in the arm is just a pain, a connected series of sensations. The associated memories of a neighbor who lost his work and eventually his arm due to cancer are stories that attached to the pain.

Physical sensations and thoughts will arise as long as you are in a human body. Belief in the stories need not arise. You can learn to be with a painful sensation or thought with patience, kindness, and spaciousness. If a story does arise, and you are with what has arisen in a spacious way, it will soon diminish. That which is aware of an arising story sees it as a result of present conditions, not as something permanent and irrevocable with which to identify.

We watch ego arise with patience, with tenderness, as just another conditioned object. We do not create a self-identity around it. As you work in this way, you become increasingly aware of pure awareness. Ego is based in fear; awareness is beyond all fear. This is so because the ego is still lodged in a dualistic view and sees itself as separate. Awareness is beyond all dualism; it knows that nothing is separate.

So how do you get beyond this self-identity, this seemingly separate self? The path of growth, of harmony, of peace, is never to wage a war with any objects arising into awareness, but to understand them, that they are conditioned expressions that are impermanent. Just as ripples or even large waves will form on the lake surface when the wind blows and will cease when the wind stops, so these fear movements of the mind will arise under certain conditions and will cease when the conditions cease. When the waves receive no more energy, they die away. You cannot stop the waves from arising by trying to force the water into stillness. Likewise, you cannot stop the movements of mind.

Thoughts will arise. It is ego that tries to control the thoughts. Pure awareness just watches it all come and go, like waves rolling onto a white, sandy beach. Awareness does not contract around what comes, but it does attend in appropriate ways. If the window is open and there is a cold draft, the ego may contract with fear, thinking, "oh I will get sick," or angrily wondering, "who left that window open?" Awareness knows the sensation of cold, notes the observation that the window is open, notes the contraction into ego and anger. Then the human gets up and attends to the situation; awareness gets up and closes the window.

This ego self, this sense you have of being a "me," separate from the rest of the world, is just a habit. The fully realized human has left behind what we conventionally call the ego. The enlightened personality self remains as an expression of awareness and can be kind, playful, eloquent, reflective, and assertive as is appropriate. For those who are not yet fully realized, the small ego self will remain. Here the small ego is a teacher. When we feel it contract or hear it begin to obsess, we can just note "feeling vulnerable, feeling afraid" and bring forth kindness.

This aspect of self that we call ego is part of your human experience. It does not need to be destroyed but to be seen clearly. To attempt to destroy ego is only more expression of ego. That which is aware is no longer taken in by ego's stories. It speaks to ego with kindness much as one soothes a frustrated toddler. If the two year old is screaming, "Cookie! Cookie! Cookie!" at the top of his lungs, it does not mean that you have to give him a cookie. It does mean that he needs attention, to be heard, to be loved. It is with such hearing and loving-kindness that we transcend ego's voice and return to a sense of spaciousness.

Please remember that awareness and ego exist simultaneously; clouds of ego float in the clear sky of awareness. We can obsess about the clouds, or we can choose to regard both the clouds and the clear sky without concern. The existence of the cloud does not change the nature of the clear sky nor negate its existence. We can obsess about any aspect of mind consciousness, including ego's voice, or we can rest in awareness and know that such consciousness will fade away. Awareness remains.

You cannot resolve ego until you accept ego.
When you accept ego, it resolves itself.

Discernment

*Q: I'm confused about channeling. How do I know whom I'm hearing
and if it is really another being or just myself? I sometimes think I'm
crazy when I hear a voice of guidance. If it is another being, how do
I know if what it says is true? Another question: It seems that many
people claim to be channeling famous teachers or spirits, and
yet their answers about what to do and how to live are
so different. How do I know who is right?*

Let me take your questions in parts. First, my own experience is that there
is spirit and it is accessible to you. I cannot prove that. In the end, it does
not matter. The sincere seeker raises a question. An answer comes. Who is
speaking is not as important as whether the answer is helpful, is congruent
with your values, and offers insight beyond your prior understanding. It is
wise not to get caught in asking, "Is it real?" The answer is real. Let go of the
source.

All beings hold some positive and some negative energy. The positive
side of expression flows more freely through some people in the world and we
think of them as being very clear. Other people are more caught in negative
thought. If someone stole your wallet and you caught him, then turned to
people with the question, "What shall I do with him?" you would hear very
different answers. That is no surprise. When one answer is filtered through
the processes of a person who is able to express his wisdom and compassion,
and another answer is filtered through the processes of a person trapped in
anger and hostility, the answers will differ.

Which you would choose to believe would depend on you. If you are able
to open to your innate loving clarity, the answer, "Speak to him of your pain on
being robbed, ask for the return of the wallet, and then forgive him," will make
sense. If you are steeped in hostility and fear, "Beat him up!" will make sense.

Each person carries energy of different vibrational frequencies. When you call forth a spirit guide, there is a tendency to call forth what resonates with your present state. This is why channeled answers are so varied. Whatever comes forth, your responsibility is to ask, what you can best do with this statement? If the answer you received was, "Beat him up," that statement can be very helpful to you precisely because you reject it. In that rejection, you see the distortion[5] of your anger. Then you can ask yourself, "What is my highest intention here? Is it to get even or to share truth and to hope to bring forth harmony?" Positive energy may say, "Open your heart to the pain you both feel. See that which is afraid and seeks control. Then you will be able to release your fear and anger enough to respond in a strong but loving way."

You may find that you are led to a new question. "Beat him up" may not resonate as truth for you, yet some angry part of you might be drawn to that answer. How do you release your anger in such a way that you may truly bring forth harmony and growth? Spirit with a somewhat negative disposition may offer advice with a subtle slant of negativity. Such advice resonates with the part of you that is angry. It is important to look at intention, to discern if it reflects your deepest truth. Remember that regardless of what any being tells you, whether incarnate or discarnate, it is with you that the final choice rests.

Please remember that these positive and negative biases are all aspects of the evolving consciousness. There is no ultimate evil within the self or outside the self. It is more like a board with two ends. Even if you stand at the very tip of the board and speak from there, the rest of the board is still attached. All beings are in some place on the continuum. All are learning to express positivity, but some must move through a phase of this process in which there is a need to explore negativity for a while, as part of the path toward expression of positive polarity. You are where you are and cannot be elsewhere. Each new situation presents the next step for your learning. Which resonates as truth, the positive or negative reply? Are you willing to investigate negativity when it arises rather than either follow it or attack it? Such investigation opens the way to wisdom and compassion.

In all of this, remember that it does not matter whether the thought is from an external spirit guide or from the self. The external guide is called up

---

[5] Distortion: Aaron does not use this word in a negative sense. When a bright light hits water, it appears to bend because of the heavier density of the water. Any such "bend," where there is a shift in direction as thought or object strikes a different density of material, is a distortion. It is an energetic movement, usually the result of a contracted energy.

by an aspect of the self. All replies are expressions of aspects of the near self or extended self, since there is only One.

Please consider a pure spring. The water pours forth a short way down a hillside. There it splashes into two different pipes. One has been carefully polished; the inside is immaculate. The second is filled with rust and cobwebs. At the far end of these pipes, the same pure spring water pours forth. In one case it has picked up distortion. In both cases, the water is potable, but before you drink the water from the rusty pipe, you will wish to filter out the debris.

Within each of you, there is the clear pipe and there is also the rusty pipe. Your work is to know when perception is distorted so that you can appropriately filter it, to access that pure water. If there is anger at the one who stole your wallet and very old fear of lack of safety, those feelings distort your perception and lead you to call forth the negative views. Thus such statements are merely a reflection of your present state.

If your intention is toward harmony, peace, nonseparation, and loving-kindness, then you will be moved to question any negative response and to learn from it. Just keep coming back with questions and releasing the distortions that arise along the way. The path asks presence and courage.

Remember that the perfect pipe is not totally accessible on the relative plane. One is always becoming clear, except in the case of the fully enlightened being. When you reach that enlightened state, your doubts will have resolved themselves anyway. Until then, you are always becoming, growing.

What of people who claim to channel famous beings and offer diverse statements from those beings? It is the same thing. You must know the pipe through which the water flows. If you seek positive-based guidance, ask if the human channel feels resonant with your own highest values. Does this human seek to live his or her life with as much clarity and love as is possible? Such a person will not bring forth a lot of negative distortion. There will always be some distortion because the channeling process is a co-creation between spirit and instrument. Unless that instrument is fully enlightened, there will be subtle distortion.

Do not believe everything you hear. You are responsible to take anything that you hear, regardless of its source, and to challenge it with the words, 'Is this statement consistent with my own highest truth?'

It is possible for many humans to channel the same great master. If you have a large reservoir of water, people may come with containers. Some containers will be big, and some will be small. Some will be immaculate, and some encrusted with filth. Each person may take water from the reservoir.

You have the responsibility to decide which water is suitable for you to drink. Because these great masters have such a vast energy, they may pour through many instruments. No instrument can hold the entire essence of that master. Just be aware of what comes forth and ask the questions, "What can this teach me?" and, "Is this harmonious with my own deepest truth?"

Q: All religious systems claim to be truth. How do we tell which is really truth?

There is a Buddhist teaching that says one must not mistake the finger pointing to the moon for the moon itself. All religious systems of thought are fingers pointing to the moon. The written dharma is not the Truth; the Bible is not the Truth; the Koran is not the Truth. To bow, chant, bind one's head and arm, or face east in prayer are not Truth. They are all fingers pointing to the moon.

As you regard these fingers, these paths, one will speak to your heart. It will call you to focus your attention in such a way that you finally begin to look beyond the finger and clearly see that to which it points. Then you will have found truth. You will continue to have deep love and respect for the religious path that allowed you to see truth. You will have come to the place where path and destination are one.

Light and Darkness

My friends, many of you ask me, "Is there any such thing as evil?" You wonder about your own spiritual path and where you fit into the picture of the new world you see emerging. You ask me to define my concepts of light and darkness.

Let me first express the fact that what I share with you here is not truth with a capital "T." We each name God in our own language. I teach you only what I understand from my own experience, toward that which my teachers guided me, as their teachers guided them. We each add what we can. Remember, I am simply Aaron. These are truths with a small "T" because they're only what I see as true. That's all that I can give you. I do not have all the answers. I have more experience and a different perspective but no more inherent wisdom or understanding than each of you has. Weigh it for yourself.

The only Truths I know are God and Love.

I have described myself as a being of light, as are all of you. You each began as a spark of God and are moving on your own path to maturity. As you evolve to purer and purer light, you are ever more in harmony with the universe and with God. You have chosen this journey of so many lifetimes in order to evolve into mature compatibility with what we may call That which Is. We are all on the same journey but follow a multitude of paths. Your path is your own and unique to you. But all paths lead to the same end. Every being will find its way home.

You ask me, "What of those who are evil?" We are all beings of light—*all.* God is the center of all forms and concepts. Divinity, as the ground of all love and all light, cannot create an evil separate from itself. Thus, you must come to understand the word evil as an absence of light, not as some nonexistent total darkness.

We are all in different places on this journey, and while many beings are filled with a great deal of light, others are deep in darkness and mired in misunderstandings. From such beings, there may be real intent to harm on either a physical or a spiritual plane. These are the beings we commonly refer to as evil. Please remember that the spirit essence of a Hitler, of a Gandhi, and each of you have equal value. Although we have chosen different paths to maturity and are at different places on our journeys, we are all beings of light. We are all one. That which you call evil is just the shadow in yourself. The saint is the reflection of your innate perfection.

As you begin to understand your own spiritual nature and to connect with your higher selves, you question the purpose of your lives and where your own personal growth is leading you. First you must learn the laws of karma and understand that each event in your life may serve a purpose and be experienced for your own growth. You begin to realize the need for honesty within yourself as you understand this unfolding process of your life, for truly you cannot get away with anything. You learn to look from a second perspective, that of your higher self, and realize that those difficulties your human self took as obstruction are instruction for your growth. You learn not to blame but to accept responsibility for your choices and learn from them. Often these choices seem harsh or cruel to those with only a human perspective, but they are always made with wisdom and love.

When you have reached the level where you can usually view your life from the perspective of your higher self, then you are asked again to expand your consciousness. Can you begin to look now from a third perspective, a place where your own higher self blends with All that Is? Here is the place where each individual's growth profoundly affects the evolution of the entire universe into light.

We are all beings of light, evolving into ever purer light. There are also beings that live in great darkness and would pull us in that direction. Remembering that they are also growing into perfect light, you come to understand that their push creates no conflict unless you permit one. Can you allow a provocation to battle to become an invitation to compassion? In some distant day and time even the last being will release its shadow and its radiance will shine. No being can alter that basic fact. It is a process, which is speeded or slowed by each being's commitment to love and its courage to honor its convictions.

We are all tools for light or for darkness. You cannot have a foot in each camp. What is your intention? When you react in anger, fear, or hatred, you become a channel for darkness. When you respond with loving compassion to any provocation, then you are allowing yourself to be a channel for light.

Simply put, when you respond with love and awareness, you add light to the total light of the universe; you tip the balance of light and darkness toward light. Please remember that to act with love does not mean to permit abuse by those deep in darkness. Compassion is strong and knows how to say no, but from a place free of fear and hatred.

Perfection is not expected. You learn from your mistakes. What is asked is that you be honest with yourselves and manifest your energy as purely as possible. In this way you allow yourself to learn, to grow, and to expand your inner light and the light of the entire universe. Remember to look from this third perspective, from the place where the spirit body unites with God or All that Is, and know that each act and word is of importance to the whole. As we are each evolving toward perfect light, so the whole universe is evolving. Each being will find its way home; in some distant day, all will be perfect light. The process cannot be rushed, but your loving awareness will ensure that it is not impeded. Continue to learn, to remain open to all that is, to greet each now with choiceless awareness, and—of greatest importance—to love. Do not be afraid. Trust.

On Love

Q: What is the balance between detachment and love?

To love does not mean to possess. To love is to let go. The ego possesses. The spirit loves. In meditation you learn how the ego self solidifies, how fear leads the ego—or personality self—into desire to possess. If force enters here, as the tool used to say no to attachment, there is separation. That is not release but denial. As you bring compassion and kindness to those fears, you find more spaciousness and less need to grasp. You begin to see the deepest interconnections between yourself and the beloved and also the uniqueness of each of you. As you appreciate both similarities and differences and cultivate a spaciousness that works skillfully with fear, you increasingly approach the beloved with a sense of deep reverence. From this egoless space, you truly begin to love unconditionally and to let go.

Q: I experienced a sense of divine love through the heart opening and I'm not sure how that relates to emotional detachment.

Attachment creates suffering. One cannot love fully when there is attachment. Divine love is most directly experienced by the higher self, not the ego self. The higher-self level is an aspect of the being in which there is no heavy emotion. There are joy and sorrow, but there is no fear or action derived from fear. This level of love may flow between the being and that which it considers the ultimate divinity, or it may flow between the being and what it considers to be expressions of that divinity such as another human, a song, or a flower. It's the same divine love.

When I use the word *love*, I imply divine love. That is not to suggest that love is impossible on the relative plane, but fear must be separated out. When you look deeply at what the ego self considers to be love, you find divine love and also fear, grasping, and a notion of a separate self. For example:

you may see self loving the reflection it sees of itself in the other, loving the way the other cares for it, or loving the sense of being somebody who cares for another. These concepts inflate the self. They are ego's mimicry of love. But when you remove ego self's motives, you're left with what I can only call divine love, egoless love. This level of being is never attached. To what would it attach? There is nothing separate.

It is important to remember that both levels of love can be present at the same time. When there is self-centered love, look beneath it, deep down to the core of love. Be aware of attachment and move through it. Then you will find divine love. It is like finding the fresh water by cutting through the ice. The water is always there, but the ice obscures the experience of it. Use the mimicry of love to remind you of possibility. Then cut through the ice and find the purest level of love.

Q: What is the meaning in the song of a bird?

You do not want the scientific, technical meaning here. The deeper meaning is love.

Free Will

*Q: To what degree do we have free will and to what degree
is our journey shaped for us?*

Free will is an important element of your human journey. In your human form you are always given choices and asked to take responsibility for those choices. You can allow a frightened, fragmented self to make your decisions, directed by a brain that screams, "Do this, do that," or you can learn to listen with your heart, to find a wholeness within yourself so that your choices become increasingly harmonious with the universe. When you make such choices guided by your heart's wisdom, then your path opens before you, and the offered lessons are learned. When you fight this harmony, you often make unskillful choices, and your learning becomes more painful. Perhaps you will come to trust the wisdom of your heart and of spirit. Then the learning experience becomes a joyful sharing of love.

You correctly understand that your lessons extend out to all others with whom you are in contact. Sometimes it may seem hard to comprehend the convolutions of the universe that join each of your separate paths. Nothing is precisely planned, yet nothing is ever unplanned. You co-create choices that bring you together for shared learning. Each being's choice impacts every other choice, creating a giant tapestry of interwoven threads. When distortion results, contraction occurs, and you shrink back from your connections. Such fear enhances disharmony.

Always, your multifaceted path is laid before you. When an option arises, you are given the choice to follow or not to follow. If you choose not to follow, there will be a different path. If that option offered something necessary for your growth, your path will eventually bring you back to the same place, but the way will wander a bit, and perhaps there will be steeper hills. If you chose the hill, it's because that steepness is necessary to your unique path, because on that rocky hillside you will find the lessons that you need. Again, you have free will—to learn those lessons or to repeat them on the next hill. If you need to repeat them, that is fine. You are given all the time you need.

At times there may seem to be impossible obstacles on the path. Always these can teach you what you need to learn. Stop and look at this cliff side that looms before you. Ask, "What has brought me here?" If you listen with your heart and search out the steps with love, you will find the learning there and understand that you have brought this cliff into existence, just as you can send it away when your learning is complete. You have not invited it because you wished to climb a steep, rocky slope but because it is the necessary outplay of karma. Your path to learning is the path of balancing and resolving that karma. Your path is always your own choice, made with the wisdom of your spirit.

Please remember that every path, no matter how smooth or steep, will eventually lead you home. Where you are on that path is exactly where you need to be, and the next step before you is always just the step you need to take. Listen with your heart, and you will find yourself in harmony with the universe, and your steps will become increasingly joyous.

Sharing the Journey

Q: What I am learning about our spiritual journey is very beautiful.
How can I share it with my parents (spouse/children/friends)?

As you find your path opening before you, of course you want to share the beauty with your loved ones. That is fine. Tell them what you are learning, but be prepared for a less than enthusiastic response.

All beings are on a spiritual path, whether or not they are conscious of that path. We are all on our way home. Remember that we travel by many routes and are in different places, each on our own unique path.

You tend to want to give your own understandings to those close to you. Do you see that insistence is a form of violence against your loved one? You can open a door for another, but you cannot force him through.

Trust that each being is exactly where he needs to be. If he does not accept your invitation to enter the door you've opened, why can you not let him be? What wants to push? One may quickly answer, "Love for my companion," but more often it is fear, a natural reluctance to watch the loved one's pain. But that pain may be an important teacher for your companion.

Examine your own need here. Do you have space for his or her pain? What must you prove? What ego is there that asks for approval of your own path? Explore these questions without judgment of yourself. Simply look at what's there, with love and compassion for your own human needs. Doing so will allow you the space to see that forcing your beliefs on another is a violence to that being.

We can teach one another and lead one another, but only from a space where there is no ego need. When you lead from that place, you open a passage through which another may follow when he is ready. There is no need within you for the other being to follow. Instead, there is compassion for his pain and a sense of wholeness in yourself that needs no reassurance that you are on the right path. Your faith is strong within itself. It does not need to be bolstered by another.

From within that space you can truly teach, not so much by your words but by your very being. Your loved ones will see your growing sense of peace and wholeness. They will notice the changes in you. When they ask you, then you may share. Your loving actions will speak much louder than all your pleas of "Try this," or "Think about that."

To share is beautiful, but the only person you can work on is yourself. Each being must learn the lessons himself. You may serve as a guide, a road sign pointing the direction, but each must walk the path himself, at his own pace and in his own way. Walk your own path with love, faith, courage, and humility, and you will be a glowing beacon that lights the way for others.

Q: Hey, Aaron, heard any new jokes this week?

If I told you a good one and it was at least nine hundred years old, would you be offended? The beauty of reincarnation is that not only the spirit but the jokes get another chance.

A Perspective on Jesus

Aaron has told us that at the time of Jesus' birth he was a young child
living in the hills in that country with his father, who was a shepherd.
As an adult he came to know this master and followed him. Aaron
emphasizes that in that lifetime he was just a shepherd and not one
of the core group who were the great disciples of Jesus. Nevertheless, he
had great love for his teacher and gratitude for his teaching.
Each year Aaron has shared stories with us about what he learned
from this beloved teacher. He offers them as "teaching stories."
The stories in this chapter have been drawn from the book
Aaron's Christmas Stories.

December 5, 1989

I would like to talk to you about that teacher you call Jesus. You are in the midst of your annual celebration of his birth. Do you understand what that birth really means, who he was and what was truly given? I see much confusion between the true gift and the church doctrine that has grown up around it. I do not mean to offend anyone here. Your private and group beliefs are important to you and must be deeply respected. The beauty of this gift is such that it needs no beliefs or myths to support it. Yet, I recognize that anything said becomes just another myth. Please take my words as very loose allegory.

You are all sparks of God, evolving slowly through your many lifetimes to perfect light and to mature compatibility with divinity. Since the dawn of time, a few beings have so evolved as to become pure and radiant light, filling the universe with their luminescence. Such beings truly sit at the side of God, and the power of their light and love are inextinguishable.

Such a being is the spirit of the man you call Jesus. This spirit was the proof of divine potential, the perfect example of what all mankind can become. As such he was deeply beloved, the Son of God as you all are sons and daughters of God, deeply cherished because of his willingness and courage to express this divine perfection.

Your earth in those days was full of war, of misunderstanding, of hatred, of chaos. There were those who believed that God taught that one being should avenge himself on another, and one nation avenge itself on another. Such bloodshed was enacted in the name of God. There were those who taught that God's laws were a matter of convenience, that murder was permitted in his name. They were not people meaning to do evil, but beings filled with misunderstandings. Many of you were there. Ask your higher self's memory if that is not how it was.

Seeing the misunderstandings that filled the world, God grieved for humans. So God asked this son, who stood by God's side, to give a great gift to mankind, to take it unto himself to return to that human plane to teach lessons of love, compassion, and forgiveness. The gift was no less God's, for God was giving this beloved son unto the pain and chaos of the physical plane.

The spirit of the man you know as Jesus agreed to God's request, with gladness that he might serve the divine intention. He fully understood what he agreed to, that in returning to this physical plane, in agreeing to incarnate in human form, he was taking on all the pains of human birth. He agreed to the subtle forgetting of his true self. Although this forgetting did not reach the level that it reaches with most humans, there were to be times of deep doubt and despair. He agreed to the physical pains of the human body, of the frailty of the human form. Out of love and to give love, he gladly accepted whatever experience he might face.

He came to teach God's true messages of love and peace to a weary, chaotic, pain-filled world. He came to teach the divinity of each soul. This is the true gift of his birth and his life. He had free will, as have all beings. He could have said no, and God would not have loved him any less. Do you understand what it means freely and willingly to leave that perfect light and love? Can you understand how much this holy spirit loved mankind and God that he accepted this mission of teaching? Only perfect love could have made this choice, and only perfect love would have been able to teach such love to others. Had he said no, the world would have continued on in darkness until another being came forth, ready to perform this task.

The other gift of this season is God's. Which of you could send a beloved child to a place torn by war and hatred, to certain pain, to teach others?

As you think this season about his incarnation to become the teacher known as Jesus, as you think about the teachings of love and peace and forgiveness, think also about the gift that was given—the gift of love. Let all your gifts that commemorate this birth be gifts of love and forgiveness, each to another, so that he may see that his lessons are truly being learned. This is the greatest gift you can give him, the way you can best honor his gift—to love one another.

I love you all and wish you a happy Christmas filled with peace and the beauty of God's and Christ's love.

December 19, 1990

It would seem fitting that we talk tonight about he whose birth you will celebrate next week, he who in his last incarnation was known as Jesus. You know that all of us have lived many past lives, and there were a number of you who were incarnate on the earth at that time, two thousand years ago, as I was. I have shared few of my memories, for most fall into that category of what you do not need to know. Yet, for each of us there are certain memories that stand out through an infinite number of lifetimes. I'd like simply to share this beautiful one with you.

I'm not going to try to separate for you tonight what has been built up as myth about the story of his birth and what was real. Was such a being born near the area of Bethlehem about two thousand years ago? Yes, he was. We will not quibble over the exact date or the details of that birth. The facts of his birth are far less important than what he taught.

At the time of his birth I was a young boy of nine, a shepherd boy in the hills outside that town of Bethlehem with my father and older brother. The emotional climate of the world in that time was very different from what it is today. Yes, there is war and hatred in many parts of the world today, but there is a new word, the concept of which barely existed two thousand years ago in much of the world. That word is "forgiveness." Instead, the prevailing philosophy was that of, "An eye for an eye; a tooth for a tooth." "Do unto others as you would have others do unto you," was distorted to, "Do unto others as they do unto you." If he hits, hit him back. Protect yourself.

There was an effort to follow the Ten Commandments: not to steal and not to kill, but it was acceptable to kill in self-defense. That wasn't considered killing. If one harmed you or those you loved, it was quite acceptable to seek revenge against that one and those he loved. You may think this sounds little different from today's world. Certainly, for some individuals, it is little different. But today for most individuals and even for nations there is an effort at harmony, respect, and forgiveness. Look at your relationships today with Japan or Germany. The past is past, and hate is not extended to the citizens of those nations.

So this is the world in which I lived—a young boy sitting wrapped in a blanket by a fire on that cool evening—a very peaceful scene. My father and the other men told stories. On that night, the air grew very still. Suddenly there was a brilliant star. That much is fact, as I saw it. Below me, in the valley some distance away was the town that has come to be known as Bethlehem.

Never had I seen a star like that before. Neither had the elders, I supposed, because everyone grew very quiet. Some felt afraid, but most felt a deep sense of peace and wonder. You have all seen a full moon shining on snow, the way the world seems to radiate light. That star did the same thing. The world seemed lit from within.

I can't say the light was focused over a special building, a stable or any other dwelling. I can't say it was not thus focused, either. I didn't observe that; I was a young boy on a hillside. But there was such a sense of deep peace, such brilliance to the light. Music seemed to fill the air, not music that is heard with one's ears but music heard with one's heart.

We were drawn as if by a magnet to descend the hills. There were many people going. My father was hesitant to leave our sheep and go very far, so we did not go all the way into the town, but stayed on the hillside.

It was a night like none I have ever known before or since. The strongest memory is that of deep peace and of a profound joy that something had happened—something far beyond the understanding of the young boy who I was, something that would profoundly change the world.

Many went all the way into town. Others of us stayed closer to our flocks on the hillsides. But no matter where you were, light permeated everything. It seemed almost as if the earth itself glowed. We were awed, not just myself as a child but the adults as well. Many began to pray.

We sat there for hours. Some of those who had gone all the way into town began to return. I was dozing by this time, asleep in my father's arms, hearing just the faint words of elders whispered past me in the still morning hours: "A child is born. They call him the Prince of Peace. They say that his teachings will change the world."

Then I remember my father's strong arms lifting me and carrying me back up the hill to our fire. I slept with a sense of joy and peace that I had never known before—a sense that somehow much that was wrong with the world might be righted. New hope was born.

I give you this memory to share what his birth meant to me. As you celebrate his birth, think, if you will, of this gift of forgiveness and the positive ways his teachings changed the world.

Q: Was Jesus called Jesus back in that lifetime or did you know him by another name? You keep saying, "He who was called Jesus."

Some called him Jesus, or the variations of that name such as Jeshua or Yeshua. Some called him "the carpenter" or "the carpenter from Nazareth." Among some he was simply known as "the teacher." Yes, there were many teachers, and yet he came to be called that by many. When I say, "He whom you know as Jesus," I do that more to distinguish that lifetime, because this spirit also lived other lives. Yes, he had reached the point where he no longer needed to incarnate in human form, but to reach that point he had lived a great many lives. In naming him in that way, I am referring to that specific incarnation.

Q: Did Jesus practice meditation?

He was familiar with the practice of meditation in its many forms. It was known by some in his time that he had traveled to the East, to Egypt, to the Himalayas, and to other parts of the world and that he learned meditation techniques there. His family followed the Essene practices and he had received these initiations. So he learned meditation in many forms. He was able to move freely into a jhanic state—a state of profound concentration. He understood that practice and also understood that it could be an escape, and so he did not frequently indulge himself in it.

From my own experience with him in that lifetime, I saw him recommend prayer, various purification practices, and mindfulness meditation to others. He taught others to live in the present moment, to know the divine self and bring it forth, and not to become lost in the small self. He practiced meditation as a path to this end.

Meditation was more a part of his own training than what he taught formally to others. He taught by example. He prayed and meditated, so those around him did the same. What he taught was very simple: Forgive, open your heart, offer love in return to hatred and fear, know God's presence in the self and in each being, and relate to everything through its divinity.

Q: Were there other teachers on the level of Jesus and the Buddha?

Yes, there have been other such beings. None has become as well known, yet they have always inspired those around them, even when it was only a small group. What strikes me as important here is that an essential part of the lifetimes of the Christ and the Buddha was their intent to serve and to teach. Jesus incarnated with that intention. After Siddartha Gautama's enlightenment, when he became the Buddha or awakened one, he made the decision, "I must share this path of liberation from suffering with others."

Buddhism has a term for such a being. A bodhisattva is one who recognizes the suffering in the universe and is willing to come back to this incarnation repeatedly in order to serve, rather than finding its own final liberation. A bodhisattva is aware that as long as one being still suffers, no one can be totally free. Willingness to return to incarnation is one manifestation of the bodhisattva. Another form is willingness to remain available on the spirit plane. Such teachers are here, but you on earth may not know of them. I feel the deepest gratitude for the gift they offer us all.

Q: When did you first learn of the death of Jesus? At the time, what significance did you attach to his death? When did you learn that his followers continued to meet? Did you ever join them?

I was a shepherd but also felt myself to be his disciple, one of an outer circle of disciples. What he taught spoke directly to my heart. I followed his teachings and shared them with others. In this way, I became very much a follower of his and when my life's circumstances allowed, I was with him. I understood that my work was more to be available to those who lived as I did, than to always be with him.

I was not present at his death, but I knew he was to be crucified. People who knew he had been my teacher directed officials to question me, and I must admit that I denied him. I said I did not revere him, out of fear for myself and because while I understood the necessity of the path he followed, which included his death, from my human standpoint I abhorred that necessity. The tremendous guilt I felt about that lie led me away, as far as I could get. It was not until several weeks later—having spent most of those weeks alone in prayer and meditation—that I understood what I had done and saw what I needed to do next.

At that point, yes, I joined with those who had been his followers and who continued to share his teachings. I found that there were many others who had done as I had done and who also felt guilt. I saw that, as with me, others had learned through that guilt the true meaning of his message of forgiveness and the necessity to forgive themselves.

This was his final gift to me in that lifetime. My pain around his death, my own fear that led me to deny him, and the overwhelming sense of guilt all opened my heart to the true meaning of his message of forgiveness. It is not a measured forgiveness. That is easy. Rather it is unconditional—to forgive the seemingly unforgivable in myself and in all beings. This is the final work of the open heart. With that step of unconditional acceptance, the heart opens in compassion so that there is truly nothing left to forgive.

Frequent Questions

**Q: Where were the favorite places you
lived while incarnate?**

When I was young and lived in fertile
valleys, I yearned for mountains. When I
lived on mountains with stunning vistas
and crisp air, I yearned for valleys.
Then I matured enough to stay in the
moment and to love each for what it was
and found that each place offered its own
incomparable treasure.

Problems

*Q: I seem to have so many problems. Each time I resolve one,
there's a new one. What am I doing wrong?*

I hear your question. Many people echo you. Certainly there are issues that
need to be resolved, but you can relate to them in loving ways. First, know
that there are no problems, only situations that ask your loving attention.
If you are willing to risk being undefended in a place of pain, as you open
your hearts to these difficulties, then there is no "problem," which implies a
negative experience, only a situation that asks for attention.

Yet you habitually create difficulties for yourselves. Why do people do
that? When you have a problem, it gives you something to focus on. You feel
you can pinpoint it and say, "This is the problem, and if I can solve this, then
everything's going to be fine. Then I'm going to be comfortable, and everyone
will be happy." This gives you an illusion of power, of control, and therefore
of safety. You are attached to problem solving. When your own problems
seem well on the way to being solved, you find friends with problems so that
you can help them with theirs. One of your chief recreations is the creation
of problems and problem solving. You even collect them in puzzle books, as
entertainment!

People become attached to what has seemed a place of safety, which is
the small self and its methods of control. You are attached to the self and
therefore you are attached to your problems and treat them as a doorway
to something that you can do—problem solve. This is tricky. When you are
problem solving, it helps you to avoid feeling the pain of the situation so
acutely. You say, "Well, I'm doing something about it." The delusion here
is that, instead of really giving the situation your loving attention, you may
withhold that loving attention because at some level you want to perpetuate
the problem that serves as a diversion from the pain while continuing to

feel that you're doing something. Letting go of the illusion of control is not viewed as an option.

You live in a world in which there is so much fear. You are all exploring fear in yourselves and in your lives. You may create new situations of fear to further reflect your inner fear and give yourself more opportunity to participate in fear, anger, pain, or deprivation. Why would you do that? Doing so may feel safer than resting in an awareness that observes fear without getting caught in its stories. To rest in such awareness means to step out of self-identification with discomfort. It is to step outside of the self. True Being has no problems. From the spacious perspective that is unattached to problems, awareness can attend to unwholesome, uncomfortable, or unpleasant situations, employing that extension of awareness you know as the everyday self. But such perspective, which lets go of self, is threatening, so you maintain the problem as a way to hold on to self.

This process is very subtle. Look at it in your experience. Find an issue that's uncomfortable for you, a place where there's a lot of pain. Maybe it's about wanting a better job or a better relationship. Find something that you view as a problem. Then ask yourself the question: what if this were resolved? Take a deep breath and ask that as honestly as you can. Part of you says, "Wonderful!" Part of you shudders, "What if it were resolved? What would hold my attention then, to divert me from the deeper suffering of conditioned existence?" The real issue is that even if this relationship were more harmonious, even if this job were improved, you would still be suffering, because your suffering does not grow from the poor relationship, or job, or even poor physical health. Your suffering grows out of your ongoing battle to maintain an illusion of a self in control. It is the dilemma of the juggler with too many balls, struggling to keep them all aloft, in anguish lest one drop. What if you let them all drop, and then pick up only those you wish to juggle, putting them down easily when you are done?

Suffering grows from grasping for some final solution that you will not find as long as you keep looking in the wrong places. As long as you cannot be present in this moment and know its perfection but keep grasping at things to be different from what they are, you will suffer. "Problems" mask that suffering.

Can you see that pattern in yourself? If the relationship is improved and you are still suffering, what then? If you retain the illusion, " If only I can fix the relationship, if only I can fix the partner and all his or her inadequacies, then everything's going to be fine and I'll be happy forever," it gives you a sense of control and helps the personal self feel safe and empowered. So at some level, you want to perpetuate your problems.

You will not be free of problems until you understand that. It takes courage to allow the self-identification with the ego self to dissolve so that the true essence can shine forth. It is very difficult to be that honest with yourself and see the addictive patterns. But this is the route to freedom. In the expression of Being, problems cease and awareness attends to life's glitches with kindness and an open heart.

Choices

Q: Aaron, life is filled with so many difficult choices. How do I know what career path to take or which job? Is this partner the right one for me? When my loved ones are ill how can I know what are the best care choices for them? How do I speak to abusive anger? When do I stick with a situation to try to resolve it and when do I leave it because it is painful?

Choices are teachings. More precisely, the experience of difficulty in choosing is a teaching. When you see two or many paths before you, this is often because you hear different voices. You have not yet come to know these voices, and so they still call loudly to you—the voice of fear, the voice of doubt, the voice of inadequacy. They tend to shout at you so that sometimes you cannot hear the whispers of clarity and love.

When these difficult voices emerge, you empower them by contracting your energy around them. This contraction makes the difficulty feel even more solid, as something with which to wrestle, something to conquer. The result is to bring forth an enhanced sense of a self and an other.

With this sense of separation, feelings like fear, doubt, and inadequacy arise more forcefully and present their stories—the tales of helplessness, badness, unworthiness, guilt, confusion, and more. The story seems to take on a deeper truth, and the self that must resolve the story becomes more solid to relate to the story. One moves ever farther from clarity. It is akin to the situation of one who has left on the tap so that the sink is overflowing. He may become so engrossed in catching the spill that he fails to take a step back, see where it comes from, and turn off the tap. As you become lost in the story, the ego self becomes more solid and separate and less able to see the bigger picture.

Here is an example. If your parent or child is very ill, and the doctors say the loved one may die, the energy contracts around the situation with fear, grief, and helplessness. The fear that you will lose this person becomes enormous, including the fear that you will not be safe yourself. Anger arises, "Why them? Why me?" With each new concern, you get pulled in deeper. There is no space, no fresh air. Such fear is not bad, but to become lost in it is not helpful. It reminds me of the wonderful story of Br'er Rabbit and the Tar Baby.

In the story, Br'er Fox created a baby out of tar to try to ensnare Br'er Rabbit. He knew Br'er Rabbit's habitual tendencies quite well. Br'er Rabbit was out walking and found the Tar Baby sitting in the middle of the road. "Howdy," he said. Tar Baby didn't answer. "Aren't you going to answer me?" No reply. "You are very rude. If you don't answer me I am going to punch you." The Tar Baby remained silent. Br'er Rabbit gave him a hard punch in the face, and of course his hand stuck there. "You let me go or I'll punch you again." No answer. He punched again; now both hands were stuck. Br'er Rabbit was furious. He screamed, "I'm going to kick you! Let me go!" No reply, so he kicked, one foot and then the other foot. With a final burst of rage, he butted the Tar Baby with his head. This was a very stuck bunny! Does it sound familiar?

When there is a difficult situation and many voices of fear and confusion arise, if you recognize those voices and allow a spacious presence around them, they lose solidity. When you allow that voice to lead you into an increasingly solid story, and a solid self forms to accompany the story, it is very hard to get out. Let us imagine Br'er Rabbit stuck here in the hot sun. The more anger grows, the more he pulls and the more stuck he becomes. If instead he takes a breath and relaxes a bit and notes his situation spaciously, it reduces the contraction of anger. Simply taking a moment to look at the actual circumstances, repeating to himself, "stuck, stuck" as a way to slow himself down and focus, lifts him aside a step to see how fear is dominating his actions. Here is the physical experience of being stuck, but instead of a "somebody" who is stuck, awareness watches the phenomenon—the uncomfortable physical sensations, the fear, the contracted energy—that come together under the label, "stuck."

Sadness may come, but the fear lets go its hold. He realizes the tar baby has no personal vendetta but is just being tar. He didn't have to punch the tar baby; that was his choice. He is now experiencing the result of that choice. He has participated in creating this situation. When he understands the situation, then he may relax further. That which is aware of being stuck is not stuck itself. Where there is "stuck," there is also "unstuck." As he sits patiently, present with his own discomfort, no longer creating stories, he will find that the sun melts the tar somewhat. The tar baby shrinks away. It is impermanent. The body comes loose. We can see that the less energy he gives to fear, the less solid the story feels, and the less hold the tar baby has.

Even from this bigger perspective, there may still be fear, "Br'er Fox will find me here and eat me." But the fear is just fear. That means it is just another object, an emotion like sadness or pain, unpleasant but impermanent. It is big enough on its own; he does not need to make it bigger through stories.

The words, "Br'er Fox will find me stuck here and eat me" could be a fact, something that could happen, and it is also a story. "My loved one could die" is both a fact and can become a story. The fact is the truth of impermanence. That is not a morbid statement, simply real. All conditioned things are impermanent, subject to decay and dissolution. There is nothing we can hold on to on the relative plane. "Why is this happening to me?" is a story. "I feel sad and afraid," is a fact. Can you feel the difference?

Only when you recognize this fact and come to an ease about it are you free to hear a clear voice that can see the situation and respond from a place of love, not fear. This does not mean that fear ends, only that one has learned not to indulge in fear's stories. "My loved one may die," is heartbreaking. There will be sadness, discomfort, feelings of helplessness and anger. Whichever of these difficult visitors come, recognize and make space for them. There is nothing to fix. Fear may continue to murmur in the background, but its voice no longer holds your attention. Now you can hear the voice of loving-kindness and clarity.

You can see there is no simple answer to your question. The first answer seems simple, to choose love and not fear. The next question is what trips you up. How do I choose love? How do I not get caught in fear? It is difficult, yet it is what you are incarnate to learn. The difficulties that offer choices are not problems but teachers. Understanding that also invites spaciousness. There are no problems, only situations that ask our loving attention.

When you feel bounded by fear in its many voices, it is very helpful just to pause and note, "Here is fear." Ask yourself, "What is my primary intention here?" For example, is it to save your loved one or, urgent as that choice may feel, is the primary intention to help to bring forth whatever is for the good of all beings? But at this time it is not given to you to know with clarity what is for the good of all. Therefore you must relax, not try to push when you cannot see the outcome, but to act only in ways that are fully harmonious with intention.

The second question is, "Is what I am about to say or do consistent with this highest purpose?" Here is an example taken from recent experience. The ill loved one was at home. Doctors had determined that the health situation was untreatable and that death would come soon. The loved one had requested that no heroic measures be used. There were trained attendants, but they did not have authority concerning care. The loved one's breathing became very labored.

The spouse said, "I wanted to rush him to the hospital. It was so difficult to sit by his side and watch this struggle, but I could see that it was my own fear that said to seek medical aid. Love said to just sit there." She told me, "Aaron, I sat for many hours. At first I cried and said, 'I cannot do this.' Then I relaxed and began to do the breathing exercise Barbara had taught me, breathing with him and releasing a gentle 'Aahhhh' with each exhale. His breathing calmed. It was still strained but the fear went out of it for both of us. I was right there with him in his final breath. I have never felt so close to him. It was a precious experience. And I know that was so for us both."

When there is a difficult choice, ask yourself, "Where is love here?" If fear's voices are too loud to hear love's voice, can you be present with fear? What is the experience of fear before the stories start? Can you feel the fear in the body, such as tightening in the jaw or heat in the belly? What happens with fear when you are thus present? As fear's energy dissolves, you will be able to hear love's response.

Remember that there is often no one right choice. Life is like a maze with many paths that open out into the destination. Some paths will be shorter but they may lead you up cliffs you may not know how to climb.

A different path may be longer yet carry precious learning. Either way is fine. Consider the poem, "The Road Not Taken": one path will lead to another and yet another. No path is a dead end. With thanks to Robert Frost, "Yet knowing how way leads on to way, I doubted if I should ever come back." And yet you do come back, not to that precise spot, but to the dense woods, again and again. Whatever your habitual tendencies, karma will draw you back to re-explore until those tendencies are resolved. This is your path. This is your work. Do not be afraid to walk it with faith and love.

Energy

Q: Aaron, in the past you have often spoken about energy and how we can work with it skillfully through spiritual practices. Can you summarize what is useful for us to know about energy?

You are energy. Every cell of the body is energy. The mind is energy, and you exist in energy. The earth under your feet, the air around you—it is all energy.

You bear an energetic relationship with everything with which you come into contact. Because everything is energy and yet seemingly there is a self, you learn how to create boundaries for your energy. Then you forget that the boundaries are a construction created to serve you and take them as an ultimate reality. It is not the move into self that creates difficulties, but the belief in that state as ultimate truth.

As you become increasingly aware of energy within your human and physical experience and in the universe around you, you will begin to see certain patterns. Energy in its natural form is balanced. There is both spaciousness and contraction. It is not frozen into either extreme. All distortion comes from imbalance. When you note imbalance, be aware that the balanced system is still there; you have just misplaced it temporarily. You do not need to fix the imbalance so much as to release it and return to balance.

In one lifetime I was a practitioner of an energy practice akin to shiatsu. That is certainly not the only practice that addresses imbalance, but it provides a clear vocabulary with which I am familiar. In this tradition, one observes that energy is either *kyo* or *jitsu*. When it is balanced, there is a smooth alternation of kyo and jitsu, each flowing into the other. Kyo energy is still, quiet, and without contraction. Jitsu energy is moving, engaging, and contracting. Here is a simple illustration.

Hold out your hand, palm open, while a partner holds an object to place in your palm. Can you feel the subtle jitsu tension, waiting to receive? There is a contraction in that energy field. Feel the release of that contraction as the object is placed into the palm. The energy field quiets itself: kyo. Then the thought may arise to bring that object in towards the body, closing the fist, drawing the hand inward, closing, contracted: jitsu. The closed fist comes to rest against the body: kyo.

Another example is seen in nature. The jitsu energy of the wave pulls it into a froth as it tumbles over itself, rushing to shore. There is a moment when it hits the beach and comes to rest: kyo. Then it begins to withdraw, pulling again into a fierce tumult. It is jitsu. That undertow and the incoming wave meet with forces of equal resistance, and everything stops. That is kyo. Then the outflowing water either rushes out to sea or joins with the incoming wave in a new jitsu expression. Your own breath offers a very parallel example of kyo and jitsu.

Parts must be in balance or there will be distortion. If there were no kyo resting place in the waves' cycle, they would overrun the shore. If there were no jitsu contraction in the breath, you would fail to take the next inhale or exhale.

There is one more aspect to this pattern. Imagine a river where logs are being floated into an area with a large dam. The current carries the logs, which crash into each other with much jitsu energy. At the dam they jam up, and their motion seems to cease. It looks like the situation has become kyo. This is an illusion of kyo. The logs are not truly quiet but merely so jitsu that the motion can no longer be expressed. If you offer additional energy to true kyo, it begins slowly to move. If you offer additional energy to this overly compacted illusion of kyo, it just becomes more compacted. We call this state *hyper-kyo*. If you release true kyo it remains still. If you release these logs by creating a small opening, they will spill out, expressing their jitsu nature. Hyper-kyo is a traditional label, so I offer it. Remember that it is really a jitsu state.

Everything in your universe is expressed as energy—kyo, jitsu, and hyper-kyo. When energy is in balance, there is peace and harmony. When it is out of balance, there is distortion and discomfort. This is true on the physical, emotional, and mental levels. Balance is the natural state. Many situations bring imbalance. The work is twofold, to recognize and release imbalance and to know the experience of balance and how to return to the balanced state. Note that I do not suggest avoidance of imbalance. You cannot do so. What you can do is to attend to it.

Let us look briefly at common areas of distortion. Your bodies move easily into imbalance. Chronic fatigue syndrome is an example of a kyo distortion. Energy is blocked. Tendonitis is an example of a jitsu distortion. Often by the time tendonitis has developed, it is hyper-kyo. Anger is a jitsu distortion. Extreme passivity is a kyo distortion. Remember that the mind and body do not separate here. If there is a jitsu or kyo emotional imbalance, it will have a physical expression. And the imbalance will exist even on a cellular level.

There are many ways to attend to imbalance. Most importantly, although the imbalance exists on the relative plane, there is no imbalance on the ultimate level. One then works to know the ever-perfect balance that exists on the ultimate level and to use that ever-present perfection as a template or reminder to invite release of the distortion and return to the ever-perfect. The second part of this work is to attend to the distortion on the relative level. That may be done in meditation and through work with body-energy practices or through work with the elements. Note that one is not fixing what is broken but attending to the distortion because such distortion is painful, and it is compassionate to attend to it. If one attempts to fix distortion, one gives it more energy. When one attends to it with kindness, one recognizes its impermanence and does not create solidity around it.

One might be tempted to work only on the ultimate level, seeing only the ever-perfect. Compassion leads us also to attend to the relative. If you have a broken leg, you will stabilize the fragmented ends to relieve discomfort and to aid the re-expression of its wholeness. You will also wish to visualize the ever-perfect leg and know its ultimate wholeness. If you feel intense rage, you will attend to the bodily and mental expressions of the anger in suitable ways, such as simply noting, "Here is anger." You may be led to take deep breaths or take a short walk to help release the contracted energy. If you make release into a goal however, you will bring more attention and more energy to the rage and thereby stimulate it. The rage must be attended to, but not feared. It is important to notice that right there with rage is that which is not angry. That which is aware of the anger is not angry. This is the observer, which knows the rage but is not caught in it. We sometimes call it "awareness." You may rest in that awareness, in that deep peace and kindness.

Remember you are connected energetically to everything. It is sometimes skillful to shield against external negative energy, simply by visualizing a barrier and holding it in place. Allow the negative energy to flow past you and visualize your own energy field as having no breaks where the negative energy could enter. This is not a move of fear but of kindness, such as putting on sun screen to protect the skin from burning.

When negative energy is emitted by another person, it helps the negativity resolve when you offer the counterweight of kindness rather than the jitsu state of fear. Do not use shielding to create separation of self and other. Be attentive to your energy. See if it is balanced and take care of it if it is imbalanced. You are responsible for what you put forth. If distortion comes forth, judging and condemning yourself is a further distortion. The balance for the contracted state is the ease and spaciousness of loving-kindness.

Pain

Q: This week I went to the funeral of a six-month-old baby who died suddenly. The whole family was in terrible pain, especially the grandmother. How do we deal with such pain?

This is a difficult situation for you. You are asked to do two things simultaneously, to respond compassionately to the suffering of those around you and at the same time to keep your own calmness and not become emotionally involved in the stories prompted by the pain. Yet it seems a conflict for you. If you don't become involved but are detached, you fear the heart has separated and you wonder how to respond compassionately.

A mixture of two vital elements is needed here. There must be awareness that makes you sensitive to others' pain. Within this awareness is compassion that allows you to feel deeply your oneness with every being and to know that your pain and theirs is the same. The second element is equanimity, a deep inner calmness and balance that comes from a knowledge that all phenomena and feelings are impermanent, like passing clouds that briefly hide the sun. Equanimity also grows out of a trust in each spirit's wisdom to have entered the situation it needs for its own learning and acceptance that sometimes the learning situation will be painful. This is not detachment but wise presence.

Your lives weave a complex tapestry. Every life touches every other life. For whatever its reasons, this child has moved on. Of course this death affects family and friends. You spoke of the intensity of the grandmother's pain. Certainly one cannot say that the grandmother has chosen the grandchild's death for her own learning, and yet certainly she has a chance to learn something that her grandchild is able to teach her.

When your life touches another's and that person makes a choice with his or her own free will, you are also touched by that being's choice. You may feel threatened by the choice, and fear may arise. Your ability to accept another's decisions and make space for the outplay of another's karma is what allows you to respond with calm awareness and give love. To do that, you must be aware of any feelings of threat or fear, and open with kindness to them. This is the start, to note turmoil in the self with wisdom and spacious kindness. Then bring attention to the outer situation.

Here the elements of awareness and equanimity must work together. Where there is awareness without equanimity, you will be overwhelmed by all the pain that comes past you. Where seeming calmness is based on separation, you dwell in a center of self, calm within yourself but insensitive to the world around. That is not true equanimity, but it is fear that walls off the pain. There is a semblance of calmness, but it grows from a closed heart, not an open one.

When you cultivate both awareness and equanimity, you can learn to respond to others compassionately and truly to serve them from a center of love. You become able to accept their pain into yourself and know that you are big enough to hold it and not be afraid. Then it ceases being their pain or your own pain and becomes our pain, the shared pain of mankind, borne with love by the heart we all share. To do this you must let the pain pass through you and acknowledge it without holding on to it. I am not saying that this is easy, but you may hold it in mind as a goal.

It may help you to think of a being who has served others who are in pain, such as Mother Teresa. Such a being gives selflessly to others. She does not break down and weep helplessly amidst the suffering but copes with it calmly and accepts it without approving it. You truly can absorb these qualities of wisdom and compassion into yourself by thinking about them in a being you admire and understanding them at a deeper level.

When people feel great pain, it does them no good if you break down and weep. I am not saying it is wrong to cry. If your tears are natural to you, that is fine. They will pass. But if you go to a place that has been ravaged by war or natural disaster and all you can do is sit and cry over the pain you see around you, you cannot help.

Let us reflect on this being sitting and weeping at others' pain, perhaps in a war zone or with a friend by their loved one's grave. You wonder, is it sensitivity that leads to continued weeping? It is not sensitivity so much as fear. The being that weeps at seeing death and brutality but eventually stops weeping and works to alleviate the suffering is aware and sensitive but not caught in the small self. The being who keeps weeping is not responding to others' pain but to his own suffering, which grows out of his own fear and feeling of helplessness. This is what I mean when I say weeping may come from a self-centered place.

You must be honest with yourself. Are you weeping for another or yourself? When the distinction between self and other is dissolved, there is no longer your pain and my pain but our pain, and together we are strong enough to bear it. When you personalize it and claim it as your own, then your fear grows. It becomes impossible to respond with love when your life is ruled by fear.

Each being who works with others who are suffering must confront this fear in the self. Unless you acknowledge it, you cannot move beyond it. There is nothing to criticize or blame here, just your own very real feeling, "What if that were me?" Let the fear in and look at it without judgment. Then you will be able to transcend the pain and, in doing so, your own strength and calm will lend peace to others and allow them also to move beyond it. What you are asked to do here is to allow love to replace fear, so that you are freed from the negativity, and your own natural compassion can take hold.

The more you are able to offer love to pain, the less hold it will have over your lives and the more your own compassion will serve as a guide and inspiration to others. Love is a very potent tool. I urge you to try it.

Q: Isn't it natural to grieve?

A feeling of loss is natural. When you lose something dear to you, there will be awareness of loss. There will be sadness. The direct experience of sadness is made up of turbulence and contraction in the physical, emotional, and mental bodies. It doesn't offer stories such as, "It could have been," or, "If only...." It is like feeling a snowball against the skin and having a direct experience of cold. If the mind begins to race at that touch, asking, "How long will it last?" or, "How can I get revenge on this person pelting me with ice?" then it is creating stories and may barricade itself from the direct experience, using the story to maintain separation. The wise being will not lose itself in the stories that sadness prompts but will know the direct experience of sadness and that it has arisen naturally out of conditions and will pass. That being will treat itself with kindness and accept kindness from others but not dwell upon the sadness, thinking it needs to be fixed. Sadness is just sadness, a normal response to loss.

Grief is different. Here we may enter into a semantic question. Many people see grief as a deep or intense sadness that comes following the loss of cherished loved ones or cherished ideas. Grief can become pathological and dwell in "if only's" and in "poor me's," but many people would say grief does not always become pathological in this way. In order to speak with clarity, I choose to distinguish grief and sadness, perhaps to an over extreme degree. Grief, as I understand the word, implies fear and grasping. Grief is attached to things as they were. It comes from the small self that cannot let go of the story "if only" or the story "poor me." Sadness comes from a place of love, grief from a place of fear.

If there is grief, one must not strive to ban the grief, which action only solidifies the self, but to acknowledge the fear or anger that is at the root of it. When seen clearly and with compassion, this fear or anger will pass, leaving sadness, free of old stories.

We touch here on the issue of the difference between pain and suffering. Sadness is painful, but there is no necessity of suffering. Grief and suffering come together. We will talk of this at another time.[6]

Q: Do you feel pain where you are?

I feel no physical pain; I have no body to ache. I feel pain at times but do not personalize it as you do. Instead, I allow it to flow through me, as part of the energy of the universe. I feel the pain of all beings that suffer and send them love.

---

[6] Pain and suffering: see Appendix A, "The Universe According to Aaron," for more detail.

Violence

Q: Will you talk about the violence in the world today?

There seem to be many causes for violence. If we take some issues and trace them back to the causes behind the causes, we eventually get to the misunderstanding that there is a separate self. A being immersed in this misunderstanding becomes involved in service to self, believing the needs of self and of other are mutually incompatible. The self, experienced as needy, demands what it believes it must have for its own safety and comfort. This could be a craving for personal satisfaction that leads to an act such as stealing from another, or a craving for ideological satisfaction where a being may commit violence against another in the name of a belief. In either case, the action grows from the notion of a separate self whose needs can only be satisfied by disrupting the essence of another.

Is this person satisfied? In truth, no. There is always a continuation of the wanting, on either the personal or ideological level. Let us trace back farther the source of this sense of wanting. It grows out of a feeling of incompleteness, of lack of wholeness. Indeed, the being that sees itself as separate can never find wholeness, for your wholeness grows out of your understanding of oneness. In separation from others there is also separation from your self. The acute pain of this separation leads to an attempt to fill in the emptiness, not by reaching out to others with love, but by taking.

At some point all beings are asked to make a choice between service to self and service to others. For a time, both choices are possible, as God is within both self and others. Service to self can be service to God. At a certain point in the journey, the vehicle of service to a self seen as separate from others is no longer viable, but the being involved does not understand that. The more a being pursues this service to self, the more deeply enmeshed he or she becomes in misunderstanding. I believe that this choice of service to self is what led beings like Hitler to commit violence to others while strongly believing their acts were righteous.

Service to self is service to God until it infringes upon another being. Then misunderstanding grows from the deepened misconception of the separate self. Not knowing the oneness, the being mistakenly believes he can enhance himself and God through damaging another. The problem for you in the physical plane is that so many beings are enmeshed in this mistaken idea of separateness and they have no idea how to get beyond it or even that there is a beyond.

As with all issues, the only work that you can do is on yourself. When you see beyond your own separateness, then personal violence is no longer possible, but you cannot dictate this belief to another without doing violence to him. Many have been killed in the name of such righteousness. Your only option is to use your own life as a demonstration to others that there is no separateness and that violence is not necessary. This is certainly one of those cases where actions speak louder than words. You are all teachers and have wonderful ways to demonstrate through your own lives that violence is not a necessity.

There are so many secondary sources of violence—prejudice, anger, hatred, pain, humiliation, and hunger. If you examine these, you will find that each traces back to this idea of a separate self. The question then becomes not, how can we get rid of violence, but how can we move beyond this misconception that the self is separate? No act that violates the essence of another can truly benefit the self.

Q: How can I teach this idea in the context of my current life?

You can teach this idea simply by affirming the truth that violence is not a necessary or an inescapable part of our lives. Contrary to popular belief, violence is not inborn in human beings but is learned behavior. It arises with fear. You may have no choice but to experience the fear, but there is choice as to how you will relate to fear. Your free will enactment of that choice is the teacher for others.

Violence to another is not confined to physical aggression. Forcing your own ideas on someone is a form of violence, as are anger and even impatience. There is no being on the physical plane, no matter how pure or how careful, who does not occasionally commit violence against another. When such violence occurs, the being who is deeply committed to nonharm will stop and look. What are the causes of this violence? From where did it spring? Here one may see the pattern of violence in one's reaction to one's own violent thoughts. Is there condemnation?

Please understand that your anger, or any heavy emotion, is not bad in itself. It is simply a feeling, just energy passing through. It is your relationship with your anger that creates the problem. Acknowledge your anger to yourself without judgment. As you do so, realize that there is no need to force that anger on another. It is enough to simply acknowledge it. Be honest but compassionate with yourself as you examine the ego needs that have led you to anger.

When your ideas or needs conflict with those of others, acknowledge the discomfort that this conflict causes in you and compassionately open to their ideas and needs as you continue to express your own. This open consideration creates a better space for listening and communication than does struggle. When you approach any situation as a battle, you create a battle, even if it is only a combat of ideas. Battle cannot exist unless you allow it to exist. You always are given the choice between responding with love and compassion or with hostility. Remember that a battle of ideas is also a form of violence against another human being and is truly not necessary.

Your life choices can be a much better teacher than any words that you may use. As you strive to speak and act in wise, loving ways, be compassionate with yourself and your own errors. You are not asked to be perfect. If you had reached the level of perfection where you never made mistakes, you would not need to be learning on this physical plane. Allow your mistakes and learn from them. Simply be honest with yourself.

Remember, anything that violates the essence of another being is a form of violence toward that being. The reverse of such violence is inherent in the concept of *ahimsa*, a Sanskrit term meaning harmlessness, or more completely, "dynamic compassion." Implied in this concept are not only nonaggression, but healing.

True healing grows out of forgiveness and, even more important, love. We cannot speak of transcending violence without mentioning these states of being that provide a balance to violence. Open your hearts to yourselves and all beings and practice loving-kindness and compassion. Deep looking and understanding is the vehicle. That is the most important lesson.

The Imperfect Body

*Q: Aaron, why do we have bodies that age
and become ill or disabled?*

Many factors determine the nature of the body. Karma is only one factor. Genetics, environment, and culture play a part. Thus one may also ask, why do I live in a difficult environment or culture? It is circular, and there may be no dominant reason. Nothing is haphazard, but one may not understand why circumstances have offered this particular body, family, or place. Not knowing, the best we can do is be present with what is, with an open heart, and take it as a situation for learning. The mind that seeks to blame or grasps at knowing *why* cannot open to things as they are. Let the question not be so much, "Why" as, "What good can be made of this situation?" That said, let us look at a small part of the situation of incarnation into a body that does not function as well as would be wished.

What does *imperfect* mean? This body may be uncomfortable or inconvenient but for this moment, it is your perfect schoolroom. Movement into the body is never determined by convenience or pleasure. You are here to learn. Much care is taken to be sure the optimum conditions for learning are available. Please understand that by optimum conditions I do not mean wealth, high rank, or even high intelligence or special gifts. I simply mean a choice of physical attributes and cultural and living situations that are best able to enhance the spirit's opportunity to open to the intended growth. Remember that the physical plane is a schoolroom for the higher self. Also remember that the higher self itself is never handicapped. With these ideas in mind, you will see that a handicap that you, in your physical form, may consider as an obstruction is actually a form of instruction.

It is important to remember that the body experiences, resultant from karma, also come with careful thought and with love, always with love. The result may seem cruel to a being on the physical plane who has forgotten the spiritual reasons for the choice. And, my dear ones, you forget so easily. Sometimes a being that experiences a difficult physical situation, such as a severe handicap, will not comprehend the reasons for this experience and may become mired in bitter misunderstanding. He may blame outside circumstances for his discomfort rather than recognizing the opportunity that is offered. When entrenched in this kind of distortion, the higher self obviously cannot make use of the chosen physical situation to attain the desired growth.

Sometimes, even with guidance, this forgetfulness and misunderstanding continues throughout the being's physical lifetime, both accruing new karma and necessitating the planning again for the hoped-for growth in another physical body in a new lifetime. Your resistance to learning is one of the conditions that manifests those experiences you need to teach you. What you are unwilling to learn in one lifetime, you will learn in another.

Even when a lifetime seems to have only increased the distortion, you are learning what you need to learn so that you can face the lessons you are avoiding. For example, the one who cannot walk may wish to ask what it means to stand upright. The deaf one may be led to explore what it does not wish to hear. This does not mean a specific fear caused the distortion, but the inability leads one to examine all the possible contributing factors. Each lifetime brings new light to areas that previously were dark. Sometimes it is only a glimmer, at other times a brilliant glow. Always, awareness is growing back toward that light which is its source and its home.

There is one more situation in which a being may move into a handicapped body. This choice involves both the spirit's own growth and its willingness, in love, to become the fulcrum for another being's growth. Occasionally a being may incarnate in a body that is so severely mentally damaged that little personal growth is possible in that lifetime. This may be done to aid another or others, perhaps the parent or a sibling, who in relationship with the handicapped being is able to gain important understandings, usually about love and selfless giving. Here, the handicapped being acts as a catalyst. Although love is the force behind all learning, the decision to incarnate in such a body is not entirely selfless. Remember that during this stage of repeated physical reincarnation your learning is not just on the physical plane. You learn on another plane while between physical incarnations. Thus, a being that has entered incarnation out of love and service to another has expanded his own capacity for love by the giving of his own self in love.

How can you work with the situations when you feel lost, bitter and afraid? Try this: picture yourself on a stage, your life just as you experience it, with the harshness of the disability. Now picture yourself lifted to a balcony where you can see the players come and go, on and off the stage. See this body return to an undistorted form as it exits the stage. See the whole picture.

You must take both parts: the player who deeply experiences the distortion and the audience who sees the entire spectacle and understands that the distortion is a difficult but useful illusion, brought forth for a reason. Can you trust that reason and re-enter the stage scene?

It may take a being many lifetimes to learn something that has become difficult for that being. In each new lifetime the optimal learning situations are chosen, and you may try again. There is never any rush. You have all the time that you need. With each lifetime you add light. With each step you find your way, guided by love, when you are able to open your heart to that love. You are all on this path together. While each of you walks a unique path, the process is the same for all beings and is one of those things that unite you. Be patient. Find the reality of love and follow it. Be as aware of your choices as possible and be responsible for them. Be assured that every being will find its way home.

Q: What you say here is beautiful but feels inconsistent with what I've read and heard about karma and the bardo state [the state between incarnations]. Specifically, Buddhism traditionally doesn't speak of such choices or of a being who makes such choices, just a pull of karma. Will you speak to these differences?

Each religion attempts to explain the process in its own way. I fully agree that ultimately there is no self and thus no soul in the sense of a lasting, separate entity. That does not mean that this aspect of being is nonexistent. Each drop of water that falls into the sea becomes indistinguishable from the sea, yet if there were no droplets, what would form the sea? The drops are the sea. The drops are also not "self" but are made up of what we could call "non-drop elements." They are made of water vapor, clouds, wind, and much more. The sea is greater than the drops, just as divinity is greater than any personal expression of divinity. In the same way, in Buddhist articulation, the Unconditioned constantly expresses the conditioned, that which arises out of conditions and ceases when the conditions cease. All conditioned objects are existent. They are "real." The lower bodies, which are "not-self," still are real or existent.

As you progress through the densities,[7] the heavier bodies fall away. These bodies—the physical, emotional, and mental bodies—are all conditioned. In the incarnate phase they are active. Only when we come to the spirit body do we enter the realm of the Unconditioned. This aspect of Being does not make choices; such choice comes from the lower bodies, and the karma is carried there, in these aggregates[8] of self. When I speak of a being that makes the choices, it is the aggregates or the heavier bodies that make the choices, led by karma. But there is intelligent awareness within the mental body, and there is some choice as to how the karma will be expressed.

Choice means many things. If I constantly choose meanness to others and do them harm, when they eventually attack me, I have in some way chosen that attack. I may have chosen meanness unconsciously, out of fear and the thought to protect myself. Nevertheless, such meanness became habit, as did fear. If it is not "I" who has chosen meanness, then it is habit and unconsciousness that have. Perhaps you may be more comfortable saying that you have invited or allowed what arose. In any case, you have participated in its creation. Since there is no "you," we could say that the various physical, emotional, and mental factors of karma have participated in the creation of the next moment. However you phrase it, the result is the same. We co-create each moment, on the basis of our karma.

Q: If I have a choice, am I not responsible for creating my illness? Why did I do that?

It is not helpful to reflect in this manner. To seek a place to lay blame for illness is just more negativity. Ask instead, in what way may this illness serve my own growth and serve all beings? However difficult the situation, what can it bring forth? Eventually you may understand some of the factors that led to the expression of this illness. If such insight comes, let it be the fruit of love, leading to the release of old holding and distortion, and let there

---

[7] Densities. Traditional metaphysics speaks of various "densities," using this word to describe the vibrational frequencies of the various bodies. A lower density has a heavier vibration. As the bodies purify, the vibrational frequency is higher. See Appendix A, "The Universe According to Aaron" for more information.

[8] Aggregates: these are form, feelings (of pleasant, unpleasant and neutral), thoughts, impulse, and consciousness.

be gratitude toward that which was a catalyst for such purification. Such openhearted compassion to the self is difficult yet may be the greatest fruit of painful experience.

Earthquakes and Disasters

Transcribed from a channeled tape made in reply to an anguished phone call from a friend in San Francisco, October 19, 1989, immediately after a severe earthquake.

Q: Why has this happened? What are we meant to learn from it? There is so much suffering. My home is destroyed. Why? I am terrified by the instability.

Greetings, my dear one. I send you my love.

You have been through a terrifying experience and a painful one, and of course the pain has not yet ended.

You have seen great suffering, seen your world turned upside down in a moment. Of course you wonder why such horror is permitted. And you wonder at your own feelings of terror. Let me talk about these separately.

You know that no natural disaster is meant as punishment. We are simply contending with energy here, the forces of the universe. They are neither inherently good nor bad; they simply exist. Yet, as with anything else in our lives, we may use these forces to teach us.

Everything in your life is part of your learning. In an experience such as this, people have died, people are in physical pain from their injuries, and people are homeless. Any person with a caring heart screams out, "This isn't right. How can this be permitted?"

Who is permitting it? Some may say, why does God permit it? But "God" is not one who chooses. Conditions come together to co-create each moment. Sometimes we can understand those conditions, and sometimes they are beyond our understanding. When this happens, people raise the question, why did God permit it?

Always, you make the choices for your lifetime; God cannot protect you from your choices. I do not mean to sound harsh when I say that those who choose to live above an earthquake zone have made a choice, but that is quite obvious. Similarly, those who have chosen to live in a war zone have made a choice. In the wisdom of each being's higher awareness, the being is always where it needs to be for the next lesson it needs on its journey.

Of course there are those beings that seem to have little choice, whose poverty shapes their lives and prevents their leaving. There are children who live there by their parents' choice. Each of them is there for a reason; there is something for each to learn. Trust the wisdom of each higher self to be where it needs to be, to experience what it needs to experience. If that experience ends in great injury or death, that happening is part of the lesson and is the result of karma. I do not wish to sound cruel, but try to look at it from my perspective for a moment. You live so many lives. Each one is precious. I'm not denying that. But also each life is like the blink of an eye.

This is not to suggest that one may shrug off another's suffering, or even one's own, as karma, and say, "It is fated." Perhaps it is his karma to have a building collapse around him and yours to rescue him. We must always attend to suffering, never just presume that because everything has a reason, we should leave suffering to fester.

You are asked to keep both perspectives simultaneously, to attend to the suffering of everyday reality and to develop the equanimity, which knows that at the ultimate level, everything is just the way it needs to be. I know this is difficult, especially when there is suffering. You can best help to relieve the suffering by maintaining an equanimity that accepts the experiences that come, not with rage and blame, but with a deep trust in the wisdom of each higher self and its choices. Trusting that knowledge, your love and compassion allow you to work to relieve suffering in any situation while accepting that it is and will be part of human experience.

There are other lessons to be learned here. I have previously spoken about this in terms of those who died in concentration camps, who gave their lives in great love to teach others. They did not choose this at the conscious level, but from the level of their deepest wisdom.

There will be more shifts in the earth and fiercer earthquakes, not just in San Francisco, but all over the world. I mentioned free will before. Humans live on an unstable planet where there are tornadoes, earthquakes, and volcanoes. They must learn to live with this instability if they are to survive. This is one of your universal lessons.

That highway could have been designed to withstand an earthquake. If the earthquake had been a force 9 rather than a force 7, thousands of people would have been killed along the whole length of the highway. Can you understand the gift of these people's lives when seen in this light? Had nobody died, do you think it would have been taken as seriously? As rebuilding is begun, a tremendous effort will be made to better understand the engineering that is required to prevent loss of life in the future. Do not feel sorry for those who have died. Rather, thank them with all your heart for the gift of love they have given to teach others. When they return, perhaps the world will be a safer place.

Let us talk about your own fears here. You cannot get past your attachment to wanting comfort, to wanting the continuation of your home, until you understand where your true home is. Then your present home will be seen with a clearer perspective. I understand how painful it is for you to lose the security of this home, to have to find a new place to live. Go deeper. What might you learn here as you examine your attachments? Try to let go gracefully. Open your heart in trust and faith that the learning that will come from this will be good and will be a positive step on your own path. Look at the now rather than holding on to what is past.

I have little to add to what your heart's wisdom already tells you, other than to assure you that you do understand what is happening to you. For those such as you who understand it, this is a very deep lesson in impermanence. Highways, bridges, and buildings that seem so strong and permanent are gone in an instant. You can never count on anything to be the way it was a moment ago. All things are impermanent. It is a reminder, and a strong reminder, that we must seek true peace in ultimate reality, not apparent reality.

Open your heart to that which continues forever, not that which may be gone at the snap of a finger or the shaking of the earth. This lesson is the gift this earthquake gives to all beings. Bless it for its teachings and go on to the work of caring for those who have suffered, rather than raging against that which you cannot change. Allow its lessons into your heart with forgiveness and love.

Marriage

Q: What is the purpose of marriage?

What is the purpose of anything in your lives? This earth is the schoolroom for your higher self as you pass through this human stage of your journey. As with anything else, your marriage has the potential to teach you the lessons you seek to learn. They are often lessons of love, of giving selflessly, of sharing with another, of hearing and allowing yourself to be heard, of knowing and being known.

You have also chosen marriage because of the support you offer to one another. You are both on parallel paths, whether consciously or not. Your recognition of each other's efforts teaches you both. Ideally, your marriage partner is one with whom you can be honest about both your needs and your dreams. You can help one another see with a broader perspective, lifting each other beyond the earth plane to see the path more clearly.

I say ideally. Obviously, many of your marriages are not ideal. There is anger, blaming, bitterness, and pain. Yes, I hear you wailing, "It's not my fault." Stop your blaming for a moment. I ask you to pause and see why you have chosen this. I must remind you that you are always responsible for your choices. You are never in a situation that you have not agreed to, at some level of your being. Just as the person who aspires to run a marathon agrees to the arduous training, so you have agreed to participate in those situations that teach you, even if they are difficult. Your intention is to learn. When the learning process has been slow, the teacher may become more forceful to grab your attention.

Quiet yourself and look within. There must be no self-judgment, just clear seeing. If there is self-judgment, let it be and look beyond it. What are you learning from this situation? You have made this choice, consciously or unconsciously. If you do not understand why, if you continue to cry, "It's not fair!" and place all the blame on another, then you will not learn what you came to learn. So quiet yourself and look, compassionately but honestly, at what's there.

What did you come to learn? I cannot answer that for you, but you will hear the answer within yourself, within your fear and pain. It may not be pretty to see your misunderstandings. It may be painful. Treat yourself with kindness, and forgive yourself for your mistakes. Then honestly try to grow from what you've learned. The same misunderstandings will occur over and over. Learn to greet them with a lighthearted, "Oh, you again," a gentle reminder to reexamine and see where you have lost the path.

You are here to gain maturity and assume responsibility for yourselves, so that you may ever more fully express your divine essence. Your past lives are your higher self's infancy and childhood. Many of you now are adolescents. You long for the freedom of adulthood, but fear to relinquish the dependent child in yourselves. While one part of you longs to grow up, another part of you trembles in fear of the responsibility.

Marriage is one of your tools here. You cannot learn lessons of responsibility and love in a vacuum. The closeness of a living relationship with your spouse, your children, or your parents provides you with an ample place for practice. Before you can practice you must know what you need to practice. Most assuredly it is not blaming one another. Look within yourselves for the answers.

Are you ready to leave a painful marriage? Stop a minute and ask yourself two questions. "Did I learn what I needed to learn?" If so, perhaps you are ready to put the pain behind you and move on to new learning. If not, perhaps you are running away from the pain, but you will not leave it behind with the divorced partner. You'll carry it with you into new relationships until finally you are ready to face your own responsibility for your misunderstandings. Then ask the second question. Is it too painful? Perhaps you know that you have something to learn, but simply cannot face the pain of the situation. It is not wrong, in any moral sense, to move on. Know that you have these lessons still to learn. Perhaps in the next learning situation that you choose you'll be more ready, and the road will be less rocky.

Let us return to those marriages where the love outbalances the pain. You say there is no pain? You are not being honest. You are suppressing those feelings. No matter how much love there is, there is also occasionally pain. But the love in any close human relationship can far outweigh the pain. It is a much more pleasant way to learn.

Your learning does not need to be painful. When you face the same lessons over and over and do not listen to your inner voice, then the lessons become stronger to invite your attention and direct you to focus on the needed learning. When you are in harmony with yourself and in touch with the voice within, you develop the courage and honesty to face your issues and misunderstandings. Then, truly, your learning can be joyful.

A loving marriage between two beings in harmony with themselves provides the foundation for deep learning. The lessons of loving-kindness, generosity, and compassion are the most important for you on this physical plane. When there is judgment and bitterness toward others and toward the self, there is the continued practice of negativity. When kindness blossoms, negativity cannot be sustained. This ending of the attachment to negativity, the resolution of the habit of negativity, is the primary lesson. Love enables you to transcend ego, to move beyond the needs of self-interest, and to serve others. It is a path to the understanding of your oneness with all other beings and with God. Although there will be occasions of conflict in even the most loving marriage, you will both know divinity in the other. Both beings will stretch themselves to become all that they are capable of becoming and will support this effort in the other.

Death, Rebirth, and Karma

Q: What happens when we leave the incarnation?

What is the immediate death experience? Is there a heaven? Is there a hell? One person who had a near-death experience says she knows there are light and spirit guides who come to meet you. Is that heaven? No, it is just light and loving energy. Why give it a name so laden with concept as heaven? Heaven is not a place but a mind state. Is there a hell? Not as a place in space. Hell is being so blinded by fear that you cannot see the light, nor feel the presence of your guides at the time of death. Hell is also a state of mind.

Humans see death as a dark tunnel. They see an abrupt doorway and experience fear of the unknown because they do not know what lies beyond. This loss of memory of transition[9] is the nature of human experience. If you were utterly annihilated by death and could not move through it as part of the ongoing process of your being, none of you would be here. If death ensnared you, trapped you, destroyed you, none of you would be here. Although you cannot remember it, death precedes and follows life. It's a process, a continuing. Dying is safe. You have done it many times.

Life is change and death is part of that change. Do you want to be stagnant in a changing universe? This is not to suggest that you should choose to leave before it's your time, although some do make that choice, and I will speak to such decisions in a short while. Death is not to be feared, but neither is life to be feared. Embrace life and live. Then eventually, you come to that inevitable time when consciousness is ready to part from the body.

---

[9] Taking birth we forget our true spiritual nature. It is as if a veil of forgetfulness has descended and cut us off from the clarity of what we are.

Consciousness[10] continues after death, until full realization is reached and the decision is made to release everything and move into seventh density.[11] The essence of Being can never cease to exist. The personality self,[12] the ego self,[13] and the physical body, of course, will cease. Eventually even the mental body will cease, leaving only the spirit body, which finally will cease to hold itself as any separate thing.[14] Using different spiritual terminology, this is the movement from sixth density through eighth density.

Let us return to the death of the human, the third-density being. Mind and emotion, both of which are elements of consciousness, continue on both the causal[15] and astral[16] planes. The physical body as known on this material plane ceases but it continues energetically. On the astral plane, the physical body expresses as light. Unresolved physical, emotional, and mental distortions are still carried within this light body. This karma is carried on a cellular level and takes rebirth in the next body. In this way, unresolved areas of trauma in the body show themselves again in a new body. The energetic manifestation of the physical body does not fully cease until all karma of that body is resolved.

So the heavy physical body ends. Your light-energy essence expresses itself on a different plane. A certain level of consciousness continues, but identification with the past small ego self dissolves, sometimes partially, sometimes thoroughly. The greater the degree of clarity, of realization of true Being, the less identification there will be with thoughts or emotions beyond this transition.

Within each incarnation, there is a certain confusion that you seek to resolve. It is this confusion, as contracted energy, that expresses as karma.

---

[10] Consciousness: body consciousness ceases but mental and emotional consciousness continue. Spirit consciousness, which we call 'awareness' also continues.

[11] Seventh density: See Appendix A for an explanation of densities.

[12] Personality self: the expression of mental and emotional bodies into the world.

[13] Ego self: the inner expression of the mental and emotional bodies.

[14] Buddhism describes this condition of nonseparation by stating that for the arahat, or fully enlightened being, there is nothing left to create any separation from the Ground of Being. All karma has been resolved on all levels, and everything simply releases.

[15] Causal plane: that plane of being still involved in cause and effect, in karma

[16] Astral plane: an energetic level. This level may or may not be beyond cause and effect. A being on the astral plane but beyond the causal plane still offers expression of energy, but free of karma.

Certain experiences shape your path and this shaping grows karmically from past lives. If a wolf's bite brought death in a lifetime, and at the moment of death there was great fear and hatred of the wolf, those contractions of fear and hatred will be part of the karmic heritage. In the next lifetime you may find yourself in frequent contact with either a literal wolf, or a figurative one, in the form of a human with wolflike qualities. Hatred may arise. As compassion develops for yourself and the other being, the mercy you seek to learn is accomplished and hatred is resolved.

Some of you have complained about the system and said that as you mature, you start to figure things out, feel more stable in your lives, and then you get old and die. My dear ones, you are not here to figure it out, just to live it. To "figure out" is to seek to control. Fear that controls can never know true Being. Only awareness, which rests in total nonduality with All that Is, can know true Being. You are here to embrace life, to live it with love and, above all, to learn.

What you understand before death has profound implications for the way you move through the death experience. If you cultivate an open heart in life that greets the unknown and change with spaciousness—not prohibiting the fear that arises, but inviting fear itself into the spaciousness—then you will be able to move through the process of death in the same way. One develops either wholesome or unwholesome habits and they remain with you through transition.

Your life is a series of thousands of little deaths, little losses, little places of darkness, places of subtle or profound fear that you must enter on faith. All your life you are practicing how to enter that which is just beyond your prior limits. In each moment where you stretch yourself, you come to an edge and are asked to let go, again, and yet again.

Each exhalation is a little death. Do you think that in the entry to death you could experience open mind states that you could not allow yourself to experience in life? Some of you enter new places with force. For example, when jumping from a high diving board, you hold your nose and push yourself: "I must leap!" There is no joy in this leap into the unknown, only a sense of dread. If you are angry and afraid in life, do you think you will cease to reflect those mind states as you die? Some of you have learned to greet the unknown as a growth opportunity; something to open you still further and challenge you to be more than you thought you could be. If you have nurtured the spacious heart and the mind of unknowingness, that heart and mind will cross into death with you. So, your first experience as you cross the threshold will depend precisely on how you have lived your life. If you have nurtured awareness, you will greet death with awareness.

The light is there. Angels, or heaven-realm beings, are there. Can you feel them in incarnation? If so, you will certainly see them as you move into the discarnate state. Does your fear or shame serve as a blinder against knowing spirit while in incarnation? Then it will continue to do so. There will always be loving energy and light surrounding you. You may or may not recognize this light. You may even find it intolerable if you have preferred darkness all your life.

The astral plane has no linear time. Therefore, we can't say it takes thirty hours, thirty days, thirty weeks, thirty years, or thirty thousand years for awareness to open. It takes as long as it takes. If your heart is shut, how long does it take to open? If loving energy surrounds you, how long before you recognize your true nature and All that Is? It takes as long as it takes.

Those beings who have dedicated their efforts to doing inner work, purifying their energy, living their lives as lovingly and skillfully as they can—those who have made real effort to be skillful with their fear and be open to the light of the universe—such beings will feel this light immediately on the next plane. Those who have lived unconsciously but with loving-kindness will also see the light, but awareness of its nature will take a bit longer.

Others will carry their isolation and fear with them and create their own dimness, darkness, or hell. Although they may not experience the light, the veil of forgetting of the incarnative state lifts and there is nothing to prevent them from knowing this light except their own fear. They are surrounded by so much love and such deep caring energy that it's difficult to maintain that fear for long, as measured by your linear time.

When these beings awaken from darkness, even if they spent many centuries of your time in this state, the darkness seems distant. They are aware of an extended darkness lifting and the instant they wake up, even just a bit to the presence of light and of love, the pain departs. There is true grace in this. Separate self is clearly seen as illusion. It's like a nightmare—in the light of the sunny and clear morning, the dream doesn't grip you anymore. You see clearly that the darkness was a dream, and here you are in the light.

The first stage of death is this opening into light and truth. The being may not open fully, but the illusion of the ego self is shattered and one's energy opens to the brilliance of the universe. Again, this process takes as long it takes.

After this stage, you begin to review the life past. You no longer identify with your past self or with any belief that you are that person, but you still have a clear memory of having lived the incarnation and of your incarnative hopes and fears. You may still feel some attachment to the incarnation or anger or shame over situations that developed during the lifetime. With the help of your personal guides and loving teachers, you will look at what one might call a blueprint that you created before the incarnation, a blueprint based on intention and karma. What learning opportunity was afforded in this lifetime? In what ways did you hope to grow and to serve yourself and others? Then you overlay on that intended path what you actually did.

Perhaps you see that you intended to learn deeply about sharing and generosity. You truly learned not to be afraid that your physical needs wouldn't be met, so there was material sharing and letting go, but you were often distrustful and impatient. There was not sufficient spaciousness to allow for trust and emotional sharing.

In this way, you begin to see what was learned and what was not learned, to understand the karma that arose and how the impulse of that continuing energy will create the map for the next incarnation. For some beings, this process of insight is very fast; it may happen in what seems like a matter of days in your time. For others, it seems like years before they are even ready to begin the process. Please remember this longer time is of no concern; there is no rush. There is no sense of linear time.

After looking at this blueprint and understanding how the life unfolded, you begin the process of letting go of the recent life. At first you see yourself still clothed in the body and the clothing styles of the past lifetime. You see your guides in similar bodies and similar styles of clothing. But, of course, these beings are just energy, just light, as are you. You typically maintain the image of self longer than you maintain attachment to seeing your guides and peers as human. In other words, your guides come clothed in familiar faces and bodies; as you become familiar with their energy fields, you cease to need the outer mask and, suddenly, you realize that each of your beloved friends and teachers is truly a swirling energy of light. Then you look at yourself and say, "Ahhhh, it's time to take off the costume. I am also light." This is a moment of great freedom, of letting go of the self.

What happens next depends on the individual. Some beings may race into a new incarnation very quickly. Those who have died sudden, traumatic deaths at a young age are more apt to move into an incarnation quickly. Some may spend a considerable period on the astral plane. Each of you has special areas of focus, special areas of interest. Some of you have been musicians in many lifetimes; some have been dancers, scientists, or healers. You're not stuck in one type of work; you may have many different skills. But there may be something you deeply aspire to learn and you may plan to carry it into the new incarnation. This results in a carrying forth of knowledge and practical skills. It all can be stated in terms of karma, not will, but the effect is the same.

There may be clear seeing of the need to develop more patience, generosity, clarity, or even assertiveness mingled with compassion. As you find the area in which to hone practical skills, you also hone these inner qualities. So, the energy, the light which you come to understand yourself to be—energy expressed as light and consciousness—moves into a learning-serving phase. It is never just one or the other. "To learn" and "to serve" come together. You stay on the astral plane as long as necessary.

In ways I will not detail in this talk, your energy and karma eventually lead you back into a new incarnation.[17] Sometimes there is a sense of readiness to take these outer and inner skills back into incarnation and see how they are expressed within the veil of forgetting. Sometimes there is more sense of hurry, usually imposed from within. Then the skills may not be as evolved as might be hoped. But one can wait overly long, seeking certainty, afraid to take the leap. This pattern is just another distortion. You always have free will. You are not pushed into incarnation by others, but move into

---

[17] The various Buddhist traditions are highly conversant on the topic of death and the resolution of karma. But there is one difference of opinion that recurs even among the Buddhist traditions. It centers around the question: When a being is fully realized, can that being choose to retain the mental body and either return to the earth plane or remain available on the astral plane, as a servant, as a bodhisattva? Some traditions say that what is gone is gone, and there is no choice about what happens after full realization. Other traditions state that the realized master may still return. The idea is that the master refrains from fullest realization, from full arahat status, and thus the bodhisattva vow states, "so long as beings suffer, I will not seek full release." I believe the difference of opinion is partially semantic, relating to the term arahat, and partially derives from an incomplete understanding of this phase of transition.

My own experience is that both are true. What goes, goes and cannot return. That is what I call the move from sixth to seventh density. Once the mental body is dissolved, it is never restored. It's gone. The energy does not cease to exist but becomes like the ember returned to the fire, enriching that fire with its extraordinary radiance, or like the pure drop of water returned to the sea, enriching the sea with its purity. But beings have free will and may hold themselves in the highest level of sixth density, with the mental body still available as a tool and may thereby remain available as a servant, as a bodhisattva. Is such a being an arahat? This debate is meaningless, since all that holds one back is the intention to remain available as a servant rather than go on, also as a servant. One path is not better than the other. One being is not more advanced than the other. Each serves in the ways that best suits its nature and the needs of all beings.

incarnation as you are ready for it and as karma leads you.

Some people hold a belief that there is only karma and no assertion of free will choice involved in the movements into and out of form. Others believe that it is entirely free will choice. My experience is that it is a mixture of both. There is always free will. Because of the complexity of karma, certain streams of karma come to fruition as the result of the free will expression of intention. Sometimes there are seemingly conflicting intentions, such as to serve and learn, and to be safe. At such a time, the prevailing karma determines the movement. Then the being who sought safety may discover that to seek safety through fear, greed, or selfishness cannot truly provide what was sought, and a new intention for service to all beings and for the good of beings may come forth.

You may wonder why descriptions from different traditions conflict. I can only tell you that what I have described is my experience. Perhaps it not so much contradicts as goes beyond what is commonly said. What I have just described is something I seldom speak of. It falls into the category of that which you do not absolutely need to know in order to progress on your path. Yet, for many of you, it is helpful to hear these things so that you can lay aside worry and speculation and refocus on the work you came to do. Much of what I say here is not really important to your work. In the end, all that matters is that karma draws this energetic stream into a new incarnation. Even the idea of rebirth doesn't matter. Let it go. We have rebirth from one moment to the next to work with. That is enough.

I can rephrase what I've said above in a different way. It is all karma. Whatever you have practiced and developed in the incarnation will come forth beyond the incarnation. If you have practiced kindness, beyond the incarnation that kindness will be accessible and will shape your decisions. If you have practiced fear and control, those will predominate. Most have practiced some of each. Any action or rebirth is the result of a variety of karma. Remember that each moment is a kind of rebirth. That which comes from a clear and loving place does not pull you back into distortion. That which comes from a distorted place will thusly draw you back. If lustful sexuality and violence pull at you, then consciousness will be drawn into a new moment or a new body based on that pull. If you have released the roots of grasping, craving, and lust in the incarnation, then the new moment or birth will reflect that release and will draw consciousness toward spaciousness and clarity. If deep loving-kindness and respect are primary, consciousness will seek that as rebirth.

Please understand that it is not the personality self that makes these choices. Consciousness is karmically drawn into its future and this is a kind of choice. Here is a simple example. If you always favor sugar, indulge in such a diet, and choose never to clean your teeth, then at some level you are choosing tooth decay. This distortion is a result of your choices. Your body is drawn to tooth decay because of prior choices. If you have chosen lust and greed, have never addressed these movements in the self nor acknowledged the painful results of this grasping energy on others, you have planted certain seeds. Consciousness is then drawn to situations based on this habit. Whether the situations are within the lifetime or in the bardo state, the state between lives, is irrelevant. The prevalent consciousness draws itself back to replay the situation.

Returning to the progression of experience, some beings choose to stay on the nonmaterial plane for what, in your linear time, would seem a very long time. Fear and love may both be part of the impetus for their stay. Some beings are aware of what they need to learn on the incarnative plane, and of the difficulty in maintaining the level of clarity they need while incarnate. They've karmically boxed themselves in and they are responsible both for creating that tight spot and for moving out of it. They will always receive all the help they need. No one ever moves into an incarnation in which the learning they hope to do is impossible, but some incarnations are more difficult.

For example, if one has been a murderer in many lifetimes or has beaten and abused others, one will move into a lifetime that helps one learn how to be compassionate and live in nonharm. Such beings need not move into a lifetime where they will be directly abused. That is a mistaken interpretation of karma. The patterns of self-absorption and self-centeredness, which caused someone to seriously misuse others out of fear, must be addressed. Karma must be balanced. One does not need to suffer during the process of addressing and balancing. But because of the nature of habit energy, one who brings this fear and self-centeredness along is likely to manifest it and create more difficult and painful life situations, no matter how loving the initial incarnate situation. This is free will, the choice to act out or release the habit energy that invites pain.

On the astral plane, these patterns are understood, but one must balance the patterns during incarnation. This is like the difference between learning to swim from a book and jumping into the water. You read how to do the strokes but eventually you've got to get wet. On the astral plane you understand the confusion, but you have set up such a habitual pattern that it's quite possible you will move back into the old ways when you move back into incarnation. Consciousness is drawn back into an incarnation that seems to address itself to awareness of the pattern, thereby allowing you to change the pattern.

There is not a conscious prebirth decision, "I'm going to change this pattern. This time I will be kind," which carries through into the incarnative state. Rather, because the energy has habitually patterned itself in certain ways, it simply repeats the old pattern. In order to change a pattern of harming others, one must first learn deeply on the physical plane the lessons of interconnection and the insubstantiality of separate self. Although one knows the truth of interbeing on the astral plane, one must still come to that truth as human.

One of the characteristics of karma is that it is habitual. To give a simple example, if somebody pushes you and you move into a rage and push back, then you do it again and again, your energy has set up a certain pattern: when you are pushed, you contract and push back. When you move into a new incarnation, you may be treated lovingly or you may be treated cruelly. In either case, the self-centeredness and the fear of being hurt that caused the pattern of pushing back will still remain, ideally leading you to begin to look at the question, what is this self that you've assumed to be so solid? Sometimes, resistance to change leads one to need to be hurt quite badly before one is finally willing to let go of that solid and separate self and begin to investigate the myth of it.

Because of resistance, you may remain discarnate for a longer period, until you are free of identity with the incarnation. You begin to know the small self as a mere tool, as illusion. Loving energy surrounds you. You dwell in the light. The guidance you need is always at hand. Confidence grows in the possibility of change. When you are ready, you will move into a new incarnation.

When I say that you dwell in the light, please understand that there are degrees of light. You dwell in light which is comfortable and tolerable for you. The frequency vibration of the light body is most comfortable in a certain light or vibration, and it seeks out that vibration. As the vibrational frequency rises through learning on the astral plane, awareness seeks out higher vibration. It's all differing degrees of light. No one feels superior to another because it has a higher vibrational frequency. There is profound respect for the work that each being does at its own level.

Can one continue to live in darkness? Not after taking the first steps out of darkness and looking at the blueprint of the life just past. For some beings these first steps may be very slow, though. Can you choose to reincarnate without having passed through this stage of shedding the darkness? Yes, you can. This is a movement of fear that leaps ahead without pause, not wishing to confront ancient conditioning. The results usually lead to more pain.

How long is the being newly moved to the astral plane available to you who are still incarnate? There is no single answer. A being who has let go of its identity with the past incarnation may choose to remain connected to you; it may become a guide to you. It has free choice. It knows itself to be energy and light but may make the decision not to move deeper into the light or into a new incarnation so that it may serve as a guide to you either temporarily or throughout your entire lifetime. In the latter case, it would be available to you at any time.

If it does not make this choice, it may be available to your awareness for a short time, from a few days to a few decades. If it should find itself deeply in darkness, it would not usually be accessible to you. It will first become available during the time after it has looked at the blueprint of the past life and before it lets go of the solidity of the past incarnation. In some cases it is still available once it has let go of that solidity but, otherwise, it will move off in its own direction. This does not mean you cannot experience its energy, only that it will be less immediately available, truly of a different vibrational frequency.

I say "usually." The one exception is the earthbound spirit that has not accepted it's transition, but clings to the life just past. Such a spirit will be available, not as a guide, but as one who is lost and seeks direction. It will attempt to thrust itself upon those who remain in the incarnation, seeking attention and help.

I want to make it clear as I talk about the continuation of awareness that, as the being moves into the light phase of its being, there is an increasingly pure awareness which parallels the pure heart-mind of which we often speak. Identification with the old self is released. One sees oneself as an interdependent energy, part of everything and not separate. Personal consciousness fades except as it is maintained as a useful tool. For instance, if a being who was a healer moves into the light phase and works with certain techniques of healing, it will maintain enough personal consciousness to retain the intention to carry those techniques back into a future incarnation to the extent that it is able. But the new incarnation is not a continuation of Person A. Person A died and no longer exists. It is a new person who will manifest the karmic stream and retain a certain level of the awareness carried by Person A. Everything wholesome and unwholesome of person A is included in that karmic stream. Nothing is ever lost, including the loving deeds and speech.

Q: What of those who leave the incarnation by suicide?

When they first begin to open to the light, however long that takes, they will experience some sadness that they let go of the opportunity for learning—not anger at the self, just a sense, "Here was a learning opportunity, and I turned my back on it." But, along with that response is a certain respect for the being that was and awareness, "Now I see from a bigger perspective, and I see that the being I was could have stayed there and learned, but it did what it felt it needed to do." There is acceptance, "I am responsible for the choices of that being that I was." There's no condemnation, but a growing compassion which helps the being move further into the light and eventually into a new incarnation with a sense of hope rather than fear.

Sometimes, when you hurt too much, you just need to come home. Have you ever been sick when far away from home, sick with a high fever or a bellyache? Remember how much you may have wanted to come home. Sometimes it is the kindest thing to do, if the sickness feels overwhelming and you feel that you cannot move through it. Just because you die, it does not mean that learning ceases. There can be profound learning on the astral plane, sometimes learning that was not possible during the incarnation because you were so blind and caught in your own misery. But, of course, there is still the loss of that opportunity—a very precious opportunity—to be human, to balance karma and to learn in incarnation. The learning that now occurs on the astral plane still must be carried into incarnation. With few exceptions, only in incarnation is karma fully resolved.

So, the being who has taken his or her own life will usually feel sadness and deep compassion. It is very likely to move into a profound learning experience. This may not be so for a being who was killed through the anger of another. If that being carries its anger over, the sense of rage and blame may entrap it and hold it in darkness for a long time. The suicidal being who intended no harm to another but simply chose that path out of fear and misunderstanding seldom stays locked for long in darkness, while the being who raged and blamed may find itself in considerable darkness. But, at the end there is always light, learning, healing, growth, and readiness to move back on stage again. Give it another try, here are your lines. Raise the curtain. You're on.

Q: What about assisted suicide with someone who is terminally ill?

It's very much the same situation. Perhaps learning was possible. Perhaps if one could have tolerated that state, made more space for the pain, a certain opening of the heart would have been possible. On the other hand, with the choice to depart, hopefully there is a kindness and sense of compassion toward the human who found its situation intolerable. So, there may be sadness, and also a letting go, a resolve to look with compassion at the being that it was and simply let go and move ahead.

Q: Aaron, you have said that a soul doesn't leave a human experience one moment before or after it wants to and that includes suicide. Does it also include murder and all kinds of accidents?

Yes.

Q: Even murder?

Even murder. Some of you are going to be uncomfortable with this. When there is a murder, at some level, the one we think of as the victim has agreed to participate in losing its body. Please remember that there are many planes of being. The conscious level will probably scream, "No!" At that level, you really don't know what's happening.

On one plane, there can be an intention to be safe and to be happy. On a different plane, there is a deep spirit-level intention for a certain kind of learning. These intentions sometimes conflict. Safety means different things at different levels. On the relative human level, safety means not being harmed. On a deeper level, the spirit is always safe. In so many situations you think you're doing one thing, and what you're really doing is something very different. Safety, in the deepest sense, is in learning what you need to learn and resolving the karma that led in the past to unskillful choices and pain. So which safety are we following, that of the higher self or of the relative human? The relative human thinks it knows what it's doing, but it is not truly in charge. Deeper wisdom makes the choice. Therefore we must trust beings and the choices they make for themselves, even when there is disagreement with the choice.

Q. Are you saying death is never an unskillful choice?

Let us not confuse "unskillful" and "painful." On the relative level the choice may create much pain, even suffering. It may seem very unskillful. But on the ultimate level, there is never a fully unskillful choice. Even choices made from a place of fear and hatred are part of the needed learning experience. If you did not need to make that choice in that moment, you would not do so.

---- ⚜ ----

Q: What does it feel like to die?

It is the way you feel when you have stayed underwater just a bit too long. You emerge into the fresh, sweet air that fills your lungs with gladness, and into the sun's warmth, which fills spirit with light.

Looking Within

Q: You talk about the sanctity of all life. I was driving and accidentally killed a squirrel. How serious is this? I feel very guilty.

What does this experience teach you? Was your mind completely on your driving? Could you have been paying closer attention? Guilt is a negative emotion; it will not help you learn. Open your heart to life's lessons compassionately and without judgment. Learn what you need to learn. And thank this small being for its great gift. It has given its life to teach you something important. Perhaps this gift of love was its life's purpose. Thank it with all your heart, and send it your love.

Eden

Q: You've said our lives don't have to be so painful if we learn to pay attention when there's no pain, and I understand that intellectually. How do we learn to pay attention without pain? Can we ever live in perfect peace? If, as you say, things are far less cruel on this planet now than thousands of years ago, and if we continue moving in a positive direction, can this planet eventually be the paradise it has the potential to be? Or must there be pain for growth? In short, can this world ever be a Garden of Eden?

It would first be useful to ask how you define Eden. By this term do you picture a totally pain-free environment where all is provided in abundance, where there is never anger, never illness, never any discomfort of any sort? How can this be? Within the limits of this physical environment, the rain that allows food to grow to abundance also may be disturbing to those who wish for sunshine. Had you in mind a planet where it only rains over growing vegetation, perhaps only from 11 p.m. to 5 a.m.?

I understand what you mean by Eden, but I am not certain that you do. Suffering may be eliminated, but can there ever be total freedom from physical, emotional, or mental discomfort? Can Eden include such discomfort?

Defining Eden in a more realistic way, can your earth ever be free of war, of starvation, of most disease, and of the general suffering of human beings? I answer this with a resounding yes. It is indeed possible. Will you still be able to learn? Again, yes.

You must come back here to the difference we've often talked about between pain and suffering. Pain is just that, pain. It is the physical hurt of the injured or ill body. It is sadness at the loss of a loved one. It is the ache in the heart when one sees the effects of pestilence, war, and famine over the earth. Yes, pain hurts.

Your suffering is created by your conflicts and struggles with pain and all else that arises in your lives. It grows out of resistance to life. Let us use an obvious example here of something that you cannot avoid as long as you are human. No matter how advanced your medical technology, no matter how far you move beyond war and disease and even accidental death, no matter how long you are able to extend the human life, there must still eventually be an end to that life.

For most of you, the idea of this inevitable death causes suffering. Does your Eden include eternal life? Might you not grow weary of this earth or this body and long for change? Would your Eden include the miracle of being able to move into a fresh new body, to return with your loved ones to a new learning situation? My dear ones, that is exactly what you have been given.

Does this opportunity to leave the body and continue on your path need to cause pain? Does it need to cause suffering?

When you struggle with what arises in your life, there is suffering. You want to control life and cannot. You feel helpless and angry. Here is a major source of your suffering. Can you imagine growing old peacefully, knowing that the ending time for this physical existence approaches, and not struggling with that fact? Your difficulty is this: the higher awareness that knows death is safe has been suppressed, and the small self has been given authority. The small self must fear death; that is its end. True Being has no fear as it passes through various phases, but you have not learned to open to that Ground.

Take this to the other areas of your life. Can you imagine being at peace with the knowledge that there is not and cannot be perfect agreement between you and another being? Can you accept that there will be differences as long as there is self-awareness and free will? Your neighbor wants to plant a row of lilacs between your properties as she has a great love for this shrub. You want to plant evergreens. Need this situation lead to anger and then to suffering?

When mindfulness is lacking, there is a clear progression from self-awareness to fear, fear to separation, separation to the need to protect and the arising of emotions such as anger and greed. Can an Eden include such emotions? Along with the physical body on this earth plane there is an emotional body. As long as you are human there will be emotions, no matter how evolved you become.

I have said this many times. It is not the emotion that is the problem, not the emotion that causes suffering, but your relationship to it. Can you see that there can be an Eden and still be feelings of anger or greed, if you can relate with love and openness to those feelings, not contracting around them, not needing to act upon them, but observing them and responding with compassion to the self and to other selves?

What is Eden on earth? It is not a place where there is never anything unpleasant or discomforting but a place where all is recognized to be just as it needs to be.

Let us say that all beings have learned such trust and have let go of the need to struggle. No one is suffering. How do you learn these lessons of love, compassion, and faith? You learn them the same way you do now, but without the added pain of distortion caused by movement toward separation. The faster you can notice separation and respond skillfully, the more your energy flow is harmonious with the flow of universal energy. Then you are learning through love and awareness, not through pain.

So let us redefine Eden. There is nothing given that cannot be gratefully accepted as a source of teaching, as a gift. Thus, there is no suffering, but only a joyful embrace of each moment of learning. The difference is in your perception of what you receive. Small mind says "bad" and you contract. Already learning is limited. Your resistance to the experiences of anger, fear, and greed create distortions that lead to increasingly painful learning for all. Without the fear that leads to greed, would there be any starvation? Without the separation that leads to hatred, could there be murder?

This is your Eden, an earth where each being has developed the skill and love to respond as if there were no sharp delineation between self and other. Eden is not a perfect place but a state of mind where everything is known to be as it needs to be, where there is trust and love.

In that state of mind there will be no famine because when drought or some other natural condition creates less food in one area, others throughout the world will respond with their plenty. There will be no war. There will be increasingly less disease as technology advances to transform diseases, all the while respecting that even the virus or bacteria has a place in the scheme of the world.

The next question is, how will you learn? You do not need pain to teach you, only awareness. You may see separation arising that will lead to fear and then perhaps to anger and greed. When you are able to be aware of the first arising of that sense of separation, then loving options are present. Instead of fearing your neighbor's lilacs and building up a rage at her so that you plant a thick wall of evergreens that will shadow and kill her lilacs and shadow and kill any hope of harmony between you, you will notice the separation and you will communicate with each other. You will do so with love and respect, each hearing the other, each feeling the other's needs and preferences as clearly as your own. Then together you will plant your yards in such a way as to bring both physical pleasure and increasing respect and love into both your hearts.

You ask, "What if we can't agree? What if she's so rigid that she won't hear of my evergreens even while I listen openly to her lilacs? Do I always have to give?"

Here we are speaking of group karma and group learning. You can only learn for yourself. If you have truly learned, then while you may feel sadness at the lack of your evergreens, you will not hate or despise your neighbor but will forgive her and accept that she is not yet as ready to open her heart. You will wish her well on her journey, help her to open her heart as you help her plant her lilacs, and plant your evergreens elsewhere in your yard. Was it really that important that they were planted right there?

How can you help another being learn to listen, to open, to love, when you meet him with resentment or fear? You have a choice about how to respond to this neighbor. What message do you offer in your response? Love can never grow from hatred.

Each being that accepts love and compassion as its responsibility, that takes the care to notice when separation arises, that responds to every provocation as lovingly as it can, is teaching love. As more and more of you do this, the behavior patterns that are considered acceptable slowly change. There is still torture in this world, but there are groups like Amnesty International that work against it, work to bring such inhumane treatment to the attention of the world. A thousand years ago such treatment was taken for granted, and no cry was raised about it. This is but one example. You are all evolving. You are learning slowly, but you are learning.

So when does Eden arrive? It is already here. You just have not noticed it because you have been too intent on self and its fears to pause and look around. When a sufficient percentage of you learn enough, become responsible and loving enough, and learn to master your own minds and emotions, then Eden will be apparent. Like all else on the earth plane, it is a process and not an event. Open your hearts to the possibility of Eden's emergence as you each learn the lessons of love.

❦

Q: Could you talk about the plight of the homeless people in the world?

To which home do you refer, your spiritual home or the house you build to maintain your illusion that the body is all that needs a home? In truth, you are all home. You have never left. The pain of the illusion that you are homeless, in separation from God, is in itself what drives you to pierce that illusion and understand your oneness.

Perhaps the physically homeless have gone one step farther in penetrating the illusion. We cling to material possessions and to the body, not seeing our true selves. Those who face physical homelessness may come to understand the nature of their true home faster because of that homelessness. During severe illness some people have the same experience, as they come to see that their true home is not in this body.

Climbing With an Open Heart

The question has been asked, how do you choose between staying in an old path that has many opportunities for learning but is very painful and moving into a new path? When is continuation a voice of fear rather than an expression of harmonious movement? Does one struggle with what is or find a more harmonious path? This is an area where there's a lot of confusion. I can only offer guidelines, and not hard and fast rules.

No matter which choice is made, there will be pain at times and there will be joy at times on any path. It is as if you walk through woods and emerge in a clearing where there is a sign that says, "Spiritual growth, maturity, and peace: that way." Ahead are the openings to six or seven different paths. Where do you go from here? You start down one of them, because it had attractive flowers growing along it. After a while, the ascents and descents become steeper. The rocks are sharp and frequent. Some of the ascents require real climbing. Your fingers start to bleed. Finally, you say, "I have had enough of this path. It's too hard," and you return to the clearing.

Now there are six more paths. Here's one with beautiful, leafy branches overhead. You start down, and, oops, here's a river. "How do I get across?" You find a raft and start poling. But the current is fierce, and you're afraid. You pole your way back to the shore and walk back to the clearing.

Try a third path. You may think, "The prettiest paths did not work out; I'll try the ugliest one this time. Here's one that looks brown and muddy." A mile farther on, it still looks brown and muddy. Another mile, it's still brown and muddy, flat, messy, ugly. You are bored with this one. It's passable, but not very interesting. You return to the clearing.

You look around. "I avoided this one because it starts off with a steep hill; maybe I'll try it." After you climb the hill, there's a spectacular view on top Then there's a cliff, a sheer descent straight down. There's a rope ladder. "No!" Back to the clearing. Is there any one path that will take you through without formidable obstacles, with continued interest and beauty? If it is there, I've not found it, but we must remember that "obstacle" and "beauty" are states of mind.

Let us say you've explored all these paths, and you're back in the clearing. What are your options? You could forge a new way through the woods, steering clear of any path at all. Perhaps you can skirt around the mountain and around the mud, or find a shallower place to cross the river. Or you could just pick a path and follow it. What about that steep descent? Can you climb down that ladder? How about the river? Surely, if there's a raft there, there must be some way to get across. Can you do it?

To what extent is fear dictating your choice to seek a new path? What is the fear? How aware can you be each time fear arises? How clearly can you assess your own skills? You don't need to climb down a sheer drop on a rope ladder when you know you are incapable of that and that halfway down you will fall and get hurt. If it's too hard, you do not have to do it that way. That's why there are so many different paths.

Let us come back to real life experience. Perhaps you're in a job or relationship that is painful. What are you learning? Have you reached a point where you have worn all the skin off your fingers trying to climb? Your hands are bleeding, you are truly in pain, and you say, "I can't live with this pain any more. There must be a clearer way through." Where are you at that point? Do you hate the pain? Do you hate the catalyst for the pain? Is there much anger at yourself? Then fear is at the root of seeking that easier way.

Or, does the "that's enough" come from a place of self-respect and respect for the other as well? Such respect allows an acknowledgment, "If I'm in this much pain, this being who is the catalyst for it is also in great pain. We're heaping hatred and anger on each other, and it's reached a point where healing feels impossible right now. We need not live with it any more." The clear heart doesn't feel the separation of "that being or situation against me." The open heart says, "I can be more gentle to all beings, including myself." Can you see that the same choice to move away is then made with love, not with fear?

What if there is fear? Can you acknowledge that and greet it with mercy and not disdain? Can you extend love to this being who is afraid?

Of course there is another possibility, that it is painful, but along with the pain, you're aware of a sense of joy because there's so much growth happening. Then it seems possible that you might continue.

Again, I come back to rock climbing. I don't know how many of you have done this. When one scales a steep cliff, there is often a point where all of the limbs begin to tremble, where you literally feel, "I cannot move another inch. I've got to get myself from this handhold over to there and I can't do it!" Panic may arise, "I'm going to fall!" Or simply discouragement, "There's no further way up. It's beyond my skills."

At that point, you may simply stop and rest a few minutes, acknowledge that this mind-body has been pushed as far as it can go at that moment, and touch it with mercy.

Suddenly, in that stillness, a whole new direction may appear. "There's a handhold I'd not noticed; I feel a bit more energy; if I can get my feet set against that rock and push up, then I can get to that handhold, and there's a little ledge up there on which to rest." Five minutes later you are perched on the edge of a narrow resting space, looking out over a vast valley, feeling exhilarated with the grand view and clear air. You have the sense that you've done something that was just a little beyond your prior limits and you feel a deep sense of joy. Maybe I should take all of you on a rock climbing expedition.

Your daily life situations are exactly the same thing. You reach a point where you say, "I can't do this any more." If there's only grief, fatigue, and a sense that, "I've got to do it because I should, to prove something to myself or somebody else. I hate what I'm doing," then nothing is being learned. At that point you are totally out of the flow of harmony with the universe. The wise thing to do is to step back to a place of self-acceptance and kindness, and at that point ask yourself, "What was it that made me push myself into so much unkindness?"

On the other hand, if you stop, take a deep breath and look closely at your situation, look closely at the places where you're being unkind to yourself, and ask, "Can I keep going?" with kindness rather than contempt, you may find that there are new openings that you never had considered, just as the climber did. You may suddenly find yourself with that exhilarating success of having worked through a serious obstacle in your relationship with your work, with a loved one, or whatever it was that challenged you.

It is a process. You must be constantly aware of where you are in the process. Where are you approaching it from a closed-hearted place of "I should, I must," driving yourself like a slave driver with a whip, and simply increasing the hatred, friction, and pain? Where is there a sense, "I see that growth is possible. I aspire to that growth. There's still love in this relationship, there's still joy in this work that I'm doing, and so I will gently ask myself to stay with it."

You do this not from a place of force, but from a place of love. You notice when love is no longer there, stop and take a break. If love doesn't return, then it's time to climb back down. But the constancy with which love returns to the open heart may surprise you.

Q: Aaron, I am uncomfortable when you use the word touching to mean bringing the mind or awareness to a situation. It strikes me as New Age-y, precious, and imprecise. Who or what is doing the "touching," since there is no physical contact between any physical forms?

I appreciate your question. There are five physical senses and the mind. A body organ touches an object. For example, the ear organ touches a sound. We might say it contacts the sound, and then consciousness arises—in this case, hearing. The mind contacts or touches a thought, resulting in thinking, planning, knowing, and more. Certain qualities of mind, such as awareness, also touch or contact an object. Sometimes the object is a more solid object, like a precise thought. Sometimes it is a more vague object such as discomfort, impatience or sorrow.

In all of these cases, both physical and mental, I literally see the contact energetically. Contact or touching occurs. Regardless of whether the contact is of sense organ to physical object, mind to thought, or awareness to any quality of being, there is an energetic convergence; touching occurs.

To touch with mercy is to bring awareness of the merciful heart and of the difficult situation together. "Mercy touches the pain," is a shorthand way of saying, "The mercy that lies within the heart is drawn forth by awareness and loving intention and brought into contact with the pain." That seems like a mouthful. I prefer "Mercy touches the pain."

Compassion, Nonseparation, and Responsibility

Q: Some people say we should not intervene in others' lives. What we perceive as their pain should not control events or people across the world. If they live with war, that's their karma. If this is so, then what about compassion? What is our role? What should we do about war or famine across the world, if anything? Are we responsible for resolving it or our action that deny others the opportunity to learn responsibility?

There are two issues here, the nurturing of compassion and the balancing of responsibility with nonattachment. Let us take them one at a time. You have said, "What we perceive as their pain should not control events or people across the world." My friend, there is no "my pain" or "your pain." Your lives are totally interwoven with each other. Look at a room in which someone smokes. Others inhale this second-hand smoke. Do you think second-hand pain is any less potent?

Across the world are people living with war, famine, and pestilence. You sit safe in your own corner of the world and wonder, if it's their karma that's led to this pain, why do you need to get involved? There are a number of related issues to explore as we answer this question. Let us look at one at a time.

First, "their pain." What leads us to this illusory space of separation? I am not condemning you for that thought. Thoughts are neither bad nor good; they simply are. But it would seem useful to explore how this thought grows, because the sense of separation does dictate your choices.

Separation grows out of fear, fear that you may be hurt, or that your needs won't be met. You must first understand that there is nothing bad about such fear. It arises because of conditions, among those being a perceived threat and a sense of solidified self. The threat may be real. Perhaps someone wishes to harm you or to take something from you. When you see this, fear arises. The fear is uncomfortable. It leads the everyday mind, associated with the ego self, to want to retaliate against the catalyst for fear. Mind moves into anger, into grasping. When such mind states are present, it feels like "me" against "them" and you feel separation.

When you bring awareness to the way that sense of separation arises, you begin to find more space. That which is aware of the anger is not angry. This awareness is the big mind, as contrasted with everyday mind. Awareness is free of ego, while everyday mind comes from the small self. You see how your identity has connected with that which is angry, and that anger was not who you were all along. You notice there is a point when the heart closes and the illusion of separation becomes solid. You see that this is also just a movement of conditions and not self, just process. From that spaciousness, you begin to notice not just the anger or grasping but the fear behind it.

Here is an important moment. If you are very aware and can see the fear before you move into anger, you may notice the heart closing. The armor pulls across to shield you from pain. To notice takes courage and a willingness to move away from the seeming safety of past patterns. At that moment, if you can allow a small bit of loving acceptance into your heart for yourself, for this being who feels fear, and if you can notice with kindness any judgment of, "I shouldn't feel afraid," or, "I shouldn't feel anger," then you open a wonderful door.

As you allow in a bit of compassion for yourself and acceptance for this being in pain, you allow the possibility of compassion for the catalyst to that pain, be it an individual or a situation. You begin to form a new pattern where arising fear does not need to lead to anger or grasping but can be a reminder for compassion.

When the heart stays open, even if only a crack, there is no need to flee into the illusion of separation, but if such illusion does arise, awareness notes it as "separating" and doesn't buy into its stories. To allow your connection with All that Is means to remove the armor so carefully girded on for protection and allow yourself to be vulnerable. From a place of connection the heart is open; the undefended softness of the heart reaches out to the world.

Of course you may not be able to maintain that state. If fear gets stronger, at some point the heart may close, and the shield draws back into place. Can you accept even that movement with compassion for yourself? When you do, you leave space for the heart to reopen. You see separation as an illusion needed for protection even as you move into it. Then you're back again to fear as a reminder for compassion.

Coming back to your question, when you are clear of this illusion of separation you know there is no such thing as "their pain." You see that label for what it is, the heart's desire to protect itself against pain that seems likely to overwhelm.

Something wonderful may happen here. As you see the whole movement with clarity and come back to nonseparation, as the heart opens, you find a new space you never knew was there. Within this heart we all share, the heart of infinite mercy, is space for all pain. This is not "my heart" or "your heart" but the infinite expression of mercy in the infinite heart of truth and loving-kindness. When you open your own heart, you open to the flow of limitless space and energy. You may still have an occasional fear of being overwhelmed, but deep inside you develop the trust that this will not happen.

Your willingness to allow yourself to be vulnerable makes you far more invulnerable than all the shielding in the world. Can you see that? You can pile on one layer of armor after another, and pain will still creep through and threaten to overwhelm. Look at the sores developing under the armor. How can there be healing? When you allow the pain to move through, when you acknowledge that pain is both inescapable and safe and that you need not hide from it, that acceptance finally allows true compassion to emerge: not "my pain" or "your pain" but the pain we all share, the pain of the universe and all that dwells therein.

When you open to that, you also open to the light, the joy, and the beauty of the universe and all within it. They come together, pain and joy. You cannot close your heart to pain and remain open to joy.

Let's go on to karma. There are those who believe that, because people move into the situations that they've created for themselves in this or a past life, they ought be left to find their own way out of the troubles they have landed in. To give an extreme example, there are those in some cultures who, if a child should fall off a boat into the sea, will not reach out to save that child, but say it is that child's karma to drown. This is a total misunderstanding.

Perhaps it is that child's karma to fall into the sea and your karma to be present and able to reach out and save him. Please never allow another being to suffer without doing all that you can to alleviate that suffering. If you see another being suffering, that suffering is your responsibility, whether you turn your back on it or not. Always. And, yet, attending must be done without attachment. This is subtle, and it's hard.

Some of you work with people who are physically or emotionally impaired, who have serious problems of one sort or another. You have learned that no matter how hard you try, sometimes you can't help that person make a change in their physical or mental condition. Does that mean that your effort is meaningless? Of course not. The meaning is found beyond the physical plane.

I see all of you as light. Just that: light. Some of you give out a very brilliant light, and some of you have a quieter light. You are all evolving toward perfect purity of light. Each act of helping another being, each act of love, of forgiveness, of compassion enhances your own light and adds to the light of the universe. Part of that light is felt as energy, a positive energy that can be felt and experienced by all beings. Of course, each action that comes from a place of fear is felt as negative energy. Each of you has felt this at some time, when you've been with somebody that was very negative and you really felt that negativity. It made you draw back. When you've been with somebody that's very loving, you relax into that love. You feel yourself embraced by it. It's a very wonderful feeling. So perhaps you're not physically able to help a person, and yet, the love that comes from you in the sense of caring does add light to that person's experience and to the whole universe.

It is not always given to you to see the direct results of your actions. Remember, among other lessons, you are here to learn faith. Can you serve, and trust that as you allow yourself to be a channel for love, this love will touch where it is needed?

You may be working with a person who's suffering terribly, and you cannot alleviate that physical or mental suffering. If you become attached to the outcome, saying, "I must make this person better," you create more suffering. Do you see the ego in that "I must. . ."? Yes, perhaps as a physician or mental health counselor, you have the ability to direct that person into healing or to aid that healing physically with your hands. But ultimately, you cannot learn for another person. You cannot heal another person.

Some of you may know of someone who recovered from a disease only to go on and develop another related illness, if there was no emotional or spiritual learning about the factors that brought forth the disease. We see that the person co-creates illness for some reason, perhaps because wholeness is too frightening, perhaps just as habit. All you can do is point out the more wholesome choices, hold open the door, and suggest that he may walk through. That is all you can do. So you must learn to work with nonattachment.

Nonattachment does not mean less caring or compassion, but full acceptance that you cannot learn for another person. You bring your skills to bear, but the person must allow the healing to enter. You still must do the best that you can, just because that's what you must do. Otherwise, you can't live with yourself. This is what you must do. The love that is given is as important as the immediate results. The mind and body are related. Often, that love is enough to lead him to seek the healing he needs.

Now, let's take that to a world situation, a war. Here both individual and group karma are manifest. There are beings that choose to incarnate into a potentially violent society because they have something to learn there.[18] At some time in your many lives, all of you have lived amidst such violence. Several of you are saying, "What about those from this society who are sent to a violent society?" At some level they have agreed to that; they also have something to learn by being part of that situation. Indeed, your whole world is now a potentially violent society, but in some places the flammable material has been ignited, in others the flint has not yet touched off the conflagration. Perhaps it need not.

Those of you who are not living in the situation of political imbalance must learn to approach it in the same way as one working with the being who is very ill. War is an illness. Perhaps you can help heal the illness and perhaps not. But you cannot turn your back on it. In what ways can you help? In what ways can more love be given? In what ways can you add to understanding in the world?

Perhaps the best way that you can help is to find peace in your own heart. There can be no peace in the world while each of you is individually at war. So that is where we start. That doesn't mean that one must just sit and meditate or pray and ignore the rest of the world. There's a balance to be found. You have twenty-four hours in a day; that's enough time to go inward and to move outward. The balance will change for each of you from day to day.

Work simultaneously on many levels. Work on yourself to soften the shielding, open the doors of compassion, create that inner peace. Work politically or through social channels, or whatever ways feel appropriate to you, to touch the world. There is no separation. The world is within you and you are within the world.

Working with the homeless in your own city may not seem to relate immediately to the situation in the Middle East. But think how war comes about in the first place, What are the real issues in a war? You don't need to

---

[18] More in-depth discussion of karma is found in the chapter "Death, Rebirth and Karma".

go halfway around the world to find people who are starving or have a great need. This giving has an effect beyond the local scene. Very often, those who receive need the experience of receiving in order to learn how to give of themselves. Then your giving may multiply, moving in many directions. You have no idea where it will end up.

Let me return to a war situation. I have said very strongly that it is unskillful to turn your back on any being that is suffering, to say, "It's their karma, they created the situation." To turn your back and say, "Well, I didn't create war for myself, and I won't be involved in it," is no different.

You are not your brother's keeper; you are your brother. Pain felt in any part of the world is felt in your own heart, and you can't escape that. Yes, you can escape it by hiding your head in the sand like an ostrich, but eventually you have to face the reality that there is no "my pain" or "your pain," just pain.

You must practice to learn to respond lovingly to that pain, both here and on the other side of the world. But you need to do so with nonattachment, What of a young man whose legs were blown off? Can you accept that you could not shield him from that horror? Can you trust that no matter how painful, it is also an opportunity for him to learn something. In doing this, you do not deny the real pain. At the same time, you need to know that if you can prevent such violence from happening, then it is necessary that you do so. As with the child who almost drowned, perhaps you are the one who is meant to reach out and aid him.

As you do the inner work that enables you to move beyond separation you will begin to notice that skillful action does not arise from a space of, "What should I do?" but from an open heart prompted by deep inner wisdom and not driven by fear. The heart knows how to act. When there is no self-identification with the voices of fear to create confusion, the heart acts without measurement. Choice grows from a place of clarity and love. When fear arises, you may greet it without judgment, invite it into the heart, and explore it. In this way, you will find increasing capacity for skillful, compassionate, and wise action.

Release from Habitual Stories

You humans have many habitual tendencies that are reinforced by the stories you tell yourselves. One very common habitual tendency is the desire to be the one in control. That need to control is a story based on feeling fear, feeling unsafe. Here I differentiate between a story and direct experience. First there is the direct experience of the physical or mind sense. Then there is the story that is the result of that direct experience plus old conditioning. Feeling unsafe can be both a story and a direct experience. In other words, there may be a very direct experience of feeling unsafe. And then the story that comes out is, "I am the one who is unsafe." When one realizes one is separating oneself from the direct experience, one sees how the story serves to enhance that sense of separation and thus offers an illusion of safety. Feel the difference; it's subtle. The one who thinks, "I am the one who is feeling unsafe," is creating a somebody. He or she has already separated from the direct experience of threat. The armor comes up!

I'll give you an example that comes from my final lifetime, when I was a Buddhist monk in Thailand. There were tigers in the woods where I lived. Once, when walking through those woods with my teacher at a time when I was not fully mature, I heard tigers snarling and I felt fear. But my teacher was just walking. He looked very peaceful. My mind began to spin out stories about how the tigers might attack my teacher and I would save him. They would attack me and he would save me. They would attack and kill us both. These were the stories of one who did not feel safe.

Aware of the stories, I kept asking myself to let go of them, but they were obsessive. I would see a stick and plan how I could beat the tiger with a stick. Then I would think, "No, I became a Buddhist monk, and now I cannot beat a tiger. What am I going to do?" My mind was racing. I was young, a newly ordained monk, and I had not previously lived in the north where there were tigers. We came to the end of our path and settled down to meditate and to rest under some netting that we carried. My teacher looked so at ease that I took heart from him. I decided he couldn't be that at ease if the tigers were really dangerous, so it must be safe. Then I was able to put the thoughts of fear out of my mind.

We rose in the morning and walked on a distance, to a village where we could receive alms. In the village we were offered food, and took it aside to eat. Then I said to my teacher, "This was my first experience with tigers. Your sense of utter safety reassured me."

He said, "Me? Feel safe? I didn't feel safe. I was experiencing a very deep fear."

I said, "Well, how did you do it, how did you keep walking?"

He said, "Well, there was just fear. In fear there are not tigers attacking. In fear there are many of mind's stories running rampant but they are known as stories. There is the physical contraction and the wild mind, and we call the experience fear. What happens to fear when one does not believe in the stories? I saw my fear, and breathed in and out with my fear. I know this fear has arisen from my conditioning, from seeing myself and the tigers as separate. I know it has arisen from listening to stories about tigers attacking people."

This explanation let me see what was possible: that there could be fear, even mind obsessing about fear, and still one could stay centered and not act from fear.

In a sutta,[19] the Buddha offers a teaching to sit with fear and dread and allow the experience of it until it dissolves itself. When we are present with any direct experience, it will dissolve. It is all impermanent. We can work with the great wisdom, "Whatever has the nature to arise has the nature to cease,"[20] including fear, including anger, including greed. With the direct experience it's always workable. It can be very intense. It can be very difficult. But it is workable.

Stories can go beyond workable and overwhelm us. Then, depending on your karmic tendencies, you may find it hard just to sit with the fear and allow the experience of it until it dissolves itself. Your mind runs off with the stories and then into the idea of being the powerful one in control, or the helpless one, the victim. Then you act out the personal expressions, your particular way of being in the world. If you do it often enough, you are convinced that this is who you are: the victim, the helpless one, the hero, the

---

[19] Bhayabherava Sutta.

[20] This line is from the Buddha's first discourse, the Dhammacakkappavattana Sutta.

powerful one, or the one who has to save everybody. It's very difficult being stuck in those narrow niches. What a burden, always to have to be the victim or the savior, the good one or the bad one.

So our first step here is to get to know the stories as stories. When the stories arise, we ask, "What is the direct experience here? Can I stay with that?" The direct experience is in the moment. Fear is about the envisioned future or the remembered past. Stay in the moment.

You don't have to know exactly why the story came, at least not at first. You just need to recognize, "Here is a story." One useful question is, "If this story were not here, what might I be experiencing?" The monk that I was did not want to experience his vulnerability. He did not want to experience the fact that he was just one creature walking through the forest. It made him feel weak and unprotected.

Instead of being present with the fear as his teacher had been, his way of dealing with fear was to create stories that made him feel powerful again, powerful either in killing the tiger or even in being killed by the tiger, because if he is writing the script, he is in control, even if he gets killed in the script. Interesting.

When there are stories, know they are stories and ask your self, "If this story were not here, what might I be feeling?" Another part of this is to watch the habitual tendencies and get to know them. Watch how you react in a very patterned way in different kinds of circumstances. For example, as one of you experienced today, somebody walks up and begins annoying you. You're trying to sit quietly and meditate and he starts asking you questions. "What is this place? Who put the animals there? Did you see all the geese in the lake? What are all these people doing walking around silently? Nobody's talking—a bunch of freaks! What's going on here?"

So this person is pestering you. The tendency might come up to push him away. You refrain from pushing him physically, but you snap at him. You tell him, "Shhh! This is a silent retreat. I don't know anything. Go away." Your heart is closed. You snap at him.

So he leaves and you sit back on your bench, and a few minutes later there are some mosquitoes nipping at you. Now, you're sitting by their lake. To them, you're lunch. They're just being mosquitoes. But no, they're picking at you, and they're annoying you just like that man did. Just as you didn't literally slap him but expressed anger, so you may not slap at the mosquitoes, you may just brush them away, but with irritation.

You come inside where it's screened and you sit. The mosquitoes have left some bites, and there is itching. Noting, "Itching, itching, itching," and,

"Tension, tension," as anger comes up. There is rage at the mosquitoes for biting you. There is annoyance at your own skin for being inflamed. There's no compassion anywhere. This is a habitual tendency that has developed, a way of being in the world when you feel violated in some way.

Maybe it had some roots in your childhood. For example, maybe you had a bully living next door. You were three years old and he was four, bigger than you. He came over and pulled away all your toys. You learned to grab your toys and run inside as soon as you saw him, before he came close and did anything. You would see him come into the yard and say, "No! You get out of here!" If you yelled loud enough, sometimes he would leave. So maybe that is the way the seed was planted.

Let's look at another person. She's also sitting on the bench here trying to meditate. Our same driver with a carload of little children drives up. "What's going on here? Why the animals? What are these geese doing here? What are all these people doing here?"

Now this other person has a different kind of habitual tendency, to withdraw completely, stifling any irritation she feels. She feels she has to be pleasant, so she smiles at him and says, "I don't know. This is a retreat. The animals live here. It's a wildlife refuge." The anger is really almost not felt.

He goes on, "What about all these people walking around and nobody's talking? Weird people. What's all this?"

"Oh, they're meditating."

She's not really being kind, she's imitating being kind. She's squelching her anger. She wants to say to him, "I'm meditating too. The public animal rescue compound is across the road. Please go there and let us be." But she doesn't know how to say that. Maybe she had the same bully as the neighbor; maybe she lived on the other side of him. When he came to her yard what she learned to do was be meek, to hide her feelings. The only way he wouldn't hit her and take her toys was if she swallowed her feelings.

The man goes away, and the mosquitoes come and they attack her too. She sits there sweetly and says, "Oh, I just ought to let them bite me. After all, they need to eat." But her heart's not in it. She's separating herself from herself and not allowing herself to feel, "I don't like being bitten." What's appropriate? I would go get a long sleeve shirt or some bug repellent. But she has a different habitual tendency.

When she goes into the meditation hall, the mosquito bites itch. She continues in denial and withdrawal. It's very unpleasant, almost painful, but she can't acknowledge it.

I'm giving you simplistic examples. Of course, situations go far deeper.

One who was abused as a child, for example, wanted what all children want, to be loved, to be valued, to be heard. The abuser hurt the child and told the child, "It's because you're bad." Perhaps intense rage came up in the child. But the child could not express that rage. In order to feel valued in any way, she had to go along with the abuser, to be the one who was bad, "Yes, I'm bad." It wasn't safe to feel the rage at the abuser so she turned it on herself and became convinced, "I'm bad." Now every time there's a trigger, something that arouses anger, she cannot go to the direct experience of anger. Instead, the idea comes up, "It's my fault. I'm no good." Depression may set in, even organic distortions in the body. So this is the way her habitual tendency expresses itself into the story, with, "I'm bad." When she asks, "What would I be feeling if I were not feeling unworthy?" the answer, of course, is anger, but she's too frightened to feel the anger.

Now, something interesting happens. Years go by. This adolescent who thought herself unworthy begins to learn new things about herself. Perhaps she marries someone who genuinely loves her and treats her with love and kindness. She has children, and they love her. She has friends, and they love her. She begins to see through "I'm bad," to treat herself with a bit more kindness. But anger is still uncomfortable, and the pattern has not been understood.

If the habitual tendency is very deep, if somebody comes along and pushes her or her child, and anger comes up, the whole flow of the habitual tendency that has not been understood brings up powerful feelings of unworthiness, shame, and despair. Although she no longer believes in the story, "I'm bad" on a surface level, she still lacks the ability to go deeply into it and say, "Here is anger." So the trigger is still working. There's no longer belief in "I'm unworthy," but she still doesn't know the direct experience "Anger is here."

Slowly she begins to allow herself to experience the anger. She may come to a point where, when somebody pushes her or her child and anger arises with the thought "I am unworthy", she knows it is just the voice of anger. It still arises, but the anger is just anger and does not bring stories.

Habitual tendencies tend to fall into two basic categories, and the way to work with one depends on which category it is in. Some habitual tendencies are rootless. For example, the one who could not be with her anger and learned finally, "When I feel unworthy, what's really happening is that anger is present," came to allow the direct experience of her anger, and yet the painful feeling "unworthy" still arose.

We don't try to fix unworthiness because no one was unworthy in the first place. When we bring wisdom in, we acknowledge that this story of "unworthy" is the result of certain conditions. If "unworthy" is still appearing, maybe it's just because it's a habit. What happens if you literally say no to it? When it appears, just say, "No, thank you. Here's unworthy right back. I don't need that today." You keep going into it. It takes a lot of patience. You might be the one who needs to be in control, the one who needs to be right, or the one who feels helpless. All of these are old stories. Just let go of them again and again and again.

Sometimes you will find there still are roots. An example would be if unworthiness keeps coming up and you keep saying, "No, I'm not going to buy into that story line today," and yet mind keeps obsessing. When you touch deeply upon the anger and allow yourself to feel the anger without judging it, if the unworthy sensation has no roots, it will go. If it stays, there then there's still some kind of root, maybe a judgment, "I shouldn't be angry," or a fear, so that you are not able to let yourself experience the anger but only the concept of the anger. Maybe there is some hidden, painful memory from childhood. So there is something there that needs to be looked at. This is what I mean when I say it may have roots.

If when we look at an object with spaciousness, wisdom, and compassion, and it doesn't dissolve, then one might assume that there is something there that needs to be investigated. But don't investigate the resultant story, which is the unworthiness. That doesn't get you anywhere. Investigate the conditions, the direct experience, which is what gives rise to the result. If you go to the result, you're just trying to control things, to get more comfortable. You can do that forever, and nothing is resolved.

Go to the direct experience with kindness, with gentleness. You are not trying to fix yourself or fix anything. You're not trying to fix unworthiness because nobody was unworthy. You're not trying to change the anger, fix, control, or get rid of it; you are just bringing attention to things as they are. It is in this clarity that freedom can be found.

When you see how things are, that the sense of the badness of your anger is from a thousand memories of people saying, "Shame on you for being angry," and how you used "unworthy" as a smokescreen, then wisdom has an opportunity to develop. You see how you believed this thought to be a personal truth, although it was just created by the flow of conditions. This gives rise to that, giving rise to this, giving rise to that.

Here is where we come to understand not-self, not me or mine. This is a shorthand way of stating that what arises in this mind and body is the result of conditions and not the fruit of one separate ego. When fruit grows on a tree, it is not because it is a good tree, but because all the necessary conditions of seed, soil, water, sunshine, and more were present so that the fruit comes into being. When fruit fails to grow it is not a bad tree; the necessary conditions have not developed. I am responsible for what arises in me, but what arises is not identified as the result of a self. Whatever has the nature to arise has the nature to cease and is not me or mine. With that knowledge I still laugh and weep. But with that knowledge there is enormous spaciousness and freedom. It is not a freedom built from convincing yourself of something. It's a freedom based on truth, on direct experience of how this conditioning of mind and body work. What happens is that pure awareness creates a large container in which all the shame, grief, fear, and anger can float.

Habitual tendencies may continue for a while even after there is deeper insight into them. You can't chase them away; the attempt just gives them energy. It is like trying to hit swarming bees to make them leave. Your action just stimulates their reactivity. If you sit quietly, they will go. When you have attended to the conditions out of which these results have grown, there's nothing left to feed them.

It's like taking a tree and cutting off its roots, not cutting at the trunk of the tree but destroying the root itself. I cut all its roots. I cut the conditions out of which fear and negativity spring forth. When I know that my fear of the bees stems from earlier painful experience of swatting and of being stung, I cut the root of that fear by bringing awareness to it. As the fear dissolves, the impulse to swat the bees lessens. Finally, there is only compassion for the bees.

Habit energy is like the tree, which may have enough root structure to stand up, but there's nothing to nourish it any more, and so eventually it dies. Because you are still incarnate and experiencing, the trunk of the tree is not cut, but this awareness and presence cuts the long taproots. The habitual, karmic results have no more nourishment, and they die. It is in this way that we abandon the unwholesome mind states, abandon anger, greed, and so forth. Kindness cuts the roots. When the tree dies, all that's left is kindness.

Working with Depression

Q: Why am I depressed, Aaron? What do I do about it? If my learning doesn't have to be painful, why is it painful? I think I'm paying attention, but there's still so much pain.

My dear one, you are light. Each thing seeks its own kind: light seeks light, darkness seeks darkness, joy seeks joy, and sorrow seeks sorrow. When you're fully able to enter into the experience of yourself as light, everything seems lighter around you. You know yourself to be part of that Ground of all love, call it God or whatever you prefer.

If you have a beautiful flowering houseplant with lush green leaves, and you put it in a dark closet and forget about it for several weeks, except to open the door and pour in some water, what happens to it? Will it thrive? Each of you takes yourself for hours or even for days at a time and shuts yourself off into a dark closet. Your fear and anger are walls that enclose you and shut off the light. Then you ask me, "Why am I depressed?" How can the light get through?

What is this darkness? Your fear is opaque. It assumes solidity. You find it so hard to have compassion for this dear being who is afraid. When fear arises, it is followed by judgment, "I shouldn't be afraid." Then the fear is suppressed and you move into anger or greed with the same, "I shouldn't...." By this time the light is thoroughly walled out.

It is not the emotions that bring the darkness, but your reaction to them. To feel heavy emotions and have compassion for the being that you are, in pain, does not block light but invites it. To feel heavy emotions and dwell in those without awareness shuts out all light as effectively as if you were the plant in a closet.

Connection reconfirms light. Separation enhances darkness. When judgment against feelings arises, it separates you from yourself and, of course, from the light.

Can you begin to see the depression not as a cause but as a symptom, so that you begin to recognize the process? "I'm depressed, I need light." Perhaps that recognition can lead you to see the walls of fear, anger, shame, jealousy, judgment, or greed with which you've surrounded yourself and to ask yourself, "How can I open some window shades and allow light in here?" You can do that, but in order to do it, first you've got to recognize that the shades have been drawn, that the walls have gone up. For many of you, that is the most difficult thing to do. The judgment is so thick. The darkness offers an illusion of a safe hideaway.

Why is it so difficult? If we are beings of light that yearn for the full experience of light, what is this attraction to darkness? In your pain, you seek that which will confirm your feelings. When anger arises in you, and you judge that in yourself, saying, "I'm no good, I shouldn't be feeling anger," that "I'm no good" seeks to confirm itself through experience. It actually makes you reach out and find those experiences that prove, "Yes! See? I really am no good."

As you judge your heavy emotions and deepen the anger at yourselves, the walls get thicker. Not even a glimmer of light can shine within.

It is as though you hide in a safe tunnel, putting up strands of protection in the doorway. They wall out all that you fear would harm you, and thus serve to defend, but they also wall out the light. For example, feeling another's judgment, you move into anger. Anger protects you from the pain of feeling judged and from all your self-judgment. It separates you from yourself and from the one who judged, and it blocks the light.

You can begin to dissolve these protective strands of anger, greed, and so forth. You must do it with utmost gentleness, recognizing that each has been placed for the purpose of defense. You need not tear them all down and stand naked and vulnerable in the blazing sun. That action would be brutal. Instead, slowly allow yourself to acclimate to the light so that it warms but does not burn.

Work gently. Lift one item at a time and examine it. Regard the wall. "What is this fear? What is this jealousy? Do I still need this judgment? Might I not lift it from the doorway and leave it here beside me? I can replace it if necessary, and I can see how it feels to allow the light to enter, the light of truth."

There is desire for the light. Is there also fear of it? Do you still cling to the darkness for protection? Do you hide your soft and vulnerable heart behind anger, jealousy, or greed?

What if you really are as good and as beautiful as I keep saying you are?

Many of you felt a bit of fear as I said that. Can you start to see what that fear is about? You have each experienced the pain of rejection and defeat so many times. There is such yearning for the light. The thickness of the armor in which you have imprisoned the heart bespeaks the sensitivity of the heart. How badly it has been wounded to seek such heavy protection. How soft and vulnerable it is.

It becomes less painful to believe the light to be unattainable than to reach out yet again and experience defeat. It is the process of "You can't fire me; I quit." You defend yourself by wrapping yourself yet again in your fear and wearing it as a shield.

Each of your higher selves yearns to move fully back into that light, to re-experience that which truly is your birthright. And yet, each of you knows, with deep wisdom, that you have work to do, and that's why you're here. So you move into a misunderstanding in which you see the light, and the very pain of your yearning causes you to push it away. It is what the Christian mystics call "the dark night of the soul." You create situations to prove to yourself that you are not good enough to be in the light—the precious light which you so desire and without which you wither away. It is a very poignant human predicament.

Can you begin to notice the arising of depression and see it as a symptom of yearning to move back fully into the knowledge of connection with light, rather than as proof of your unworthiness to know light? There's a world of difference in that, because when you see it as a symptom of your love, that immediately opens the window shade, maybe just a crack, but enough to let sunlight come in. It reminds you of who you are.

Let us explore other factors in depression. Barbara received a letter from a friend who said that every morning when she wakes up, she does a number of things to remind herself that she is an angel here in a human spacesuit. Depression is a symptom of the claustrophobia of that angel. One feels hemmed in by this spacesuit at times. It feels unworkable. Nothing is as easy as it should be.

Somewhere beyond the conscious mind are real memories of the ease of moving in the light body and the joy of being fully present in the light. Of course incarnation feels claustrophobic. Can such discomfort become a deep reminder of who you are and lead you to appreciate the perfection of the journey? Even depression, fear, and anger are gifts to help you learn love.

There's one more aspect of depression I'd like to talk about. When you seek to confirm a heavy judgment you've laid on yourself and move into increasingly more difficult and painful situations, the heaviness of your anger invites in negativity. There are beings of positive and negative polarization on all planes. And there are mischievous spirits, not beings that are very negative, but beings on the astral plane that are a bit bored. They're young beings, for the most part and they like to participate in chaos. Your negativity is an invitation to them.

There are also beings that are deep in misunderstanding and feed on anger and pain. Your anger and fear invite them in. So, when you move into depression, it's like opening the door and saying to all the negativity, "Come in, welcome! We're having a party." This is no different than seeking out another depressed friend when you feel depressed so that you can feed each other's depression.

I'm not suggesting that you say, "I won't feel depressed; I'm not going to let in negativity," because that in itself is negative. When you're feeling depressed, somewhere you have got to open a window shade. That which knows the experience of depression is not depressed. That awareness never becomes depressed. Where does identification lie, in the consciousness that is depressed and sees this depression as self or in the awareness that observes with kind, spacious attention? One way to open the shade is to deepen presence, to invite awareness to watch the depressed self and not be caught with self-identification in such a feeling.

Humor helps. Perhaps you could have a set of Groucho Marx glasses and mustache and you could go and look at yourself in the mirror. Just stand there and stare at yourself for a few minutes until, finally, you have to laugh. "Am I taking myself too seriously?" Anything to lighten the moment, to begin to penetrate the density of those walls that you're pulling around yourself, walls that separate you from the light.

Humans have short memories. As soon as the light is cut off, it's gone. It's so hard to remind yourself, "I really am an angel in an earthsuit, and I really am as connected to spirit as I am to this body."

Think about the ways that you can bring light in when you're emerged in darkness. Each of you will find different ways that will work for you. One may find it wonderful to go outside in the sunshine, take a walk, and reconnect with trees, grass, and flowers. Another may find an outlet by listening to music, or exercising your body in rhythmic ways: dancing, doing yoga, playing ball. A third may seek loving companionship. There's no one best outlet.

When you feel depressed, please remind yourself of the flowering houseplant that has been put in the closet. Ask yourself, "Wouldn't I, in compassion, bring those flowers out into the sunshine? Can I not do at least that much for myself?"

Anger and Other Heavy Emotions

Q: I feel peaceful while I meditate. Then, a short time later, everything seems chaotic and I find myself feeling furious or anxious or some other uncomfortable emotion. What do I do with these feelings?

First you must be willing to look at the real difficulty. The emotion is just an emotion. Why should it not be there? If the conditions are present, an emotion or anything else will arise. Why should you be the exception to this rule? But you believe it should not arise, and attack it or try to avoid it, and there lies the ground of your suffering. Humans are so hard on themselves. You condemn feelings and fears within yourself that you would meet with compassion in another. You are human. You are subject to the arising of thoughts and sensations out of conditions. The perfection to which you aspire will rarely come forth, and if it does, it will surely not last long. Be loving to yourself. Forgive yourself for what you judge as imperfections. Simply use them as a signpost pointing the way to what you need to learn.

Look at the constant turmoil within yourself. There is so much pain, so many ego needs that grow from your sense of imperfection. You see yourselves as flawed, and constantly try to patch the flaws. You grasp at nearly anything as a possible patch, and then put patches over the patches when the first ones don't fill the gaps. At one stage you grasp at material things as patches. Then, when you see that a new car or better job won't do it, you grasp at spiritual things. You think perhaps more prayer or a new yoga posture will fill the gap. Or perhaps enlightenment is what you need. Even a little bit of enlightenment and you'd really be there; then the pain would go away.

You are driven by fear—fear that you won't get what you need, fear of trusting, fear that others will notice that you're not perfect. You cannot put patches on your fears and pain. You must allow them to heal from within. Only then will you discover that you are whole and have always been whole.

In your essence you are perfect, complete and unlimited.

You take all that you find unacceptable about yourselves and hide it beneath the surface. There, suppressed, it smolders—a slowly burning fire that gives you no rest as you race in circles, trying to escape the heat. Meditation provides a firebreak, a clear space to look at what's burning.

As you lessen your identity with the turbulence in your mind, you begin to notice the fears, resentments, and pain that have been buried there for so long. This is like a personal compost heap. You take all those heavy feelings that have been lying hidden for so long, turn them with the fork of mindfulness and allow air in. Slowly the "garbage," all that you have discarded beneath the surface, becomes the nutrient for growth.

First you must allow for this process of looking at what's been hidden. This must be done with no judgment. Simply notice what is there. Accept all of yourself. Do this mindfully, not just while you sit but throughout the day. This is your first task. Stay with it. Open to yourself with love and compassion.

As this ability for presence deepens, you will notice what is there with greater ease. There will be less need to hide parts of yourself from this scrutiny. This process of looking will lead to some purification, an ability to simplify your life and release those unnecessary burdens that cause you pain. From the greater space of deeper concentration and a purer lifestyle, you will find some wisdom, some understanding. Your increased understanding and freedom from some of the excess baggage will allow you to move to even deeper levels of meditation. And on it will go. It is a process. You must simply allow it to happen by having the courage to accept what you see, without condemnation or self-blame.

After a while, noticing these heavy, uncomfortable emotions with spacious awareness will have become a habit. Now suppose you have just finished meditating and are feeling very peaceful. Suddenly your spouse rushes in with an overdrawn check statement from the bank. He or she is furious. "Why didn't you realize the account was low and put money in?" In the past you would have become defensive. That feeling of being flawed would have pushed you to deny your blame and point out that your spouse wrote the check. There would have been an angry encounter.

This time you approach it with a new feeling of space. You feel angry and notice the feeling. You feel guilty; it is your job to balance the checkbook. You take a deep breath and notice, "Feeling angry; feeling guilty; feeling I want to deny my responsibility; feeling I want to lash out and hurt someone."

Suddenly you understand that these emotions do not define you and do not need to control you. They are not solid; they are just energy passing through. It is not the emotions that create a problem; it is your reaction to the emotions. Instead of lashing out, you're able to handle the situation with greater maturity and responsibility. That does not mean you will not feel anger, only that you will not react mindlessly to that anger. You have more choices and a great space of freedom from which you can choose a skillful and compassionate response.

You may be able to point out that anger is not going to resolve the problem of the overdrawn account. Your calmness will help your spouse settle down. You find yourself able to acknowledge your responsibility for neglecting the paperwork. Calmly you are able to discuss what steps need to be taken to handle the issue. There is no need for blame and anger. At this point you may even notice that you are no longer feeling anger.

Suppose your spouse continues to be angry and blames you. You still have this space from which you can note the feelings—anger, ego need for approval and to be right, frustration that he or she does not seem to hear you. From this space you can notice the continuing anger and realize that there is no need to strike back. You understand your spouse's pain and anger and can relate to it compassionately. Not condescendingly, but compassionately.

Everything that happens in your life is meant to teach you. When you have co-created a situation of anger, you may ask yourself, "Why am I in this situation? What am I able to learn?" Perhaps it is a situation where you truly feel you are not to blame, that you are being victimized. I remind you that nothing happens to you without your agreement at some level. Always your karma draws you to these issues and always you have something to learn from them. It may be that habit draws the situation to you, but as soon as there is awareness of the pattern, your awareness can turn the occurrence into a gift.

Learn to accept yourselves at ever deepening levels, noticing what is there. Do this first in meditation, and extend it to your entire day. Before you can love others, you must learn to love and accept your entire self, including the emotions that cause discomfort. This is a basic step on the spiritual path, learning to love and not to blame.

I am not saying that it is easy. It takes faith and courage and honesty. But you can do it, and your lives will grow increasingly harmonious. Love is the strongest force in the universe. Allow it to be a part of your life. Do not be afraid of your feelings. Accept your whole self with love, that your love may then reflect outwards and shine light upon all beings.

Q: What is the relationship between fear and love?

Love is the natural condition of your being. Fear obscures it. Attend to the fear and you will again experience love. This is not the grasping mind that sometimes passes as "love", but the fully open heart, which is the loving heart.

Anger and Forgiveness

Q: You talk a lot about forgiveness. I'd like to forgive, but I feel so
much rage, I can't get past it. How do I learn to forgive?

Please remember that forgiveness does not mean that you condone what has been said or done. It means that you deeply understand that this unskillful act or verbal statement is the result of many conditions. The person who acts out anger exhibits some misunderstanding. The expression is unskillful. The person is stuck. To forgive him or her is not to say, "What you did is okay," but "I forgive you for being human, for being stuck and expressing your confusion in ways that have hurt me. While I ask you to be more responsible for the expressions of your feelings, I do not separate my heart from you and consider you evil for these expressions. Instead, I attempt to approach this pain with compassion." Thus, compassion is a doorway to forgiveness. The closing of compassion leads to further separation and the arising of hatred and blame.

Forgiveness comes from a space that becomes accessible within you when you have moved past self-identification with your rage and past the impulse to perpetuate that rage or blame it on another, so let us first talk about anger. Anger is thought and energy. It is never bad to experience anger, but we recognize that the anger does create pain for ourselves and others, and so we must be responsible and take care of anger. What is anger? Have you ever stopped to look closely at it? Sometimes rage feels like a solid wall that never be gotten past. Is it really as enduring as it appears?

Anger is a protection. It is your way of feeling less vulnerable or of striking back when you have been hurt or seen harm come to another. Within anger is fear—fear of being hurt, of being out of control, of not knowing how to change a painful situation, and of acknowledging your own part in a situation, because with that acknowledgment you must assume responsibility for your acts. There is often grasping or aversion within fear. Both are part of wanting things to be different from what they are. It is all these ingredients that make your anger so painful.

When you only see anger, it seems like a solid wall. So much rage—what do you do with it? Can you break it into its parts, and see the aversion or the fear separate from the rage? Next time you feel rage, take a deep breath, dive back in, and see what's really there. Fear: where is it coming from? What, exactly are you afraid of? Grasping: are you angry because another has what you want, and it doesn't seem fair? Aversion: this relates to fear as well. What frightens you that you must push it away so strongly?

Fear is not an enemy and it is not bad. Fear lets you know you have moved beyond a safe and familiar place in your experience. Each time you cross the line into the unknown, there will be fear. Let fear teach you, not frighten you. Take it as a marker: New Territory; Be Present.

Do you begin to see that your anger is not solid but is made up of many components? All of them are workable, and none of them is self. They are merely the results of conditions. Therefore do not focus attention on the anger, which is a result, but on the conditions that give rise to that result. Do not feel you must take on every component at once. Just open up a bit and begin to be aware of what's there. You do not need to stone these emotions to death, just to allow them into your merciful awareness—compassionately, nonjudgmentally, gently.

On many levels, acceptance is one ingredient that is missing in most anger. You cannot accept the situation, and you cannot accept the arising of strong emotion in yourself and so you separate your heart from yourself and the emotion. This separation actually feeds the emotion. Anger does not arise simply because of nonacceptance, but because the separation resulting from nonacceptance supports the further projection of anger.

Anger is filled with blame. There may be no room in it for accepting one's own responsibility. That's too frightening. If you are responsible, then you have the ability to make changes. Are the changes more frightening than the anger-causing situation? It is like the prisoner who, being set free, heads back into his cell. There's too much space; he's not ready to handle it. Be honest with yourself, and look to see if that is part of your experience.

Let's stop a moment here. We started with forgiveness. Can you see how impossible it is to forgive while there's still so much rage, so much fear and confusion? So you blame yourself for not being forgiving—just another place to judge yourself inadequate, something else unacceptable that enhances the fragmentation, separating you further from yourself.

No single one of these ingredients is the cause of anger; they are all conditions that may contribute to the growth of anger. Sometimes one will predominate, sometimes another. So where do we begin? What is the way out of this trap of self-blame and rage? The answer is love and you must bring it first to yourself. Let yourself back in to your heart. Sit down with yourself and your fears. I ask you again, what are you afraid of? Let it in. It is not as terrible as it seems. Just notice where it's coming from. What is it that you want and cannot have? What has been done to you that isn't fair? What are you are afraid of doing to another, in the passion of your rage? Take all this emotion that you've labeled unacceptable and buried and let it out; let the sun and air get to it.

Do you see how you get caught in the story to avoid looking closer at the emotions? "But it's his fault …," or "She started it.…" Yes, that's fine. But now what do you do about it? You can blame and rage forever, and perhaps the other being will acknowledge its responsibility and perhaps not. That is irrelevant. The question is not who is to blame but where is healing to be found. It is fear that wants to hold on to the stories, blame, and contraction. A deeper wisdom asks you to step past these old holdings of mind and body and open to new possibilities.

Healing can only come from within you and you can only heal yourself, not another. Do you want to continue on in rage? Do you enjoy the suffering? It's your choice. Nothing ever happens to you without your agreement at some level. Why are you in this situation? What did you come to learn here? Are you finally ready to learn, or do you choose to go on with the blaming and the anger? It is always your choice.

When people have wronged you and you feel hurt because of their unskillful acts, let your pain be a reminder to love. Allow another's anger to be an invitation to return compassionate understanding for their pain. Look at your fear and anger and hurt and make a decision that you can move beyond it, that you can choose love, first for yourself and then for another.

Remember that compassion is strong. It does not ask you to allow yourself to be abused by another. Compassion knows how to say no, but it speaks from kindness, not from fear. It says no in order to serve and to heal, not to control or destroy. Remember also that anger is energy and can be used to support such attendance to abuse without enhancing hatred. Kindness knows that it must not sit back and tolerate abuse, for that is a way of participating in the abuse. Anger is not a necessary force here, but if anger is present it can be transmuted to skillful use.

How does forgiveness begin? Since blame involves separation from yourself, first you must forgive yourself. Accept that you are not perfect. If you have made mistakes and have acted in unskillful ways, those errors are part of your learning. Let them teach you, not about hate and blaming but about acceptance, forgiveness, and love. We are not talking here about suppressing the anger, the feelings of unfairness or hurt, but of finally acknowledging that these feelings are real and that dwelling on them enhances them and causes more pain.

You must first acknowledge the pain; love yourself enough to move beyond it. You cannot transcend what you do not accept, and you cannot accept what you've feared to acknowledge and buried. We are talking of honesty here, of opening to yourself, not of closing down.

You are all so afraid of all that you've found unacceptable in yourselves, all that you've had to bury. The fragmentation has torn you apart. You are at war with yourselves. Now it is time to see through this skillfully. Decide to end the war, to create peace, to allow room for love and forgiveness.

Having reached this point, sit down with yourself and, saying your own name, tell yourself, "I love you; I accept you; I forgive you; I welcome you back into my heart." You may continue, "I am whole and am a being of love, a being of light. All the emotions and fears that have made me put myself out of my heart, I acknowledge and accept and forgive. There is nothing that is unforgivable, if it is opened to with love." I recognize that the verbal statement does not bring forth the opening of the heart. It merely states the intention that smoothes the way for the possibility of the opening.

Now reach out and repeat this statement with the being who has hurt you. Feel the space in that potential for forgiveness. It does not matter who was to blame—that is beside the point. Feel all the space that surrounds your intention to forgive. There is no wrong or right here. That is not the present issue. Remember that forgiveness does not mean condoning what was done, only letting go of all the stories about the incident or the words, releasing blame a bit so as to see how the painful situation arose out of many conditions. The only real issue is whether you choose anger and fear or love. That choice is always yours. But know that where there is love, there is healing, and that is what you came for.

Q: Is my anger bad or wrong?

No, my dear one, it is never wrong to feel. It is immature and unskillful to use your emotions as an excuse to injure another.

Anger as a Catalyst for Compassion

Q: Please talk about anger. Is our anger ever useful? If not, how do we
get rid of it? It seems that without righteous anger, we'd let many
more social problems go unsolved.

Your anger is not good or bad, it's just anger. Let's start with that. Anger
contains energy that can be transformed into skillful and loving action,
but first you must understand your dislike of experiencing anger or any heavy
emotion.

You ask, "Isn't anger bad in itself? When I'm angry, I give off negative
energy, and that can hurt people." That is true; when you're angry, you do
give off negative energy. Are you going to stop the arising of negative energy
in yourself by saying, "I'm bad to be angry?" Can you stop a river from
flowing? Can you stop a cloud's movement across the sky?

You can control the flow of reaction toward another, but can you shut
off the feeling of anger in yourself, really get rid of it? Or do you merely
suppress it? In terms of energy flow, if you suppress it, it's just as present;
it's simply hidden beneath the surface. Yes, it would be skillful to transform
it into positive energy, but such transformation will never happen through
judgment and suppression. As long as you try to rid yourself of your anger,
you are still controlled by that anger.

It is not helpful to feel you must eradicate all anger, greed, jealousy, or
pride, because as long as you are in a human body, there will be catalysts that
arouses those emotions. I'm not suggesting that you simply allow anger or
greed in and act upon it. Can you develop a different relationship to them?
There are more than two choices. You need neither to act upon them nor to
suppress them; just bring gentle awareness to them.

When someone speaks or acts in such a way that anger arises in you,
can you stop and look? What is this anger? Ask, "Does it relate only to

the catalyst or does it also relate to my dislike of this emotional turmoil in myself?" It is so inconvenient and uncomfortable to experience anger. In your slang, it pushes all your buttons. You fear you'll be driven to act on that emotion, and with that fear, you judge yourself as if you had already acted. Do you see that judgment? Another way to ask the question is this: is the anger related wholly to the catalyst or is part of the anger about the fact that there is unwanted discomfort that came to you through what this person said or did? He or she left rocks in the road, and it made your cart lurch. You wanted a smooth ride.

The issue of suppression versus reaction versus simple awareness leading to wholesome action is easier to see with greed. Take a situation where you missed several meals and you're feeling very hungry. You walk into a room, and there's a child with an ice cream cone. There's a great sense of longing, "I want that, I'm hungry!" You know there's no danger that you will reach out and grab the treat from a small child. None of you is going to do that.

It's not hard for you to say, "I'm feeling hunger. I'm so hungry, I feel I could reach out and grab that ice cream cone and eat it. I really want that." You don't hate yourself for that feeling. You just note, "feeling hunger, feeling greed, wanting the ice cream." And you walk on, perhaps deciding that you'll stop and get something to eat. Here is the emotion of wanting transformed into skillful action.

Why is anger so different? You feel anger arise and you want to lash out at somebody. Most of you are not going to lash out and hit someone any more than you were going to take the ice cream cone. That doesn't lessen the intensity of wanting to retaliate. Then you come to the judgment, "I shouldn't feel this way, I'm bad to feel this way."

Were you bad to want the ice cream cone? You were feeling hunger and desire. Now you're feeling anger. Are you bad to want to reach out and hit somebody? You don't have to act on that, and you don't have to suppress it or hate yourself for it. Anger is just anger. Why make it more than that? You have not been conditioned to judge yourself for desire, but anger is another story. Can you see that they are both uncomfortable feelings but your response to them is vastly different? What is this conditioned mind? How are you a slave to it? Where does freedom lay?

As you notice the intensity of the angry feeling, you might begin to see what lies behind it. Anger is a mask. Behind it, you will often find fear. Fear that your needs won't be met leads to grasping and clinging, to jealousy and selfishness. Fear that you are going to be hurt arouses a need to protect the self. In that need to protect, anger arises with its rush of adrenaline.

Thousands of years ago, your ancestors may have felt fear, perhaps of an attacking wild animal, and a sense that they or their children or friends could be hurt. With that rush of adrenaline came a rising of the hand and a desire to kill, followed by a throwing of whatever missile was at hand to kill the wild creature before it killed them. You have had much practice with that process.

Now you've evolved to a different level, but the same habits come to bear. When fear is experienced, the body reverberates with so many echoes of past danger. There is the constant question: "Could I be hurt?" When you feel threatened, fear arises and anger often follows. In these days it's rarely a physical threat, but the process is the same.

As you observe deeper levels of the process, the solidity of the emotions changes. It's no longer a solid mass with which you must do battle. Instead, it becomes just anger. When you notice it early, just noticing the first tightness in your stomach, then you understand that it is anger arising in you, and you can be present with it with less reactivity.

Many mind states pass through you every minute. Some of them are painful, and you may react to that pain. To free yourselves from reactivity it's useful to see the arising of such mind states as part of a process.

Central to the teachings of the Buddha is a natural law called Dependent Origination. Put in simple terms, for something to arise, the conditions for its arising must be present. When conditions are no longer present, that which has arisen dissolves. Understanding the process of how things arise and dissolve isn't mere intellectualization but is vital to your lives. Even more, it's a keystone upon which you may begin to act more skillfully and to free yourselves and others from suffering.

Let's look at the process by which you move to any emotion, painful or joyful. What really happens when you feel anger, desire, or even bliss? How do you move into the experience of emotion?

To experience anything, first there must be contact of sense to the sense object and consciousness of the contact. Let's call these steps contact and consciousness. For example, your eyes touch on the object of sight; you're not separate from that object but a participant with it in the act of seeing. In this way we become aware of seeing, hearing, smelling, tasting, and touching. In the same way the mind touches the mind object, and thinking is the resulting consciousness.

You may label the experience—hearing a cough, seeing an angry face, or if mind is the sense that made contact, perhaps knowing, remembering, or understanding. We can call this stage perception, perceiving what the senses have contacted. Notice that there's still no attachment or aversion. The experience is still neutral. There is just hearing, seeing, feeling, memory. But mind usually does not stay there.

At this moment of sensation, feelings may remain neutral or there may be a move from neutral to pleasant or unpleasant feelings. Then comes the instant we call the active moment.[21] This moment is partially conditioned by old habit and partially grows from wisdom. It is a moment when awareness may overcome conditioning. It involves the habitual way you may relate to the unpleasant with the arising of aversion, or relate to the pleasant with the arising of grasping. You may experience a tightening in the belly that's the first physical signal of aversion, or a sense of expansion of the heart that may be the physical sign of joy or bliss, perhaps followed by grasping.

If feelings remain neutral, equanimity may be experienced. There may be brief contraction and that also is noted and not made into a solid self. The experience is like entering cool water for a swim. With the cool touch, there will be contraction, but it releases almost instantly. Equanimity is back.

If there is strong feeling of pleasant or unpleasant and no equanimity about the feeling, you move to mental formations such as fear, anger, or craving. This movement from contact to mental formation happens in a flash, so you may not see the steps. One wise teacher likens it to falling from a tree. You don't have time to note, "seeing branches" as you fall; there is just the falling and then, thud! Ouch! It's important to understand that the feelings and ensuing mental formations do not just happen independently, but are the result of all your past conditioning.

What's the significance of coming to see that? When there's strong emotion and you understand with some clarity how it arose you have much more choice. You do not have to react to emotion or suppress it; you can just be compassionately, nonjudgmentally present with it and watch. "Whatever has the nature to arise has the nature to cease" and is not me nor mine.

It seems important to understand that it's not the emotion that causes the intensity of your discomfort, but your relationship with the emotion. To have inner peace doesn't mean you never feel, but that you are at peace with whatever arises. It is quite possible to simultaneously experience anger and compassion. Your compassion is not only for another, it is for yourself as

---

[21] Active moment: past conditioning creates the way the present moment is experienced. This present moment is called the active moment because it is the point that shapes the future. For example, if in this moment you see rage with spaciousness rather than more negativity, that changes the way rage will be experienced in the future. It is a karmic turning point.

well. Judgment about your anger is what separates you from the deepening of compassion and from your true nature, not the contraction we call anger in itself. Can you be present with anger without hating the anger? When you hate your own anger, that's just more hatred.

You ask about righteous anger. Perhaps you've been with a prejudiced being that spoke in a negative way about those of another race or religion, and it infuriated you. There was a thought, "I've got to teach this person. How dare he speak that way?" If he says, "That's bad," and you say, "No. It's good," he can't hear you. You crash into each other. There's no room for communication, which can never come from a place of hatred.

What might happen if you hear the person who speaks with prejudice, and, as rage rises in you, you meet that contraction and touch it with a bit of compassion? Here is a simple reminder of our joint human fallibility, and of our interconnectedness. We are all in this together, both as beings dependent on each other here in this earth plane and, more profoundly, as part of the great ocean of love that cannot be separated into individuals, no matter how much we wish it could so that we could blame the other. Then you know you are both feeling fear and you see his prejudice in a new light—not, "He shouldn't feel prejudice," but "Why does he feel prejudice? What are his fears?"

Can you accept that if his prejudice arouses rage in you, you also have fear, different from his in specifics, perhaps, but still fear? Can you meet fear with the openhearted question, "What are my fears? Why does his speech arouse so much anger in me?"

As compassion leads you to hear his fear, then communication becomes possible; change becomes possible. This is the basis of compassion and unconditional love—learning to watch fear and anger arise in yourself, and asking without judgment, what is this anger, this fear? Such reflection is a movement of generosity and kindness. The practice of *bodhicitta*,[22] of generous caring for others, nurtures it. When awareness sees the arising of anger, it is not caught in the anger. You step outside your personal story and look with wisdom and compassion. Until you can be compassionate to yourself, you cannot be compassionate toward another. Such compassion is the only real basis for world peace.

So this is a vital lesson that all of you are learning, to relate differently to yourselves and to each other than you have in the past, to begin to notice how anger arises, to begin to let go a bit of the judgment of yourself for being angry.

---

[22] Bodhicitta: when we remember our basic connections with All that Is, our basic goodness, and live from the innate awakened heart, we are said to "practice bodhicitta."

I said earlier that there are two issues—the difficult emotion itself and your relationship to it. Part of what you're learning is to change your relationship to emotions, to feel equanimity with whatever is coming through. Unless you're going to go off and live in a cave, completely alone, you can't control your experiences in large part. Your lives interweave with each other. And, even in the cave, loneliness or other strong emotions may arise. There may be a longing for companionship, or aversion to the snake or spider that shares your space, or to the weather. So, you can't prevent any of that, but you can affect what happens inside when you're experiencing such emotion.

Something wonderful begins to happen as you move from feeling anger and self-hatred about the anger to feeling anger and a calm acceptance. "Here's anger. It will come, and then it will pass." We call this equanimity toward emotions.

With that compassion for yourself, you begin to see another's anger or greed in a different light. That being is feeling anger. Suddenly, you no longer need to say, "I'm not going to let myself get angry" or need to judge another for his anger. There's a shift within you.

The compassionate heart opens when you see another feeling anger and realize the depth of that person's pain. You genuinely don't feel angry. You may think about it later and say "How did I do that? I truly wasn't angry." You are breaking loose from conditioned mind and creating a new pattern for yourself, a new way of being with heavy emotions, a new way of being at peace within yourself. You're learning that your inner peace doesn't depend on external circumstances, but comes from within. And that is a wonderful piece of learning.

You are also learning that all these outer expressions of being—the aggregates of form, feelings, thoughts, and even the stream of consciousness—are not self. You need to be responsible for what arises but you need not take it so personally. As you rest ever more deeply in Being, in Pure Awareness, you see so many thoughts and sensations come and go, and they have no more substance than the clouds that pass you by.

This earth is your schoolroom. You have moved into this physical body and into this schoolroom to learn. To learn what? Compassion. Nonjudgment. Unconditional love. Grand terms, to be sure, but what do they mean? What does it really mean to have compassion for another? What does it mean to be nonjudgmental?

Think about the last hour; just review it in your minds for a moment. Was there any judgment? "That driver ahead of me is slow. I don't like that house. Why did somebody paint it that color? This road is too bumpy, doesn't anybody in this town take care of the roads?" Little opinions. I'm not talking about hatred, just little bits of judgment.

Some of you may say, "But, Aaron, if we never judge anything as deficient, then there's no force within us to try to change that which we see as lacking." To see deficiency is not to judge something as "bad" nor to invite negative emotion around that deficiency. Barbara is training a puppy. His understanding is as yet very deficient in many areas. His attention span is rather short. He has learned to sit and stay remarkably well for a three-month-old puppy, but ten seconds is about as long as he can stay. Does Barbara hate the puppy or rage at him when he gets up from sitting? Or does she simply walk back to him and say, "Sit. Stay."? She understands that having a short attention span is the nature of a puppy.

One does not need to feel hatred or even mild irritation to see what is wrong in the world and attempt to change it. Discernment does not require that you take what arises as a personal affront and become emotionally entangled with it, but just that you attend to it. In fact, one can create change far more readily and more skillfully when there is no rage. Here is where anger offers the most energy, when it is transformed to compassion and to recognition of your nonseparation with this earth and all life upon it.

So, what is the path to truly moving beyond anger? In human form, can you ever reach a point where you don't feel anger? It is what I just described; we've come full circle. You can only begin to move beyond anger by accepting anger. You cannot transcend what you don't accept. When you find compassion for all the heavy emotions in yourself, you have nurtured equanimity and awakened presence. Then you find that the same catalyst that led to rage or greed or jealousy simply leads you to an openhearted look at the situations that confront you, without judgment. It becomes possible to open with forgiveness to another rather than to hold onto anger and blame.

It is a wonderful process, and one in which you are all involved. It's not something you will choose to be a part of. You've already taken that step by moving into incarnation. You are in this schoolroom and offered the curriculum. It's your choice whether you practice the lessons that are offered. Life 101: How to live your lives more wisely. How to love more fully. And yes, my dear ones, you'll still be perfecting those lessons when you've moved on to graduate school.

The Journey from Fear to Love

The most frequent question I am asked is how to work with the terrible pain that may result from the human desire for love and acceptance and from the fear that they will be withheld. This fear manifests in many ways—as a sense of unworthiness, as greed and clinging, as the push to achieve, as prejudice, jealousy, and hatred. It even manifests as the striving to offer pure service or generosity, as you attempt to be better than some preconceived notion of what you are, so that you will be loved.

I say "preconceived notion" because very few of you realize your innate perfection. You measure the imperfections against that which you judge acceptable and emerge with a sense of utter failure.

I sometimes ask people to do an exercise where they list those qualities they like in themselves and those they dislike. The insight people may come to realize is that if they are generous ninety percent of the time and greedy ten percent, they consider themselves greedy because they see only the greed. They won't allow themselves the label *generous*. They focus on the negative trait, no matter how small a quantity is present.

Do you see that in yourself? Try it with patience and impatience. Is any one of you one hundred percent patient? Friends might consider you a patient person. But the tension caused by the first arising of impatience leads you to judge yourself as impatient, even if you are not reactive to the impatience.

You forget so quickly that within each of you is perfection. Yes. This perfection is your true nature. No matter that you cannot always manifest it in your lives; the seeds are there.

There is a lovely song that contains a verse, "Just remember in the winter, far beneath the bitter snows, lies the seed that with the sun's love in the spring becomes the rose." That is what you are, the seed of that rose, and your fear is the snow that hides the truth from view.

For the flower, the dormant stage is a time of patient waiting; the seed will blossom when the conditions are right for that blooming. The human will also bloom, although negative emotion may make it seem that the blossoming will never come. Such emotion is not something you need to hate, but a gift for your growth. After living through the dormancy of heavy emotion, joy and compassion will come. Your fear reminds you that you are moving into uncharted territory, that you are moving past the known and entering that realm where growth may begin.

In this most perfect classroom of yours, you must trust that even fear has a place. Do you know the song, "Amazing Grace?" The second verse begins, "T'was Grace that taught my heart to fear...." What does that mean? Fear is the dimension through which you may truly learn love. There is no duality. Fear and love are a part of each other. Until you can be openheartedly present even with the heaviest of fears, you cannot fully love. Can you see that?

What is fear? Many of you have looked with me and seen how fear masquerades as anger or wanting. What masquerades as fear? Look into yourselves for the answers.

There is within the human experience a craving, a deep desire for love and for ultimate safety. This is not good or bad, it simply is. Yet it is natural to you, for the higher self has its source in love, and all things are drawn toward their source.

No matter where its journey takes it, through whatever fear, hatred, ignorance, or pain, the higher self's deepest memory is of love. That is the essence of every life form.

The higher self remembers that infinite love from the spirit plane and longs to return to that original experience of total nonseparation, the place where there is no ego or self, but only the One.

But the human experiences its existence as separate. It cannot be fully one with all things because it lives in a body. The fetus still within the womb dwells in oneness, but the fetal state is a transition. With birth and the physical and symbolic cutting of the umbilical cord come separation. As human, you are born alone. You live alone. You leave this earth plane alone. From the perspective of the small ego self, no one can make those journeys with you.

Your deepest meditation experiences lead you to know nonseparation of the spirit body, when all ego and physical awareness has dissolved. Some of you have glimpsed the bliss of moving fully into the light of the eternal and knowing that it is your true nature to be one with that divine energy. But you are not only spirit while incarnate; you are body and mind as well. The meditation ends. Your limbs and organs, your thoughts and emotions are there, encasing and seemingly separating this dear spirit, cutting it off from the experience of unity that it briefly knew. Then there is only memory, and a knowing that has moved closer to the conscious experience. There is memory and grasping, wanting to come home.

My dear ones, this earth is your perfect schoolroom. You are incarnate in a body to learn. And yet you hate the lessons. This makes the learning terribly difficult. How would it be if a child sat in her classroom but refused to pick up the books because they felt too heavy? Could she learn? In this classroom of life lessons come in many forms, but you turn your back on many of them because they feel too heavy.

If the experience of this illusion of separation, manifested through the body and emotions, were not necessary for your learning, it would not be given to you. There would be no veil of forgetting with each birth. The entire human experience would be one of conscious knowing. But then how would you learn faith? Life would be a practice of self-discipline and will, which indeed it is not. This veil and this incarnate experience even with all its pains are a gift. Can you begin to trust that and to trust the glimpses of who you truly are?

The issue then is not so much that fear arises, but that there is such intense dislike of the experience of fear. There is judgment of fear, and judgment that the self is bad because fear has come. Negative reaction to your emotions and thoughts arises in part because you have not learned to trust life experiences as your teachers. Thus, you consider those that are unpleasant, like fear, to be bad, and those that are pleasant to be good. With practice, you learn to see deeply into experience and know that the difficult times do bring their own gifts. The work is not to end emotion but to find peace with emotion, and not to act it out in damaging ways.

You've heard me talk of full telepathic communication on my plane. A being sends all that it experiences and feels and another being receives all that is sent. It is not possible to share one part of an experience and not share the whole. Would you be comfortable with that now? Is there anything in your experience that you feel a need to hide? Is there anything in another's experience that would lead to discomfort?

Before you are ready to move to that plane, to grow beyond this cycle of birth and death, you must first move beyond believing the judgments mind offers so freely. Why? Because only then can you stop reacting to negativity in yourself and in others with more negativity. Only with that shift is the cycle broken. To do so, you must learn to be present with discomfort without creating a solid self. Various religions label this process differently, but all have in common this moving beyond ego that identifies with judgment. Fear is a mirror reminding you of where ego is still present.

Ego is a funny thing. It's like a jack-in-the-box. It's out of sight and all but forgotten and then something pushes your buttons and WHOOIEE, SPROING! Can you see it up there with its silly grin and waving arms?

Can you then say to it, as a friend suggests, "Hello, ego. I've been expecting you. Come in and have tea?"

There are only two basic emotions, fear and love. Fear is the closing of the heart that seeks to protect itself from pain. Fear is not the enemy but is a tap on the shoulder and the reminder, "Open up; be present." Love is the opening of the heart, which knows its ultimate connection with All that Is and therefore has no need to armor itself.

For most of your lives, you fall between the two. The heart opens, the heart shuts—again and again and again. When love is strong, when the heart is open and fully present, fear cannot continue. Fear is a result. Our concern is not directly with fear but with the conditions that give rise to fear and to the reactions that spring from unattended fear.

I am not speaking here of the arising of the sensation of fear. When the conditions are present, it will arise. The frequency of those occurrences will diminish as the heart learns trust. What I'm speaking of is the relationship to fear.

"What do I do when fear is strong?" you ask me. Dear ones, no matter whether you like it or not, no matter how much you wish it away, you will continue to experience fear on occasion. Since its arising seems inevitable, can you begin to make friends with it?

It is not fear that is the problem but your reaction to fear, your hatred of fear. Without awareness, you lump them together, the fear itself and that which feeds off fear. When fear arises and is followed immediately by the desire to be rid of it or the need to suppress it, you fragment yourselves. The thought arises, "I should not be afraid," and you cut off that which is afraid. There is such suffering in that fragmentation. This hatred of fear, not fear itself, is what leads to the illusion of separation. As you practice deeper mindfulness, you learn to distinguish between the two. Can you take this very human person who is afraid into your arms and offer him or her love? Can you touch with mercy that in yourself which you have always touched with contempt?

I've said that you are here to practice love and faith. Of course there are other lessons, but these are basic. Love recognizes no conditions. It does not say, "I'll love you if you fix this or that," but radiates love for the being just as it is—for your dear self just as you are. This does not mean you no longer aspire to grow, nor that you use your fear as excuse to harm another.

Some of you had wonderful nurturing as children; some of you missed that experience. I'm aware of the pain felt by those who lacked such nurturing, but there comes a time when the past conditioning needs to be put aside. Here is this being that wants nurturing, that cries out to be accepted. Can you do it? It is as simple as that. No more excuses about why you have not done it, or cannot. No more blaming the parents or life situations. Just this: can I open my heart to myself?

I cannot tell you how to do that. For each of you, the armor is attached in a different way. You must find that keyhole for yourself, to open the lock and remove the armor, to unsnap it, unzip it, peel it, dissolve it. But the key is always the same—love.

Every moment there is the opportunity to stretch yourselves, to go one step farther than you were able to go before. Your life is a series of edges and a progression of learning—learning to let go gently and with trust. To allow yourself that letting go, there must be nurturing by yourself, of yourself. This is the end of fragmentation and the beginning of remembering wholeness.

What keeps you from that nurturing? You say you want it, from another or from yourself, yet when the possibility for it arises, you turn away. Can you begin to see why?

You have enclosed yourselves in armor, not to shut out the light that is so beloved, but to protect the sensitive heart. It is the very vulnerability and softness of this heart that has led you to don armor in the first place. Does a rock need armor? When you pierce the tough skin of the orange, you find the sweet fruit.

I have spoken before of the inherent perfection of the spirit body. This is the aspect that is fully open, loving, generous, patient, wise, and so much more. And it is so afraid it will be wounded. The thickness of the armor is proof of the fear that the spirit beneath is tender and vulnerable.

To nurture is to begin to open the armor. How frightening that movement is. Can you touch with mercy this dear, frightened being who wants to open and dares not? Do you see what a big step it is to admit the softness and vulnerability of that which you have spent so many lifetimes trying to make invulnerable? Yet that is your next step—to allow yourselves to become vulnerable.

What of responsibility? As you begin to open and learn, you understand that you are, and have always been, responsible for everything that moves through you. And even here you must let go of self-judgment. To let go of self-judgment is to claim your wholeness and power, a frightening step. It feels impossible. "Am I ready to be that responsible?" you may ask. Then you berate yourselves again for this new fear. Your lives are filled with so many shoulds.

Can you begin to see fear in a new light, as the catalyst that reminds you to have mercy, reminds you of the sacredness and tenderness of the inner heart?

It is a constant process of awareness, watching fear arise, touching it with acceptance, watching the reactions to which fear leads—anger, greed, and such—and touching those feelings, too, with mercy. Watch each moment, in its newness; constantly look for the donning of new armor. Be aware of the judgment of "I should be merciful." Can you see that that is just more judgment?

As you learn to not hate your fear, a transformation begins. You begin to find healing and acceptance for this dear being that you are. Your actions and words become more skillful, not because you have said "I should" and denied some aspects of your experience, but because you have opened your heart to the infinite space and compassion therein.

This step is the beginning of maturity. You will not become something with no feelings, but rather, a being of intense feelings. You will have sufficient maturity, wisdom, and compassion to allow the full experience of those emotions—the joy and the sorrow, the beauty and the ugliness, not without preference, but openheartedly—no longer being reactive to those emotions but allowing them to serve as a reminder to love. This is the path you all walk, my dear ones, and it is a wondrous journey. Trust.

Passion

It is such a joy to sit here in this lovely room, to share the energy of the gathered people and the beautiful evening. I might say it brings me great happiness. Many people ask me about passion and dispassion. People tell me, "Aaron, I don't want to give up being passionate. I feel like I'll turn into a shadow, devoid of feeling. But many teachings link passion with suffering. Must I give up joy?"

The path of your maturity is not to become mere shells. Your path takes you into exuberance and a fullness of joy. This inner fire must exist or no spiritual movement can happen. I think the difficulty is that you confuse passion with an excited energy that imitates passion but involves grasping and attachment. Consider the coolness of deep wisdom, where the energy is not agitated and there is a great spaciousness and peacefulness. There is no contraction there. Now consider real passion and joy. It is also uncontracted. Grasping is not present, nor is fear.

When you're passionate about something, you often get quite worked up over it. You debate with others about it, with attachment to your view. But passion does not have to include grasping or aversion. It does not have to involve attachment to views. It does not have to include any contraction of energy. The direct experience of passion does not involve suffering; the grasping that may come with passion is the ground for suffering. But passion is passion and grasping is grasping. Don't confuse the two. I see passion as a very spacious experience, deeply joyful. Passion is natural to you. All of you are inherently passionate and alive, but many of you separate from passion until you lose touch with it. Then existence feels empty and joyless.

Could you walk along a very beautiful beach at sunset, soft waves lapping on the shore and gorgeous colors spread out over the sky and water, without a natural, strong, joyous enthrallment with it? When the sun finally sets, would there be any grasping, "I want my sun back. I want the colors back."? You let the evening go naturally. There's no grasping, and yet there is what I consider passion. This mind state is one of sheer joy; it is present, awake, and totally connected to that which stirs the passion. The sunset isn't outside you, so it cannot be lost. All those colors simply reflect your own inner light. True passion is your joy shining through.

Joy is in this moment, now. It has no past or future, and thus no fear or defensiveness. Here is the mind that is free and open, not so much letting go as never holding in the first place, but able to connect, appreciate and move on.

When fear accompanies passion, a need to control may predominate. The energy is contracted. With contraction, there is suffering. But the cause of that suffering is contraction caused by fear, not the object or the openhearted joy in your encounter with the object. If you don't see the movement from joy into attachment, you erroneously believe that with joy, attachment must also come.

Here is where it gets difficult. If you feel that to be free of grasping, you also must avoid joy, and thus the sense contact with that which is joyful, you close yourself. Then you may attack the object or dissociate from it. You may not yet understand that even if grasping does come, it's just another mind and body state. There is no need to attack it or separate from it. Let it be, and come back to joy.

The common instruction is to abandon negative mind states. How do we abandon them? You are conditioned to the idea of killing the negativity, but that's not true dharma. There's no need to kill anything. Whatever you kill, you're killing yourself. You are killing the world and all its beings.

In the dharma teachings we hear instructions to watch what arises and see how each object is impermanent and not self. We are further advised to watch the object arise and then watch any mental form like grasping or aversion that results from contact with the object. If there is strong attachment or aversion around something that has arisen, and one observes the object itself and then the attachment or aversion, each in its turn becomes the primary object. The sensation is sensation, which may be pleasant, unpleasant, or neutral. The mental formations are just that, arisen as a result of the contact with the object, consciousness, old conditioning, and lack of mindfulness. Can one experience grasping or aversion as an object, free of the conditioned concept of "badness?" What is the immediate experience of grasping before any stories arise about it?

To watch aversion is not to be caught in the stories of aversion or caught in a self that feels the aversion. All those opinions—I should, he should, this is good, this is bad, I want it this way, I don't want it that way —are stories, not direct experience. The direct experience is only a contraction in body and mind, which we label aversion or grasping.

The inexperienced meditator starts to believe, "I have to figure this out. What should I do about all this grasping and aversion?" He doesn't see that the whole question is a story. What if you just note, "questioning, questioning," and know there is a grasping tension even in the question? You see the question arise, you see the tension and the wanting an answer. Go to the predominant direct experience. It may be grasping; it may be frustration or helplessness. But these are not the stories such as "how do I fix it?" These are the direct experiences of vulnerability, confusion, or grasping. What are these experiences before the stories come?

When you are with any of these experiences, willing to watch them arise and to stay present with them, then greater spaciousness comes and, with that spaciousness, the story dissolves itself. When you hear the question, "What should I be doing about this grasping?" right there is a story. It comes as judgment. Can you just note, "judging" or even "contracting"? That's all. Just note it. The noting is not to make it go away. This is not a form of bargaining. The noting reduces the self-identification with what has arisen; it reminds you that awareness is also present. It invites you to rest in awareness.

Resting in that spaciousness you can re-open to passion. There is a feeling that you do not need to solve, fix, hold onto, or change anything. That which is aware of desire is not bound into the desire. That which is aware of fear is not afraid. There is nothing to fix, nothing to be rid of. Whatever is present is impermanent and not me or mine. The tension releases. There is still the need to attend to difficult states, but from a center of loving-kindness, not one of fear.

So the heart opens and there is a passion for the beauty of this moment.

I think it's so important to understand that true dharma practice does not lead you to become a shell of a human, devoid of feeling. True dharma practice leads you to burst out into the world with light, offering it freely, but never forcing it on anyone or anything. There is such a joy in this dharma.

We talk a lot about emptiness, and I think this is one of the areas of confusion. Emptiness of self does not mean that there's nothing there. It means there's no longer a strong self-concept that rules everything. There is still a person, this collection of aggregates, which says the words, sweeps the floor, offers the flowers. When you come into that centered space, it's no longer self that smiles, sweeps, or offers, it's simply beingness, and beingness is alive and filled with passion.

What this term *no-self* really means is that there is no independent, ultimate self. We can see this so easily in the tree. The tree has leaves. The leaves fall off in autumn. Are the leaves the tree? No. The tree is still a tree with or without its leaves, and yet if the leaves ceased to exist entirely there could be no tree. So the leaves are an expression of the tree, and the tree needs the leaves. They are not separate. Is the trunk the tree? Without the roots there could not be a trunk. Without the leaves there could not be a trunk. Maybe we could say that the little seed is the tree. But what was that seed before it became a seed? It was simply energy inherent in another tree, ready to burst into expression. The leaves, trunk, roots, and seed inter-are. *Tree* is a concept, a compilation of non-tree elements that we call tree for lack of any other word. It is a summation of parts, which includes the sun and the rain, the nutritious earth, many small insects that fertilize the soil, earthworms, compost. All of these are the tree. It has no separate, ultimate self. But certainly it does exist.

So what is this human self? It's a compilation of non-self elements, including the traditional aggregates of form, feelings, mental formations, and consciousness. Broken down further, it's all the cellular structure of the body, the neurons, the breath itself; it's all the kindness and all the meanness, all the love and all the fear; it is all these non-self elements.

Once you recognize that you are not any of these elements, then you may ask, "What am I?" You are light, intelligence, energy. You are the pure spring, deep underground and about to push its way to the surface of the earth and become a mighty river. You are the flower, about to wake up from a long winter and push its way through the soil and become a radiant bush. You are the sunshine, not yet come over the horizon, which will light up a clear day.

You are all these and so much more. Why limit yourself to being this body, these thoughts?

So no-self is not no-thing; it's very much a something, but you have to understand what it is. No-self is just a way of talking about one's true nature in the same way one uses the term *tree* to talk about all of these non-tree elements come together. Non-self includes the body, includes the thoughts, includes the spirit. They are expressions of this no-self. But what I want you most to understand, my dear ones, is that when you rest in this place of no-self, rest there deeply, you are the tree that has put out its roots to the core of the earth, and entwined those roots with every other tree in the forest.

Without the ground or sun or rain, and all the animals and insects, that tree could not exist. Without you it could not exist and you could not exist without the tree. This inter-being is the heart we all share, and it is not dead and dispassionate, not agitated, attached, or grasping, nor filled with aversion and ill-will. All those things may touch it as experience, but it is none of them. What remains? Light, presence, spacious awareness.

You will find it wonderful to come to know this deeper truth of being, of your unlimitedness and divine beauty. I think when you misunderstand or misuse the teachings as a way to exclude the experience of passion, it is really a sign of your fear, that you are afraid to be that big, that unlimited and that radiant, that you are afraid of your power. To be passionless is to be powerless; it's death. Do you want to cling to that death? What frightens you so about your true radiance? Again, I think the primary fear is that as humans you still do possess negative traits. I think you are afraid of your power because you do not feel fully in control of those negative traits. If you are limited, your negativity is limited. You erroneously think that if you acknowledge your unlimitedness, your negativity also will be unlimited, and so you believe you must think small.

Anybody who wants to express unlimited negativity can find the means to do so. All of you on a conscious spiritual path who see into the roots of negative thought have at least begun to learn the power of kindness as a container for negativity so that it does not reflect out into the world.

If negativity arises in you, can this immense radiance of being stretch just a bit farther to hold that negativity with kindness? You don't have to fix it; it will go away on its own when the conditions cease to support it. Your work is simply to remember, "I don't have to enact this. But if I do enact it out into the world a bit, I can watch the suffering that causes, can apologize and learn to be more careful the next time."

Passion is an expression of your nondual awareness, and only when you rest deeply in that nondual awareness can you express the fullness of your passion. I challenge you: What would allow you to be more passionate in your lives? Please reflect on that question and if you have some insights, please share them with me.

I thank you for your attention. I love you passionately!

Q: I sense a link between what you said about the difference between true passion and grasping or attachment that may masquerade as passion and the direct experience of sadness versus grief. Can you talk a little about this?

You are correct. Sadness comes from a place of connection, even of passion. You are sad because of your ability to love. Sadness does not contain fear. When sadness, such as sadness about loss, becomes grief, that happens because there is fear. The fear takes you out of the moment and into grasping.

Q: Are you saying that as long as you stay present there is no grasping?

Yes. In this moment there is no fear. Fear is a result of going into the future, of what may come to be, or into the past, of memories of how it was. In this moment there can be discomfort, even pain. There can be feelings of joy and sadness, what we call purified emotions. But there is not fear.

Psychotherapy and Spiritual Practice

People sometimes ask me about conventional psychotherapy versus meditation and other spiritual practices as a tool for growth. When people are suffering a lot, the first thing that is needed is a bit of space. Both psychotherapy and meditation can offer such space. Each has its strengths, and each can be misused.

The drawback to psychotherapy is that while it explores the issues that have locked you into suffering, it may solidify the self that is suffering. In the process of psychotherapy, you may come to understand that you have certain beliefs because of experiences in childhood. Such beliefs include your prejudices and world view and also how you view the self. Thus you may come to understand how you came to feel unworthy, helpless, or angry, or how you became a controlling person or a bully. But you still believe in that persona as self and suffering continues.

Meditation also has its drawbacks. In meditation or any spiritual practice, you may come to remember your true nature, to know your innate perfection. That is wonderful, but a being can also hold to this ultimate view and use it to support denial of relative reality and the emotional experience, and thereby perpetuate suffering.

The question is not so much whether the tool of psychotherapy or that of meditation is preferable, but how these tools are employed. A tool used for the denial of anything enhances suffering. A tool used to bring forth truth along with a spacious arena for that truth supports liberation.

Both therapy and meditation can be useful to reveal habitual patterns. However, if one habitual pattern is self-judgment, revelation of difficult patterns may simply enhance judgment. This potential problem is common to both therapy and meditation. How do we break this cycle?

In a balanced meditation practice, guided by a teacher, one can take the patterns that have become clear through therapy or meditation and be present with those patterns without creating more self. Remember, the process is not linear; it is a process of constant inter-weaving and re-balancing. Skillful spiritual practice and psychological therapy do not try to fix, for nothing is seen as broken. Rather, they know distortion is a result of imbalance and offer balance.

Let us use as an example a person who is constantly grasping and fearful. That person might look at the neediness of her childhood and see how she was abused or abandoned. To say, "I will not feel that grasping anymore," is useless. The grasping is conditioned; it will arise.

The person may gain insight into the roots of the distortion but the fear and grasping still arise. Through the training of kindness, generosity, and caring, this person will reveal to herself facets of her being that she had previously buried when the difficult childhood experience led her to close off the loving heart. First, there is insight into the pattern. Then the self-identification with experience shifts from being the bad, unworthy, needy one to being one who is capable of giving great love. There is still a perceived self, and now perhaps attachment to being a loving self. There can be grasping at this new image at first, for fear the old self-image will return.

But the shift has been made. These beautiful qualities of the heart, which are invited to come forth, gradually dissolve the negative self-images. Then the being can look back at the self-history and recognize not only, "I no longer am that," but "I never was that." Finally, one sees how it was all just conditioning and habit. There never was a bad or unworthy one. The old patterns such as greed or shame may still arise. But because of the spiritual work the combat has ended. The identity with arising mind states as self has ended.

A further benefit here is that in this practice of bodhicitta, of the awakened heart, one offers out that which is good and serves all beings.

Is therapy dispensable? Not always. For the person in severe pain, the support of a therapist as a kind, nonjudgmental listener can help to create a model that allows self-listening and greater self-acceptance. The trained therapist can raise questions that lead into deeper reflection and growth within the context of a safe environment. If the therapist is trained in spiritual traditions, the work together can extend beyond the traditional boundaries of psychology. If he or she is not so trained, then at the point where insight into the patterned and conditioned nature of experience has developed, a spiritual practice would be useful and, in my perception, essential as a support for growth.

One question we need to ask here: is the final intention to be comfortable or to be free? I am not opposed to comfort. I pray for all, that they may abide in well-being. I also recognize that well-being is impermanent and will shift into discomfort unless there is full liberation. Well-being is but a way station. Do not be satisfied to subdue neurotic tendencies. That is not freedom. Do not worry so much about the neurotic tendencies unless they are truly harmful and unwholesome. Rather see them as results and also as voices of your own uniqueness. Learn to smile at yourself and at all your habitual patterns. Relax. Stop being the neurotic one, which is a self. Be free; be beautiful. Let the heart open. Get to know your habitual patterns, but do not wage war with them. Rather, simply ask yourself, "What brings balance here? What may I learn here? What growth and freedom are possible?" You will find the way.

Surrender

In recent weeks, several questions have been asked about twelve-step programs, which suggest surrender to a higher power. Is it really necessary to surrender to a higher power? If you do so, what happens to your own empowerment? What does the word *surrender* mean? Are personal empowerment and surrender mutually exclusive?

Many people find the term *surrender* to be difficult, if not offensive, because they are trying so hard to find a sense of their personal strength. Added to that, for women, is the popular image of God as masculine; if you surrender to God, are you surrendering to a masculine energy? Of course God is not masculine or feminine; that is only the interpretation sometimes given to that energy. Nevertheless, having grown up in this culture, you've been repeatedly subjected to the divine father image, and it has left its imprint, so that the idea of surrender to God may be repugnant to a woman who is trying to establish her own power. The same could be said of people who were abused as children by their parents, or by minorities who were abused by the majority and view surrender as relinquishment of power.

Every act, word, thought—everything in your lives—takes effort, which comes from a place of love or of fear. Sometimes these alternate quickly, so the movement is subtle. When your choices are catalyzed by fear, you are trying to protect yourself or are grasping to ensure that your own needs are met. You experience the small ego self straining to manipulate the environment to create the illusion of safety. Many of you have learned to exert such control with great skill.

For human survival, it is necessary to manipulate the environment to a certain degree; otherwise, we'd all be shivering in caves. Even a squirrel collects nuts and other types of food and finds a warm home for the winter. That action comes from a place of love. When you've learned to harmonize your energy with that of your environment so that you and your loved ones are fed, warm, and safe, that is skillful co-creation. Choice grows out of a place of love and respect, with the awareness that you wish to take care of yourself and your loved ones. You wish to create a warm house, enough food to eat. You cannot simply sit outside in the cold and trust that everything necessary will appear. But you wish to do this with peaceful intent and harmlessness to All that Is.

When your choices come from a place of fear, you're constantly fighting what is, grasping here and pushing away there, trying to peer into an as-yet-undetermined future and manipulate it to your will. Fear leads to grasping but the resultant intake is never enough to dissolve the fear. Grasping increases, and as the person seeks more comfort, more safety, the result is suffering. One figure in Buddhist cosmology is the "hungry ghost." This is a being with a huge body and a tiny head and mouth through which it can never satisfy its needs.

You have a home, and it seems adequate. Then you notice that your neighbor's home looks a bit bigger; the walls are thicker; there's more food in the pantry. Fear takes over and says, "I need more!" Fear and more fear. Fear pushes you to manipulate, control, and grasp. But the more grasping occurs, the more distortion is created. Each being is like a thread in a great tapestry. The thread itself cannot create intricate interweaving by controlling the other threads. It can only make itself as beautiful as is possible. If one thread struggles to dominate the tapestry, the design becomes distorted, and the beauty of the threads is lost to that disharmony.

Humans are almost always holding on, which creates tension and disharmony. Holding on not only grows out of fear, it enhances fear through the practice of fear. The act of letting go, through the practice of generosity and awareness, is a foundation for spiritual growth. Letting go takes great faith and an awareness that in human form your perspective is limited, that you cannot know everything, cannot always know what is happening below the surface levels of perception.

So here are two catalysts for effort, fear and love. You have spent many lifetimes learning to be masters of your environment, and, suddenly, you're becoming aware that fear is often the push for that mastery. Love teaches you to see your connection to everything. You understand that rather than being a master, you need to be a co-creator with All that Is. You can see this lesson most clearly in the environmental difficulties of earth, all the vast problems of pollution, of the holes in the ozone layer, the diminishing rain forests, acid rain, animal species facing extinction, and plant species. All of this has grown out of man attempting to become master of his environment without having any clear understanding of the interrelationships. Now you are finally coming to the awareness, "I am not the master here. If I cooperate with my environment, then I can support it, and it can support me. When I try to control it through fear, I destroy it." This is part of the catalyst for learning faith, learning to let go.

You've been learning all these skills through this lifetime and through past lifetimes as well. Letting go is not an event, but a process. Slowly, you're becoming a bit better at it, with these constant reminders that are thrown your way, threatening the very earth itself with barrenness if you don't learn. Under that kind of pressure you are learning.

The being that feels disempowered and grasps at empowerment is living in great fear. I am not saying that person is bad in any way, only that misunderstanding, fear, and a great deal of separation are present. That being sees surrender as letting go of the safety that it's so desperately trying to maintain, because control seems the only way to survive. Often, such beings have been abused in some way or another, have felt deeply hurt by their world and felt helpless within that hurt. Out of that pain have grown the defensive patterns of control that lead to addictions. Then there is more attempt at control, to control the addiction.

We return to the spiritual perspective. As is obvious, surrender is easy for a being with no fear that goads it to be in control. If great abundance was all around you, with never any shortage of anything, generosity would be very easy. Anything that anybody asked from you, you would willingly give, because if you wanted another, it was there for the taking. What meaning would generosity have? In similar circumstances, what meaning would faith have? What meaning would surrender have if there were no fear, no pull to control?

Those who find the idea of surrender difficult because it seems to diminish their sense of personal empowerment are in that situation precisely so that they can learn true surrender through letting go. Karma has drawn them into the situation. They have a powerful catalyst to look at the issues of control and fear and may begin to transcend them. It takes a great deal of courage and awareness to look at intense fear in yourself, especially for one who has been abused, been hurt, or who has lacked that which seemed necessary for security.

As you look with greater space and clarity at the arising fear which demands control, you may penetrate a haze that has previously been opaque and open a door of compassion for the self. Then you begin to see the divinity in yourself. When we speak of surrender to God, we must remember that all of you are God, that this divine energy is the Ground in each of you. Surrender to God doesn't mean that you relinquish personal power but is a way to acknowledge and let go of fear and come back to the divine aspect of the self. This truth of divinity is what you have faith in, and it heightens your sense of personal empowerment, because you know at the deepest level that you are and have always been invulnerable. Yes, you've suffered, but spiritually, you are invulnerable. You have always had that power. It is the power of love within you. It is the strongest power in the universe.

So you begin to look at the fear in yourself, the part of you that needs to control this and change that, needs to manipulate and hold on. You begin to notice, with gentleness, the fear from which the need to control arises. You begin to treat yourself with compassion for those fears rather than with self-disparagement, to allow yourself to have fears, to be gentle with yourself. As you do that, the need to control begins to dissolve. Your heart opens into connection with All that Is. You are personally empowered because it is no longer a private empowerment. The being that knows its connection with All that Is knows its infinite power because it is not personal power, but the power of all living and loving energy wrapped together, hearts connected.

What, then, of this idea of surrender to a higher power? You are not surrendering to something that is outside and separate from you. In surrendering to that higher power, you are surrendering the small ego's fears to your own deepest wisdom. You are surrendering to the deepest place of love and connection within yourself. You're aligning yourself with divine energy, opening yourself so that this energy may move through you, letting go of the walls of fear that have blocked it. Surrender does not mean helplessness or a lessening of the self in any way. It is an expansion of the self by allowing the divine and the self to merge. Your surrender is your empowerment, and when you have reached that place of surrender, you truly know that God's will for you and your will for yourself are one and the same. When you say, "Thy will be done," you can say it with perfect trust, because that divine energy works in perfect harmony with your own deepest intention.

Ego, Nonduality, and Service

Barbara and I spent much time conversing this week, while she was on vacation. She has been pushing herself at a very rapid pace for some time and was feeling a bit of, not really exhaustion, but numbness. It took a day or two for that numbness to begin to recede. As she skied along the lovely paths through the woods, her heart truly singing in joy, gratitude, and praise of God, she asked me the simple question, "Aaron, why am I here in incarnation? To do what? I feel such love and joy simply being outdoors like this. At other times, I feel such pressure and stress that I sometimes lose track of the joy. Should I not choose that in my life which leads me to be able to express joy? You say we're here to bring light where there has been darkness, but sometimes I feel like I'm increasing that darkness." Yet can you avoid stress in your lives, even on vacation? The light is always within you. How do you practice so as to allow it to shine, no matter what the circumstances?

We spoke about the fact that in past incarnations Barbara, like most of you, has lived monastic lifetimes concentrating deeply on the spiritual, but she often lived in countries where the teachings of spirit emphasized renunciation of the world, where there was deep poverty, where the focus was so strongly on the spiritual that little attention was paid to the material side of life. Even today, many in those countries still lack the basics for a healthy life. Spiritual practice in such circumstances become an escape from the realities of physical existence.

In your Western society there is material plenty and spiritual impoverishment. Your technology has brought you out of harmony with spirit and the environment. You, in your Western culture, are looking for deep spiritual traditions, while those who have been raised with those traditions are looking for Tupperware. They are looking for more than that too, but they are grasping at material goods that they increasingly see in the world around them and which their culture often lacks. Yes, it is wonderful to live simply, but not when that simplicity involves disease, hunger, cold, and lack of the barest necessities. Think of the wonder of a bowl with a sealed lid that keeps insects from your flour and thereby helps keep your children free of disease.

Those of you presently incarnate in cultures that are not physically deprived are in a wonderful place. Your efforts and love may begin an actual transformation of the world into a Garden of Eden where all beings know their true spiritual nature and where all beings also have food, shelter, clothing, medical supplies, books and educational materials, music, poetry—all the material necessities to live physically with minimal pain. This is the time for drawing together of form and spirit, for transcendence of that presumed duality.

It is valuable to sit in meditation. It is lovely to walk in the woods or on a warm and sandy beach and enjoy that beauty and sense of connection. Your joy at those moments offers light. It has real value. But at physical levels it does not touch the fundamental deprivation in the world. How can you allow connection with spirit to work through you to transform the world?

This does not mean you should not take holidays or do your solitary practice, but you need to remember that your work is in the world. How do you bring joy and love back into stressful situations? Would you worship a hollow god that stands above the world, superior to the world, that will not get its feet dirty? Would you strive to pull yourself up to those heights and leave the world to suffer in the dark alleys? Or would you give your love to a loving God, less absolute perhaps, but not seeking to enhance itself by diminishing others, a God willing to partake in pain through entering the human illusion?

This is why Jesus' life speaks so powerfully to so many. I do not wish here to promote one religious tradition over another. Many traditions have truth and great beauty. I use Jesus here only as one example with which many in this culture are familiar. The beauty in Jesus' incarnation is that it was the conscious coming of divinity to Earth. Here is God descending from the heights and touching the suffering of mankind, God offering love and receiving love. It is a reciprocal relationship.

There are two views of God. You must ask which one holds true for you. To know your relationship with the world, you must first understand your relationship with God. One view holds that because you have that of God within you, that spark of divinity, to know your relationship with God is to know your relationship with yourself and all else. Your relationship with the world and its suffering is a reflection of your relationship with God. You have the potential to express divine love through a loving relationship with the world.

Or you can choose to express that aspect of God that is absolute and all-powerful. There is a quote from the Udana scripture in which the Buddha says to the assembled monks, "There is an unborn, undying, unchanging, uncreated." God is all of that. It is easy to distort that truth to say that this absolute, infinite, all-knowing is separate from the world. You may then end up worshipping God selfishly so as to raise yourself in God's reflection. That which we name *God* has infinite power. Do you try to please God, so as to grasp some of that power? Many have done so, with the sense, God is on *our* side. The Old Testament portrayed God as a strong and even wrathful God, having dominion over all. It was to change that perception of our relationship with God, to clarify that distortion of man's image of God, that Jesus took birth, to bring the message that love is the most powerful force in the universe, and God is love.

We emulate what we worship. If God is worshipped for being superior, dominant, and all powerful, it is natural that those who worship this image of God themselves attempt to become all powerful? They may claim that power grows out of love and that they should control others because they know best what others need. Do the ends ever justify the means? Can we dominate others because we think we know what they need? In fact, this direction reinforces ego and self-service.

I once spoke about the creation of the earth and the move into negative distortion by those angels whose energy was the foundation of the world. Some of those beings moved into distortion because they sought to control out of love. Their love was so fierce that it became protective, denied free will in other beings, and became dominating. That was the beginning of negative polarity on the earth. While powerfulness and absoluteness are undeniably attributes of God, they are not the most significant attributes. Absolute power must be balanced by absolute love. This is the truth for which Jesus' life offers us a reminder. What is our relationship with God if God is love?

There was a council of bishops in the fourth century after Christ, by your figuring of years, 325 A.D. It was called the Council of Nicaea, and it produced the Nicene Creed. The debate that prompted the Emperor Constantine to call this council was precisely over this question, what is God? What attribute of the infinite God best expresses the highest aspirations of humans? What most inspires you and draws you to the expression of your own divinity and to the expansion of God? What allows you to reflect that glory back to God?

One view at this meeting was that of a priest named Arius. Arius was very angry at the Creed that grew out of this gathering, which said that Christ was begotten of God and therefore shared that divinity. The Creed says specifically, "begotten, not made…." Arius preferred the image of an absolute God. He failed to see that an absolute God who dominates everything teaches domination. There are many on Earth today who still worship Arius' God and place themselves in positions of power over others, claming religious righteousness in doing so. I ask you to see the negative polarity in this, the twist of service to self, done in the name of God.

Athanasius, a bishop, answered Arius. Athanasius said God did not make Christ as subject makes an object. Otherwise the whole universe would be one of duality. God gave of himself, bestowed the seed of divinity into Jesus and into all beings, for that same seed of divinity lies in all of creation.

The debate is not ended. This leads us to the discussion of what is called original sin versus of the idea of creation spirituality, such as that taught by Matthew Fox. Again I use Jesus here not to promote one religion above another, but only as a clear and familiar example. Jesus taught us what to do with this gift of divinity. In the Gospel of John, chapter 14, he says, "Whatsoever ye may ask in my name, that will I do, that the Father may be glorified in the Son." So God gave him divinity, and he used it to serve others. He did not reap the glory of that service for himself; he returned it to God. This is one model of positive polarity, service to others.

You are third-density beings, imperfect at service to others. Fear arises. Your desire to serve another in genuine gratitude and love becomes distorted by that fear. When you ski down a mountain path or walk by a lake taking in the beauty and peace, it is easy to feel gratitude and love. When you reach out to others, serving in whatever ways you can, there is the small voice of the ego that says, what about me? I've talked many times about how to work with that ego self and its fear with compassion, not judgment. I will not repeat those lessons here.

Your work will be far easier if you can keep these two different models of God before you. When you give and say, "What will be returned to me for this giving?" notice the fear, the desire to control, to be dominant, to keep the self safe and separate, even if there is also loving motivation to serve others. Remind yourself not only of the teachings of Jesus, but of so many who have lived the model of service, not claiming or holding anything for themselves. At first this seems a terrifying path, not to hold on to anything for yourself. Will you not be emptied and destroyed? Yes, the human may well be destroyed. The human Jesus lost his physical life. What is it with which we identify, the ego self or the divine self?

In offering himself fully, even to the death of the body, Jesus made a definitive statement to negative polarity (which, we must remember, is just an aspect of self, so he was also speaking to his own fear). The sense of his message was, "Your attempt at domination will not work on me. You have no control over me because all you can take is the body. You cannot touch my divinity. You cannot touch my soul. Fear has no dominion over the power of love."

My dear ones, you are human. The small ego self is going to arise again and again and again. I am not asking you, nor do any ask you, to go and get yourselves crucified, to become martyrs. I ask you only to be mindful of the arising ego self that seeks to dominate, to use that arising as a warning flag, and to come back to the true self.

You each incarnate over and over and over to learn to express divinity with increasing purity. In your early lifetimes, you sent out very little light to the places of darkness in your illusion. As you polish away the ego, the soul mirror of the divine shines brighter, so that divine light and love shining into you is reflected back with increasing brilliance. As you evolve, you claim less of that brilliance for yourself because self is dissolving. Instead you come more and more to emulate those pure beings that return the light fully to the Source. Then service is freely given, not bound by fear. Then much of the stress of offering such service will dissolve. Only fear holds the stress in place.

Some of you know the line in the Metta Sutta [23] that speaks of being "unburdened with duties." Remember this line does not mean that there will be no duties, only that they will not burden one who is skillful. This line offers guidance on how to serve from the open heart, where fear has been resolved. The enactment of this truth is the heart of your practice.

It is this continual process toward positive polarity that brings light where there has been darkness and love where there has been fear. This is why you are here. Remember that you are always in process. You are not

---

[23] Metta Sutta: The teaching on loving-kindness, from the Buddhist scriptures. The opening lines are as follows:

This is what should be done
by those who are skilled in goodness
and would know the path of peace.
Let them be able and upright
Straightforward and gentle in speech
Humble and not conceited

Contented and easily satisfied
Unburdened with duties and frugal in their ways
Peaceful and wise and calm and skillful,
Not proud and demanding in nature.
Let them not do the slightest thing
that the wise would later reprove.

God, but of the same nature as God, truly begotten by God or, phrased differently, partaking of God. Remember who you are, and fear will not win out over the loving heart.

———————————————— 🪷 ————————————————

Q: You tell us nothing is ever lost, but just goes somewhere else or changes form. If my ego keeps getting smaller, doesn't it have to go somewhere? Where is all the ego of all the enlightened beings?

We have a big ego bin here and recycle it. It's far more efficient that way. Often we offer it to aspiring politicians and egocentric world savers.

The Inner Garden

At times you become so lost in the fear, anger, and pain of your lives that you forget that these emotions are not who you are. We've spent much time exploring skillful ways to work with the heavy emotions. Now I want to approach it from a new perspective.

Regard your journey as if it were a river. Your energy is the water's flow. The heavy emotions are logs caught in a logjam. You've been learning how to unjam those logs so that the water may flow unimpeded. To open the channel, you may concentrate on the logs or on the water itself. If you give energy to the logs, trying to fix them, they may become more impacted. You must look elsewhere. When you raise the water level, the logs are freed. When you allow in more love and joy, the heaviness of anger and fear diminish. They become seen for what they are, artifacts of a mind that has solidified itself into fear by losing its connection with the eternal.

How do you raise this water level? My dear ones, you pay so much attention to your fear, so little to the love, patience, generosity, and caring that are a part of you. All these attributes are fragile seeds within your being. They cannot grow without your nurturing attention. Qualities such as generosity are natural to you but are also not you. They move through you when you allow them to do so. They are manifestations of the natural movement of the open heart.

Let us look at joy. We're not talking here about the momentary happiness that comes with getting something you want or doing something well. You receive a pleasing gift and feel happiness. Perhaps it's a new pair of gloves, and then you leave them on the bus. A day later you're without your gloves and feeling sadness at their loss.

Joy is not the happiness that comes from resolving issues in a relationship because even that is fleeting and dependent on things outside yourselves. You feel happiness and that's fine; I'm not negating that. But perhaps the next day there is another argument.

I am talking of a much deeper kind of happiness that I prefer to call joy to differentiate it from impermanent happiness or pleasure.

I have said that all things are impermanent. Certainly this sense of joy is impermanent, in that it is not fixed and unchanging. But when joy is not dependent on things that constantly change, then although it may ebb and flow, a sense of it always remains.

It's a bit like a perennial plant. It emerges when the sun shines on it in the spring and the days lengthen. When the weather cools, it fades, closes, and disappears. There's no sign of it above the surface through the long winter. Then it blossoms again.

I heard a lovely song. One verse is, "Just remember in the winter, far beneath the bitter snows, lies the seed that with the sun's love, in the spring becomes the rose."

That seed is within each of you, and the potential blossom lies within the seed. You can choose to be the sun that with its light and warmth enables the seed to grow. Even in winter, when joy and connection are hidden beneath the snow, you can be aware that they are there and seek ways to nurture them. So although the blossom is changing and impermanent, the seed is always there. It is eternal because it is part of the eternal light and energy of love in its ever-changing manifestations.

What is that kind of joy? Where does it come from? It doesn't depend on material things. It doesn't depend on relationships. Rather, it emerges from clearly seeing things the way they are. It grows from dawning of deep understanding about yourself and your interconnection with all else, an understanding of the nature of that which we call Spirit and of Ground of Being.

This is a joy that does not diminish even in sorrow, loss, and pain. It is the movement of the open heart that knows its most fundamental connection with All that Is and is no longer trapped in the delusion of a separate self and ego.

I ask you to discover this seed of joy in yourselves and to nurture it.

Fear grows out of your small ego self and its sense of separation. As long as the self is viewed as separate, there is need to achieve, to attain. There is much outside of you that you seem to lack.

When you begin to know your connection with all else, fear may still arise but is seen clearly for the delusion it is, and the deeper self can offer the reminder to trust. That which knows the arising of delusion is not deluded.

You may wish to work with such fear with the practice of generosity, whether material or energetic. When you follow the promptings of the open heart despite the frightened voices of the conditioned mind that arise and say, "I can't," you begin to observe from whence those voices arise. They are the patterns and conditions of old mind with its core of self. Although they must be acknowledged—noting, "Feeling fear"—they need not be obeyed. In this way, you begin to establish a new and more skillful pattern of listening to the clearer voice of loving-kindness.

Over and over again it comes to this—fear or love. Which voice will you heed? Can you have the love for yourself to acknowledge your fear uncritically and say to it, "No, not this time"?

When you look back at experiences of generosity and of fearless giving, you find a common thread. You come to feel the connection that allows joyful sharing of your energy and resources. At the heart of it is a feeling not being separate. You are a part of everything. Nothing belongs only to you, and nothing can be taken from you. There is no beginning or end, no depletion or satiation. When you know that, fear dissolves.

As you practice generosity and offer nonjudgmental awareness of fear as it arises, touching the fear with acceptance, compassion allows you to move past your prior limits and know your infiniteness. It is this knowledge of your connection, of the interdependence of All that Is, that leads to real joy and to peace.

There are two directions that mindfulness needs to take. One is the clear seeing of the arising and fading of everything, of all thoughts, feelings, sensations, of all situations, people, relationships, and material objects. This is, because that is. This is not, because that is not. Thus, one comes to understand impermanence and the absence of a self in all things.

But impermanence is not nihilism. The second direction for mindfulness is continuity and interdependence. This is, because that is.... Everything ends, and yet it finds continuance in something else. The garbage becomes the compost that nourishes the plant. The plant creates the food that nourishes the person. There is a constant flow of energy. There is such joy in the experience of knowing oneself to be part of that energy, my dear ones, much peace. This is the understanding through which one transcends birth and death.

You may nurture all the seeds within you with the same process used to nurture generosity. Each time fear arises, it is like a wall around the garden. In endeavoring to protect the fragile seed, it blocks the light. The wall is the armor around your heart, called to defend that soft center that so fears being wounded.

The wall and the plant are not separate, but interrelated parts of the garden. There is no need to get rid of the one with hatred in order to allow the other to thrive, only to touch it with awareness and gently move it aside.

It is not a wall of steel but a living wall, grown from the organic residue of the frightened heart. As you investigate its nature, you will find that it is not solid, but very workable. Trim it a bit if necessary, and gently return the clippings to the soil to nurture the new plants. Allow fear to be a reminder to deeper compassion for the human feeling such fear, such pain, rather than a gateway to anger, greed, or shame.

In this way, nurture your generosity, patience, loving-kindness, truthfulness, joy, wisdom, compassion, energy, and so much more, by constant awareness of their arising and of the walls that would block their light. Remember, there is no getting rid of. As the plant grows strong, you will not need to maintain the walls. They will fall away, dying back into the soil.

Hold forth your intention that all that you do and say should be for the good of all beings. This conscious statement will deepen your commitment and support your intention when the way is difficult.

Are there weeds in your garden? Remember that your impatience or greed grew out of the need to protect the self. You allowed them into your garden for a reason, and they have offered protection to the frightened heart. As you learn your limitlessness, you will have no more need to defend. When energy is given to the new growth of love and connection, the weeds will fall away as disuse weakens their fiber.

This is the garden of your opening heart. Treat it with love, and cherish it as it grows into the light.

A note from Barbara

When Aaron spoke of this garden to our weekly class, he asked us to do an exercise that many found of value. He suggested we each draw a garden where each plant represents some aspect of ourselves. He asked us to put in those plants that were the strongest and the plants we most wanted to nurture in the coming months, those that we felt to be weakest and most in need of loving attention.

He suggested we draw the walls, the weeds, and the entire landscape. Just how big or small is patience in us? How big is energy? What blocks this or that plant from the light?

He emphasized that our drawing skills weren't being measured. Rather, the exercise served two purposes. When one said, "I want to be more generous," the exercise allowed the person to see more clearly exactly what fears block generosity and make giving so painful. The fears lose their solidity as we come to know them intimately.

The second purpose was that he asked us to put these drawings where we could see them as a gentle reminder of our work and even to update them as flowers grew, weeds withered, and walls tumbled.

You might like to try it for yourself.

The Deepening Path of Practice

Q: Is the sky the same color blue where you are?

Truly, yes, but what I perceive is different.
I am not bound by a body and by human
perception. The blues look bluer and the
flowers smell sweeter. I perceive the reality
of things and do not see them through
the lenses of fear, or self, or expectation.
Even in your human form you can learn
to see and hear more clearly. Let go of
your expectations of the way things
should be and you will learn to see them
more truly as they are.

The Dharma Path

Good evening, and my love to you all. I hope you are well, not too tired from your day.[24] I know the first day of retreat can be very exhausting. What you do here in silence is hard work, asking yourselves to be present and awake. Some of you have been practicing vipassana for twenty years or more and some of you began today. What do you all have in common? This little word dukkha. Let's talk a bit about it.

Some of you may not know a lot about the Buddha and the derivations of the teachings we offer you. Please remember that the Buddha was a man, Siddhartha Gautama. He was born a prince, of a high family. He lived a very sheltered life when he was young. It is told that at the time of his birth, a seer informed his father, "This child will become either a great spiritual leader or a great king." His father wanted him to become a great king, so he sheltered him from the kinds of concerns that might lead him into a spiritual life.

The story goes that as a young man he went out into the city with his driver in a carriage. There he saw a man who was sick. He must have had a cold sometime or seen somebody with a bellyache, but he had never seen serious sickness. "What's that?" he asked the driver.

"That is sickness," the driver replied.

"Will that happen to me?"

"Yes. It happens to everyone."

Then, he passed a very old person. He had never seen an old person before. "What is that?"

"That is old age."

"Will that happen to me? Will it happen to my loved ones?"

"Yes. It happens to everyone."

Then he saw a dead person being carried up from the street. He had

---

[24] This talk was given the first night of a nine day meditation retreat.

never seen a corpse before. "What's that?"

"That is death, and it also happens to everyone."

He understood then that no matter what he did, no matter what his family did, they would not be spared sickness, old age, and death, and they would experience the suffering that may accompany these experiences.

Siddartha Gautama knew there must be an answer. Finally, he saw a spiritual practitioner dressed in a loincloth, with long, matted hair. "What is that?" he asked the driver.

"That is one who goes out to seek after the truth."

This final sight revealed the answer: to become a spiritual seeker. It must have been very difficult, very painful for him to leave his beloved wife and son, his parents, his friends, and all his pleasurable possessions, but he went. He became a monk, determined that he would not return home until he had resolved the issue of human suffering. Siddhartha Gautama's intent was to resolve not only his own suffering but to find the path out of suffering for all beings. It was quite an amazing undertaking.

The predominate spiritual practice in India in his day was a practice of high concentration. Holding an object tightly with one's mind, one merged self and object or absorbed into the object. This intense concentration process led to very refined and blissful states of consciousness. He found the leading teachers of this practice and studied with them until he surpassed their abilities. Each of his teachers begged him, "Stay with me and teach." But he said, "No, because while these blissful states are very beautiful, very rich, they do not lead to liberation." He could have had fame and a very comfortable life as a teacher, but he saw that this path led only to a new form of grasping. He was after nothing short of liberation and uncovering that path for all beings. He held that goal before him, not with grasping born of fear, but with dedication born of love.

So, he decided to try to live as a renunciant, letting go of everything physical. He came very close to starvation. They say that for some time he lived on just a grain of rice a day. But, actually, he was dying on a grain of rice a day, and he saw that he had no energy; he couldn't practice. He was close to death when he finally took wholesome food. He renounced that direction also and said, "There has to be a middle way between renunciation and grasping."

He saw that to focus the mind and absorb deeply into objects, thus avoiding the present moment's experience, was not the path. To be overinvolved with the movements of mind and body in this moment, trying to control what arose in mind or body, was not the path. Thus, he determined simply to be present in each moment's experience. He resolved to care for the body with kindness, not to deny the needs of the body, but not to indulge, to watch the mind that sought indulgence and to learn kindness as a response to the moods of body and mind. Notice, I use the word *kindness* and not *self-discipline.* He resolved to learn the kindness that says no to overindulgence, because certainly it is not a kindness to oneself to overindulge in any physical or mental direction. So, he learned balance and came to practice the middle way, not too little and not too much.

The time came when he felt that he was close to understanding the roots of suffering. On that famous night, when he sat down he said, "I will sit here until I am enlightened." That might seem a very immodest intention but he understood that, karmically, he was ripe for this. If you go out tonight and decide to sit under a tree and say, "I'll sit here until I am enlightened," that might not be realistic for you. You have to understand your degree of readiness. That does not mean you cannot have very profound experience of the Unconditioned, but it may not lead you to become a fully enlightened being unless you are ready. The important thing is to sit with the intention to be present and let enlightenment take care of itself. But for the Buddha, his intention was to sit until he was enlightened.

There's a very beautiful story of how he was challenged by the forces of *Mara*,[25] that is, by all the difficult forces of greed, of lust, of anger, and so forth. Whether that actually happened or not, I find it a beautiful metaphor, because every time you sit you are challenged by Mara. We sit for half an hour and think, "Oh, I'm a little hungry. Maybe I've done enough meditation. I'll go and eat. After all, that would be kindness to myself." If you were starving, it would be kindness to yourself, but since none of you is starving, if you've decided to sit for an hour and feel a bit of hunger in your belly, it's just Mara saying, "Go and eat! Go and eat! Get up and take a walk. Make that phone call. Call the lovely lad or lady you met yesterday. Call a friend. Why sit here all alone? Let's turn on the TV. How about a little entertainment? Got to wash my hair."

Ah, so many directions that your energy can go. Difficult emotions like anger, lust, and shame all have their turn. Restlessness in the body and in the

---

[25] Mara: In the Buddhist tradition, Mara is the shadow side of being. Please don't think of Mara as a personification of evil. Rather, this is our negative habitual tendency breaking through. We don't battle the force of Mara to destroy it but greet it with a kind awareness that will reduce and eventually dissolve its power. Where there is negative thought, kindness and skillful action is right there too. When we know that, we see that we can think the unwholesome thought and still not act it out.

mind will come. Sleepiness will come. Anyone who meditates can identify with what happened to the Buddha that night. All those forces came forth and said, "What right do you have to claim enlightenment?"

He touched the earth and said, "The earth is my witness; I have done what needs to be done to open the enlightened mind." By that he meant that he had paid attention; he had balanced and purified both old karma and the present mind and energies, and had brought about the balance of all the forces of faith, energy, compassion, wisdom, mindfulness, and concentration. What had to be done, had been done.

He sat through the night and learned many different things. I will briefly relate some of them. He saw the nature of this conditioned world and how it relates to the Unconditioned. When I say *conditioned world*, I mean the world that we live in, a world in which all physical and mental objects arise out of conditions and cease to exist when the conditions cease. When the wind blows the water on the lake, it ripples. When the wind dies away, the ripples stop. They may not stop instantaneously. There will be a bit of residual energy that dies away more slowly, but eventually the ripples will stop. When certain conditions are present to give rise to anger, anger will arise. When the conditions cease, the anger will cease, not instantly, but it will cease.

With anger and other heavy emotions the difficulty is that in trying to figure out how to conquer the emotion, how to master it, how to be free of it, how not to act it out, you are giving it energy. For example, when anger has arisen, you start to think that you have to conquer the anger in order to be free of it. Then your energy contracts, trying to banish anger, angry at anger. This is just more anger.

You have to attend to it or harm will result. How do you attend without making it more solid? We must be very careful. It's possible to dissociate from the emotions, to hide away in some ultimate place that's not angry and deny the reality of anger on the relative plane. That doesn't work either. There is a middle way, not lost in the anger, not denying the anger, but aware that, in this moment, anger is present in you. That which is aware of the anger is not angry. Both are true: there is anger and there is also awareness that is free of anger.

When you look in this way, you see that the anger is there, dependent on conditions, and that which is not angry, the inherently awake mind, is also present. There is an exercise that will clarify this experience. Hold up your hand, just six inches in front of your head. Wiggle your fingers. Look at the fingers move. Stare at the fingers. Get them firmly in your vision. Now, while the hand is still moving and the fingers wiggling, I want you to look through the fingers. Look up here, right through your fingers at Barbara. If you can see me, so much the better. Right there—the fingers haven't gone anywhere; they're still moving, and there is that vast ground beyond.

Your practice is not to deny one or the other, nor is it to choose one over the other. If one finger is badly cut and bleeding, you're going to need to stop and bandage it. If the fingers are pulled into a fist about to reach out and punch somebody, you're going to need to restrain them. You cannot ignore the hand and the fingers, but you also cannot ignore the vast space. This that is beyond the conditioned objects, the Buddha came to see, is the Unconditioned. His practice led him to the direct experience of the Unconditioned.

What is the Unconditioned? I've had that question from you countless times. I cannot tell you what it is. I can tell you what it's not. It is not born. It is not limited. It is not dependent upon conditions for its existence. In moving beyond our finger exercise, be careful not to think it is just the space between objects. It is everything; it is the space and also the objects themselves. Everything is the Unconditioned or an expression of it.

In the Udana scripture, the Buddha says to a gathering of monks, "Oh, monks, there is an unborn, undying, unchanging, uncreated. If it were not so, there would be no reason for our practice." He's saying that our practice is not just to realize the nature of the conditioned realm, but to look beyond and find that which has always been there, right there in our direct, immediate experience. The Unconditioned is not somewhere out there. It's not at the end of fifty years or fifty lifetimes of practice, it's right here in this moment. You may find only the barest glimpse of it, but it's here.

So, what is this Unconditioned? Some of you, in your group meetings today, talked about a fear of annihilation. I understand the fear, because I once experienced it, and yet what you fear is so different from the reality of the experience of no-self. How can anything cease to exist? When a tree falls in the forest, through the years the wood rots into the soil in which a seedling from that tree has sprouted. A century later there's a mighty tree again, an ancient tree. We can't say it's the same tree. We also can't really say it's a different tree. What do *same* and *different* mean in this context?

This collection of aggregates that you call self—those of form, feelings, perception, mental formations, and consciousness—come out of conditions, and then they go. What if you identified with your ten-year-old form, carried a picture around of yourself as a ten year old, and every time you looked into the mirror, your reflection scared you? You would say, "I've disappeared! Who is this stranger?" What if you had a specific opinion and wrote it, then learned things that led you to change that opinion, and later you read the early statement? Would you think, "I don't believe that anymore, so where have I gone? Where has the mind gone that held these thoughts? I've disappeared!"

There is a story told about the great master Ramana Maharshi. When he was dying, his disciples gathered around his bed. Some of them were wailing, "Master, Master, Don't leave us!" Maharshi opened his eyes and looked at them, and said, "Where would I go?" The body dissolves. That which Is, is.

So, that night the Buddha came to realize the relationship between the conditioned realm and the Unconditioned, directly experienced the Unconditioned, and was liberated from any delusion of owning a separate self. He also saw deeply into the truth of what he called *dukkha* and what came to be called the Four Noble Truths. The First Noble Truth is simply that dukkha exists. The word is translated as *suffering*. I like the Pali word dukkha because the meaning is very precise. *Kha* means the hub of a wheel. *Du* means off center. Dukkha is the wheel off center on the hub of the cart axle. As the cart rolls, it lurches one way and then the other. There's nothing wrong with the lurching motion. You go to an amusement park and want the ride to lurch. If it didn't, you would complain. You spent a lot of money to be tossed about. But, most of the time you want the cart to roll smoothly. You expect that it will. There's grasping to make it move that way.

Medical men of that day offered their advice using a set formula: here is the problem; here is the cause of the problem; here is the resolution; here is the manner of obtaining the resolution. Buddha presented the statement of the Four Noble Truths in just that way. Here is dukkha. The cause of dukkha is craving. There is liberation from dukkha. That is the resolution. And then he outlined the Eightfold Path, a path out of suffering, which I will not speak of tonight.

What of the statement, craving is the cause of suffering? If you have a toothache, it's very unpleasant; it's painful. The direct experience of pain is a difficult experience. When you want the toothache to stop so much that you're grasping at that idea, you cannot experience the kindness of people around you and cannot feel the sunshine on your face. You close your heart because of the intensity of the aversion to this toothache. That's suffering. Your vipassana practice will not free you from the experience of pain. It will lead you to understand the nature of suffering.

There are stories in the suttas of the Buddha having an accident and experiencing pain in the body. Even he, enlightened though he was, experienced pain if he hurt himself. As you learn to distinguish between the direct experience of pain or any unpleasant physical or mental experience and how you relate to that experience, you start to see that you can relax with pain. It's helpful to start with small pain. A big pain may be too much to manage at first. Itching is a favorite of mine. I don't know anybody who has ever died of a small itch, but it can be very unpleasant and does get your attention. A helpful fly buzzing around your head is another welcome guest. Watch the thought and contraction, "I don't want it to be this way." Then the heart opens to your situation. See how the mind creates suffering when it latches onto how things "should" be.

There is freedom, and that freedom is very wonderful. It comes in increments. Before you have complete freedom, you have little bits of freedom, but don't give up on complete freedom. You are capable of that. It's not so far away.

Awakening, the Buddha saw what he called the Cycle of Dependent Origination: that when this is present, then that will arise. When this ceases, that will cease. It's said very beautifully in the first sutta, the Turning of the Wheel Sutta. "That which has the nature to arise has the nature to cease." We add that it is not me or mine. When you understand this truth, indeed suffering will decrease.

What of the cycle of dependent arising? Very briefly, the senses of body or mind make contact with an object. Pleasant, unpleasant, or neutral feelings arise. Mental formations arise, followed by what we call "becoming and rebirth." Rebirth is not just about a new lifetime. It's about each time you swat at the bumblebee, feeling aversion, "I must swat it; it will sting me," moving deeper and deeper into fear and into separation from the bee and from your self. Each time you do that, you create the next moment of your relationship.

If you swat at a person in the same way, not using your hands, but your heart, there's a constant rebirth into a more negative relationship with that person: your boss, your mother, or your child. Each moment's choices plant the seed for the next moment.

Coming out into the fresh morning after the long night leading to his enlightenment, the Buddha was aware of what had happened, how he had found the liberation he sought. Remember that he was a man, not a God. His title, the Buddha, means only "the one who is awake." What he discovered, you can discover. He did not create the dharma, but he realized it, as you can too.

For many days he was quiet, absorbing the fruits of liberation. He thought, "Nobody will understand this. I cannot teach it. But then again," he thought, "some people will understand and so I must try to share it." Out of this courage and compassion comes the welling forth of the dharma to you today, beings hearing the dharma, learning to live the dharma and aspiring, in whatever way, to share it with others.

You don't have to be formal teachers. You share the dharma each time you open your heart to another being. Don't separate, but listen to that person and respond compassionately and appropriately. Compassionate response does not mean weak, frightened response. It may be a firm saying of "No! You may not speak to me in that way." But you respond authentically from a clear place that doesn't separate *me* and *him*. Thus, there is that balance of wisdom that sees without separation and with compassion.

I'd like to leave you with this final thought. This path has been walked by innumerable beings for twenty-five hundred years. It's not a New Age teaching. I have nothing against New Age teaching. I just want to reaffirm the deep roots of this path. Innumerable beings have found true liberation from suffering, have found the ability to enter the world from a deeply authentic, present, compassionate, and skillful place, and in this way, have transformed the world, both the outer world and their own inner worlds. You don't have to call it Buddhism. I want to give credit to my teacher, who is the one who first articulated this path. But, of course, we cannot say that he was the first person who understood it. There were other cultures, with different articulations that understood the whole interplay of the conditioned and unconditioned realms, and many cultures and religions in which it was taught to love one another, but the Buddha gave us precise instructions. If I am to love others and yet anger is in my heart, how do I work with that?

I have the deepest reverence for the one you know as Jesus, who said, "Turn the other cheek." For some who are already very close to enlightenment, that might be enough instruction, but I was a bit dense. I needed specific instructions about how to turn the other cheek and not get lost either in my anger or in being some kind of a martyr. So these teachings and path truly led me to freedom.

As you know, I have practiced many different religions through many different lifetimes. Each of them has much beauty in it, and each major religion of your earth has a deep core of truth. But this path of openhearted awareness will lead you to freedom. The nature of that freedom is that you reenter your life passionate and alive. The awakened person is not dispassionate. Nonattached does not mean disconnected. The more free you become, the more passionately alive you become— and that is something this world very much needs, people who can be passionately alive but not caught in separatist views. I deeply honor that you are here with the intention to walk this path. Not only can you do it, you are doing it. Your presence here speaks that louder than any words can. Trust your practice. Practice with courage and with love, and the path will open before you.

May all beings everywhere be free from suffering. May all beings come to know their true nature and the nature of All that Is. May all beings everywhere be happy and find peace.

Nonduality

Q: What do you mean by nonduality? (Editorial note: this question has been asked many times, and Aaron's replies have brought forth many aspects of the answer. Rather than try to synthesize the ideas, we have chosen to include excerpts of several talks, offered separately.)

Nonduality does not mean "not two" or "only one." On the relative plane there are seemingly separate beings with their own distinct forms, thoughts, and feelings. Thus we cannot say "not two" and still honor relative reality. On the ultimate plane there is only One, but it has innumerable expressions. Nonduality means that nothing is separate, in the way that your fingers are both distinct and also not separate from the hand. The raindrop of water exists but is also not separate from the sea into which it falls. The tree in the forest seems distinct, but in a hundred years it will be the earth out of which new trees grow. Even the mountain is not separate in its ultimate form. Some day it will erode away and then may appear as prairie or desert. Note that it does not cease to exist. Nothing in the conditioned realm is separate. Everything inter-exists with all else. Thus we call it "empty of a separate self." This is true of physical and mental forms, of energy, and of anything you can imagine.

There is what we might call Ground of Being or simply Being, divinity, That which Is, unborn and undying, Essence, God or Goddess, or Unconditioned. I favor this last term, drawn from Buddhist teaching, because of its clarity. *Unconditioned*: that which exists with no conditions needed for its existence. The Buddha also calls it "the uncreated." These are only a few of the conventional labels given.

Please do not think of Essence as a thing. Do not give it personalized characteristics. It is no separate thing, but everything. There is nothing else but This, in all it's expressions. It is the nature of God or Essence to express itself. Your universe is full of the conditioned expressions of the Unconditioned. There are those direct expressions that are not dependent for their existence on any other conditioned element, but only on the Unconditioned itself. Two examples are the innate sound and the radiance of the Unconditioned. The first is experienced as *nada,* the sound of silence. The second is ground luminosity, the innate radiance of All that Is. There is also an energetic vibration, a scent, and a taste that are direct expressions of the Unconditioned. Pure awareness is a direct expression of the Unconditioned.

These are the direct expressions. There are also indirect expressions, expressions that have Essence as Ground but also are dependent on other conditions for their existence. These are the billion and more expressions of your world, as forms, thoughts, and energy. A rainbow is an expression of the Unconditioned, but it cannot exist without the material conditions of rain and sunshine and certain atmospheric conditions. Ground luminosity needs no such conditions. But both are expressions of the Unconditioned. A thought is an expression of the Unconditioned but needs other conditions to exist so it is an indirect expression. Pure awareness is a direct expression. As long as the Unconditioned exists, pure awareness will exist.

Of what use is it to you to know this? You so easily separate yourselves, viewing spirit as something outside the self, and divinity as something to be attained. You separate your experience into holy and mundane and diminish the mundane, thinking of it as only mundane and therefore trivial. But it is through the mundane that this holiness comes forth onto the earth.

When you think and act only from the separated self, you lose touch with your true Being. Yet to take as real only that true Being is to deny the divinity of everything. Your work is to stay present with both, to know the Ground through your meditation and learn to rest there with stability while relating to the elements of mundane existence.

The image of a pure spring may help. Imagine pure water pouring forth from the earth. It tumbles down the mountain and, ten miles below, becomes a river filled with water and also cow dung, dead insects, and other debris. Where is the pure water? If you want a drink, there is no need to climb ten miles to the spring; just filter what is here. Where would the pure water go? It is right here.

In just the same way, divinity is not lost when heavy emotion or negative thought arises. Both are present. You do not swallow the cow dung in the river water; you know it for what it is. Cow dung is cow dung; pure water is pure water. You use a filter. It allows you to choose the pure water, even when mixed with the dung. The dung has its own uses and is not discarded.

; anger. You do not need to get rid of anger to find compassion, you need only to look deeper, beyond the anger. All the innate goodness of your heart is right there, with fear, anger, and other turbulence.

This is the prime teaching of nonduality. A major value of knowing the nondual nature of the universe is to teach you where to look, so that you may cease this separation that has been your habit. When you cease to view anything as other than an expression of the divine and begin to seek divinity right where you are, then assuredly you will find it.

What is nonduality? Sometimes on the surface there appears to be conflict, but if we look deeper, we can find the place where conflict resolves. The farmer may wish for rain, the hiker wish for sunshine. If there were no rain, after a long drought and scarcity of food, the hiker would certainly wish for it too. My point here is that there is no duality at the deepest level, while on the surface level there seem to be differing needs, opinions, and thoughts.

Here is another place where the delusion of duality appears. There are conditioned expressions and there is That which Is. There is no separation between them. There is no separation between one brilliant sunbeam falling on your face as you walk through the woods and the sun itself. There is no separation between the raindrop and the rain shower. Each raindrop is an expression of the shower. The sunbeam is an expression of the sun. When you differentiate and say, "These raindrops are bad because they wet my garments, but the rain shower is good because it waters the crops," then you create an illusion of duality. That illusion enhances the sense of separation and deepens the polarity of "good" versus "bad."

Contraction arises when you create separation with your experiences. Contraction is a symptom of separation and not the separation itself, When you contract, you energetically separate yourself from the natural flow of light and energy that would otherwise move through you. You may fight the raindrops because you dislike getting wet. With such a fight, your energy contracts. There is no need for war with the raindrops. Just put on rainwear.

The experience of the nondual is the experience of the uncontracted state. The Uncontracted does not arise; it *is*, as Ground. No matter what arises, that uncontracted state is available to you. Thoughts, opinions, sensations, and contractions arise. The Uncontracted does not cease to exist because contraction arises. Both exist simultaneously, and contraction is an expression of the Uncontracted. Each arising is simply seen as an expression of Ground of Being. Contractions will arise. That which is aware of the contraction is not contracted.

The experience of duality arrives when you contract around any given expression, thinking "this is a good one" or "this is a bad one," "this one has to be controlled or gotten rid of," "this one needs to be fixed." Then you may contract around that judgment, the small self believing it must fix a distorted expression that arose. That contraction further cements the whole experience of duality and separates you from the truth of nonduality. In other words, as you begin to take the small self's stories as all there is and become lost in them, you lose the bigger picture.

This does not mean that you would be wise to strive to live in a space that only sees the nondual and refuses to acknowledge the expressions. Such denial of what is simply gives rise to another contraction. To contract around the existence of the expression or to contract in such a way as to deny the existence are both contractions. When awareness sees this happen and steps outside of identification with the contractions, the contractions are not offered more energy and will go in their own time. I repeat, that which is aware of contraction is uncontracted.

A main point I want to make here is about the nature of the relationship between the dual or contracted state and the nondual or uncontracted state and how this relationship can become a focal point in your practice, in your lives, in everything.

How do you relate lovingly and skillfully to all these dualistic expressions and attend to them with kindness without getting drawn into a belief that they really are separate in any way?

Do any of you have fruit trees? For the tree to produce good fruit, you've got to prune it. How is it to cut off a branch, to trim the outer twigs? One could say that is an aggressive act toward the tree. And yet the intention is to support the health of the tree and help it bring forth the fruit.

I think any of you could cut off those branches that need to be pruned without any contraction, certainly without any aversion to the tree or intention to harm. You can act in a very direct way. Take your pruning shears and snip. There is no aversion to what is pruned nor to the act of pruning. There is no contraction.

I use this as an illustration. You can perform the work as necessary while holding in your mind the greater truth of the flourishing tree, the flourishing orchard, the flourishing orchards all over the world that will feed countless beings, and yet with no attachment to making anything happen, just joyful co-creation. Similarly, you can attend to negative thought without contracting around the thought, without taking it as self. There is no need to hate the thought, but you attend to it. You prune it, with kindness.

What about nonattachment? When I was a monk in Thailand, a piece of daily work was to sweep the walking paths. In front of my hut was a path of perhaps twenty or thirty feet, and I would sweep it daily with a broom. In some weather it would be covered again with leaves five minutes after I swept it. I still only swept it once a day, sweeping without attachment to results, sweeping to sweep. There was a skillful decision to keep the path walkable, but no attachment to holding that moment of perfection.

It is in this way that we learn to relate to the seemingly dualistic expressions that come as catalysts in our lives, to attend to them without contraction, without any attachment to a result, but with kindness, with patience, with love. When you live your life in that way, you can live from a place of truth that both relates skillfully to the conditioned expression and simultaneously rests stably in the unconditioned.

This is the heart of your practice—to learn how to do that. The greatest importance of the practice of balance between dual and nondual is that when you relate with tension-free effort, karma is resolved. You literally step outside the karmic field when you rest in this spacious awareness.

When something comes up and pushes at you, and you push back, you may get sucked into the vortex you have co-created Your mind starts spinning about the situation; emotions come up about it. A self develops. Very literally, the more solid the sense of self, the more compacted the whole energy field, chakras, and so forth. And the more compacted all of that is, the more you come into a self-perpetuating sense of self. The only way out is to shift back into the spaciousness of the Unconditioned. Practice teaches you this spaciousness and how to rest there when something shoves at you. Feeling fear, feeling contraction, feeling anger, you can still rest stably in spacious awareness without any denial of the feelings. None of these emotions needs to create contraction, but if any of them does, as we said earlier, it is just contraction. It came and it will go. No big deal.

When you learn to rest in spacious awareness, there are two results: one is the more skillful, joyful living of your daily life, and the other is that this gradually opening awareness—this mind that has the increasing ability to touch the nondual, the Unconditioned—stabilizes and goes ever deeper into the direct experience of ultimate reality.

I personally don't think there is any such thing as instant enlightenment, although there may seem to be. Beings that experience it are ripe, whether from their work in their present lifetimes or their work in past lifetimes. Realization is the fruit of that work. If you are practicing in a clear and committed way, there may be an explosion of understanding seemingly out of the blue, but you had already created a conscious grounding for it.

With a seemingly sudden experience of enlightenment, there comes a strong shift of consciousness. If the work has not been done consciously in this lifetime, then you must go back and do the conscious work to integrate the shift. Either way, the shift we call *realization* is the outgrowth of much past effort and learning.

Even with dedicated practice, it is possible that there may never be that extraordinary experience, just a gradual deepening so that you have increasing access to the nondual realm. You stop distinguishing so much between the ultimate and relative experience. You just look at each expression and know, "Here is an aspect of the divine." Nothing separate, and yet each expression must be attended to. Here is the enlightened mind.

I would like to offer you an exercise. Please look at one place where contraction comes up strongly for you, maybe in a work situation or a personal relationship where the other person serves as a frequent catalyst, maybe in a health situation with something occurring in your physical body, or with an emotion such as jealousy or impatience. Take just one thing in your daily life and watch it. For the first week, just watch each time it comes up and be aware of the nature of your relationship with it. How does your energy feel to you? Do you close up? Is there contraction? Don't try to figure out where it's coming from or how to fix it. Just note, "Here is a catalyst that deeply provokes the contracted state for me and leads me into a feeling of separation."

After a few days of watching it, each time it comes up begin to watch more deeply with the question, "How do I relate, not to that catalyst itself, but to the contracted state that comes after the catalyst?"

The next question I want you to ask yourself is a very specific one. "In this moment, what does moving into this state of contraction give me? Acknowledging that I don't like the contracted state, am I getting any benefit from this? Is it just habit energy, or is there a will that moves me into this contracted state for a reason?" Just ask those questions. If you see a benefit, such as that you feel safer, just note it. Don't judge it; don't try to fix anything. Just note.

And then another question a few days later. "What if I release this contracted state? What if I acknowledge the presence of the uncontracted right here and now along with the contracted? Without denial of the contraction or of the catalyst for the contraction, what if I move into that spaciousness, or am I attached to this narrow space?"

What do you have to lose? Literally, what do you have to lose by allowing yourself to see the simultaneous existence of the uncontracted and that you can choose the uncontracted without denial of the contractions? Perhaps you will find that all you have to lose is the old habit of staying in small spaces rather than allowing the self to open into its true Being.

Thank you for hearing me. My blessings and love to you all.

In the beginning[26] there was no beginning. We speak here of the birthless. Of course I was not there. I do not speak from personal experience. My understanding of it, from my present experience and from that of my teachers, is that the infinite truly is infinite. It did not begin with a big bang. There has always been energy. One can conjecture that this energy was neutral in its polarity and, through its increasing experience, moved toward the expression of positive polarity until it ceased to display negativity.

There was no duality within this infinite energy. Precisely because it began as neutral, it contained within it both positivity and negativity, but it resolved its relationship with negativity and no longer experienced or displayed it as a contracted state. If a negative thought arose, it was simply noted and released. That which Is was still neutral, and it remains neutral. Because of the intention of nonharm, it ceased to display the negative, or contracted, state. It chose to express only the positive, or uncontracted, state. Because of that choice, we label it as positive polarity.

One could debate philosophically whether or not negativity is contained in positivity. But certainly both are contained in neutral. You have heard me talk of both light and the relative absence of light. When any energy expresses as perfect positive polarity[27] the resultant expression of negativity also manifests as light. There is no longer the expression of darkness, or decreased light, no longer contraction out of which darkness comes.

---

[26] From the Nonduality transcripts, currently being compiled into a book, *Radiant Passage;* expected publication, 2005.

[27] Within positive polarity, if an impulse of "contractedness" arises, the response is one that automatically releases and transforms the contracted impulse. The result is uncontracted, positive expression.

This is an important point. Had this energy originally manifested as absolute light, one could then conceive of its essential nature as dualistic with darkness. Another important factor: its first expression was as neutral, so expansion, change, and flexibility are part of its essence. With neutrality, it is not fixed in any place, but always open. The principles of giving and receiving are not contradictory; they must both exist within a nondual energy.

We have here the core of the predicament. If this energy contains all light and darkness, "good" and "evil," positivity and negativity, giving and receiving, the human who vows to reflect only the positive must meet with failure. He cannot avoid the arisings of greed, anger, and all the other expressions of ego-based fear that are part of human experience. If his thoughts of greed and hatred are judged as "evil" and antithetical to God, then his work would be to smother those thoughts, perhaps through practices of austerity or through a strong focusing of the mind that instantly cuts off and denies fear-based arising. Doing so does not make him a more loving person or a wiser person, only a more controlling person. Thus, control and power are viewed as the attributes of the divine most highly regarded by persons who choose this solution. Judgment is predominant.

But if someone acknowledges that negative thoughts will arise if the conditions are present for their arising, then he can shift his focus away from control or denial, to creation of a skillful, loving relationship with what has arisen. It then becomes a question of responsibility and intention. He wishes to be responsible for his emotions and thoughts and holds the intention to do no harm. Is he better able to bring these goals forth through continually deeper control or by the opening that helps to resolve negative movement so that it ceases to arise? Yet while he does this latter work, he still must use self-restraint not to enact the emotion.

When one sees the divine as nondual, one does not need to subdue the arisings of fear-based ego, but only to draw those arisings more strongly into the heart of love. Just as this infinite energy was drawn increasingly to express itself in uncontracted expression until it became the epitome of positive polarity, so is the human who embraces nonduality drawn along this path.

Within every religious tradition that I have ever encountered in any incarnation, this schism exists. There are those who will distort the teachings of any tradition into a statement of the dual nature of the universe, and will state that "evil" must be destroyed. There are those who will focus on the nondual nature and simply understand that darkness must be invited into the light.

Once upon a non-time there was energy, Being. It did not begin, it simply was, is, and will be, because it is infinite and unlimited. It contains the attributes of infinite intelligence, infinite light, infinite love. It contains no self-centered thoughts; it simply is.

Awareness and nonawareness are nondual. One may conjecture that nonawareness was part of the experience of this energy. Being opened into the experience of awareness. Its nonawareness rests within its awareness, which rests within its nonawareness. Nondual. Imagine a clean, smooth piece of paper. Crumple it, then smooth it a bit. Wrinkles remain. Even when the paper is wrinkled, the perfect, unwrinkled sheet still exists within the wrinkled sheet. Where else could it be but right there? When nonawareness is predominant, awareness rests within nonawareness. Awareness is.

Because awareness is nondual, everything—change and non-change, for example—resides within it. It manifested infinite expressions of itself. One distorted but useful expression that it manifested is relative reality, the world we see around us. To phrase this in another way: what we call God manifested an expression of itself. It offered its energy to that particular bias of experience that we label relative reality. Because That which Is extended all attributes of itself to relative reality, it extended the free will for this relative reality to create itself further. Here is where we move into dependent origination.

Any bias depends for its sense of direction on the distortions of that which chooses to manifest within the bias. Some beings have chosen to manifest within the bias of relative reality as humans because it provides them a useful catalyst for expansion. Specifically, it provides them the pathway by which each mind-body-spirit expression may expand into the purest understanding of its true nature and thereby begin to manifest its energy in the same way as did that which we call God.

❧

*Q: Aaron, what happens to all the socks that disappear
from my laundry?*

They spin into the higher densities and we thoroughly enjoy them here, as we don't have the idea you humans do that they must match. They are very colorful!

*Q: Would you mind sending some favorites back? In return, I'll send
you the ones that were pairs to socks that got holes.*

We'd be glad to ask them if they will return, but you must understand that if they come back it must be through reincarnation. They will be very small, infant socks, you might say.

*Q: If time is nonlinear, can't you send them back before they get lost
and need to reincarnate?*

That would be before you've made this request, and they'll simply spin away again. To insist they not spin away would be a violation of their free will.

Q: Can you just keep sending them back?

Please note that they do not belong to you but merely agree to live with you. If they have decided to pursue their journey elsewhere, what right have I to interfere? I think you had best take it up with the socks.

Have you heard the saying, "Trust God and tie your camel"? Before you wash them, ask them if they will please remain in the machine and express your love and appreciation. Then pin them together. You may lose whole pairs, but at least you won't have odd socks. Or start a new custom of wearing mismatched socks. They really are very lovely that way. Are there further questions?

God and Buddhism: A Series of Questions

Q: Buddhism teaches that everything is emptiness. Nothing substantive or permanent exists, such as a soul or God, and therefore all things are empty by nature, that is, empty of self or "zero." I've been a practitioner of Buddhist meditation for over twenty years, yet at times I sense the existence of a soul and of God. Can you comment on this?

First we must consider the meaning of the words *God, soul,* and *empty.* On the ultimate level, there is nothing separate or permanent in itself. This is often phrased as, "All things are empty of a separate self," and as you phrased it, "Nothing substantive or permanent exists." If you consider God as something separate from all else, as something that controls all else, that idea is inconsistent with Buddhist teaching and with the nondual experience arrived at through vipassana meditation. This separate and controlling deity is a limited idea of that which we might call *God.* There is still *the deathless* but we must understand what we mean by that phrase.

That which Is—let us call it Ground of Being, the Unconditioned, or the "unborn, undying, unchanging, uncreated" of Buddhist scripture—is an ultimate reality. It also is empty of any separate self. Yet we call it "undying, unchanging." How can it be that there exists an "undying, unchanging" as the sutta says, and that nothing is permanent? This is where your practice must take you. I can promise you that God exists, but that promise will be meaningless to you until you discover it for yourself. I believe you have begun to do this and you must learn to honor what you feel with your heart.

The word *soul* usually refers to the combination of the mental and spirit bodies. The mental body is conditioned and therefore impermanent. The expression *pure spirit body* refers to that which is not conditioned and not separate. Thus, *pure spirit body* and *soul* are not synonymous. So your explorations may more correctly lead you to the pure spirit body, and not to the soul.

Empty. What is emptiness? Do you understand that everything and nothing are the same? I see that you know this in an intellectual way, but your heart will not accept it. Where does the mist go when the morning sun shines bright? Has it ceased to exist? The mist may have seemed solid, and yet it has no substance. It is an impermanent expression of the atmosphere. Its essence has not ceased to exist; it has only moved into a new form. Where does the mountain go after eons of rain and wind have pounded it into dust? Now it expresses as desert. Nothing ceases. It is undying. Yet the individuated expressions are not permanent. What seems separate and substantive are only expressions of the Unconditioned. We must understand the relationship of these conditioned expressions to the Unconditioned or Ground.

What of Ground of Being? It is everything and it is nothing. You cannot point to any one expression and say, "This is it;" you can only point to all expressions and say, "These are expressions of it." Eventually you stop distinguishing: the ant is divinity, the whale is divinity, the human infant is divinity, as is the dying flower. There is a teaching from the Christian scriptures, "The all is in the all."

Learn about this idea of everything and nothing being the same from silence. You understand when you meditate that the silence is full. The deeper you go into the stillness, the more you find there. Some people will hear nada, the sound of silence. This sound is like the evaporated mist. It is everywhere. Some people will see the ground luminosity, which also permeates everything and cannot be lost. The deeper you go into the emptiness, the more you find, until you suddenly understand that God is there.

This is not self, nor anything of form or consciousness, nor any of the aggregates of self. It is the level where there is no concept of self, as the Buddha taught. And it is empty of self, as he taught. But that part of you that is no-self, that which is part of the One, resides there. It is through your life in this heart we all share, this spirit we all share, that you find the deathless.

This is not a self with consciousness and continuity, but when you reach this level, there is simply Oneness. Truly we are all one.

Some beings rest in this space with no awareness of the conditioned. I am always in this space, but I am also cognizant of the conditioned. This is my own learning now, to teach others and grow in compassion and wisdom as I do so. It is my choice, even as your learning in this lifetime is your choice. And yet, although I have temporarily chosen to assume the cloak of personality and consciousness, I dwell in this oneness too, and it is my constant experience, as you try to make unbounded awareness your constant experience.

It is simply a matter of degree. Bound as you are by physical form, it is hard for you to go as deeply as I can. That is fine. You are always in the right form and on the right plane to learn what you have chosen to learn. Trust that, and honor your heart's wisdom. Please meditate on this. My words can take you only so far. The true understanding must come from within your own heart.

Q: You have talked about God, yet much of what you teach is Buddhism, and there is no mention of God in the Buddha's teaching. Why does the Buddha deny the existence of God?

I feel the confusion behind your questions. Let us take them one at a time. We are not concerned with an *ism* here, but with truth. You are not fundamentally a Christian, a Moslem, a Jew, or a Buddhist, but a spirit having a human experience. Through your many lifetimes you have participated in most of the major religions and many lesser ones. What is the truth that runs through all these religious beliefs and practices? The truth is love, and that which we call *God* is love. What is love? On an energetic level it is absence of contraction; it is nonseparation, the fully open heart, not-two. It is more, but these are the major attributes.

There is a form of engaged Buddhism called the Tiep Hien Order of Interbeing. It began in Vietnam in 1966 as a means to bring together Buddhism and responsible social action in the world. *Tiep* means to be in touch; *hien* means the present time, the now, which is all that is real. The essence of Tiep Hien is our relationship with each other and our world. When we are in touch with our deepest being in every moment we cannot help but be aware of our constant interrelationships with all else that is. Then the boundaries fall away, and we experience the nondual relationship of all things.

The first precept of this order is, "Do not be idolatrous about or bound to any doctrine, theory, or ideology, even Buddhist ones. All systems of thought are guiding means; they are not absolute truth." I ask you to look at the meaning here. How often do you look at an issue through your identity as a Buddhist or Christian and lose the truth behind what you see to be real, because you are so locked in to the *ism* that has become part of your identity, part of the filtering lens that shades your reality?

You can only find what is real for yourself. If I tell you that God is real,

I must also tell you not to believe me, for nothing is real until you know it for yourself from your own experience.

You ask why the Buddha did not teach of God or soul, why he said all is emptiness. While I explain this, please keep in mind those lines in the Heart Sutta, "Form is emptiness; emptiness is form."

The Buddha taught a path grounded in reality and experience. You cannot know the fullness of the Ground of Being through the everyday senses. Until the highest levels of pure awareness mind open, Ground must be felt with the heart and accepted on faith based on the intimations of it that have come, those moments of radiant lightness, clarity and sublime joy. The Buddha did not make faith a condition of freedom. He did not ask people to believe in anything but to be present in each moment and see what they found there. This has nothing to do with the reality of God. It is simply a statement of the Buddha's love and compassion.

Perfect freedom is clearly experienced by any being realizing the Buddha's path. The samsaric cycle is broken, and suffering is ended. That is as far as the Buddha saw it necessary to go. At that point one understands the meaning of God. In his great compassion the Buddha chose not to make insights into part of the path, which are clear only at the end of the path. While you are walking the path, what difference does it make whether liberation includes God and spirit or is only empty?

There is another part to the answer. Remember that the Buddha taught in Hindu India, where there was a habit of asking the gods to solve difficulties rather than taking personal responsibility for one's affairs. The Buddha sought to emphasize such responsibility and to teach a clear understanding of karma. If you don't like a result, learn what conditions led to its arising and work to resolve those conditions. Don't just pray to a god and say, "I can't help how things are." Here he aspired to emphasize the distinction between fate and karma and to lay the ground for growth.

You seem uncomfortable with this. Can you formulate the question?

Q: It's just that leaving God out of it seems a denial. And the Buddha says there is no soul.

The Buddha was a man. He lived on the human, earth plane. He had great wisdom and compassion, but he was not God and never claimed to be. That is what makes his teaching so beautiful. Wise though he was, he learned nothing that is beyond the reach of any human. To know the Unconditioned directly is within the reach of every human, and this is what he taught, but he wanted people to find the experience of that Ground for themselves, not just to worship on faith. It disempowers people to say, "There is divinity," and ask people to believe it because a wise one has said it. He understood that. As for the soul, I believe he wished people of his native land to break away from the Hindu idea of the immortal soul, or atman, as the highest level of personal being, for this aspect of being is still conditioned. Only by teaching people to reconsider their belief in the nature of atman as eternal could he lead them to find the true eternal, the Ground of Being or Unconditioned.

Q: It seems that I could prove the existence of God or soul in the same way I can prove egolessness, by my personal experience.

When you experience egolessness, you see the wheel of karma stop. You understand that you always have choice. The real-life effects are evident and obvious. When you experience spirit, it is very vague, just a feeling of oneness and continuing awareness. Your direct knowledge of God is even less. Light, love, cessation of conditioned experience, what reality have these? I am not denying their absolute reality, in spiritual terms, but I am talking about them in relation to human experience. Do you see that it is the veiled glimpse and your faith that allow you to know God? Few beings have been so graced as to know divinity's full reality while in human form. Even for Jesus a veil was laid across his consciousness when he accepted human birth.

Please return now to the teaching, "Form is emptiness; emptiness is form." As I speak, try to move past the lens that clouds your clear vision of reality. When you finally reach the place on your path where there is no self nor any notion of self, where there are no longer defined edges to your being nor any notion of separation between self and other, you may find total emptiness there. Or you may find fullness there, may find that it is a space that includes All that Is. Do you see that those two are the same thing? God, itself, is "zero," is emptiness, and the emptiness is God. It is the totality of All that Is. It is not void and it is not something, as a substantive object. Please allow your practice to take you into the direct experience of it.

Teachers

Q: There are so many different spiritual teachers and spiritual paths.
How do I know which one is best suited for me? It is difficult to put
trust into a teacher when I hear so many stories of people who have
experienced abuse by trusted spiritual teachers. How do they
learn to trust again?

First know that there is no one right teacher or path. Everything is your teacher. And everything you do is part of the path. Fear to trust is a teacher. And trust itself is a teacher. Doubt and confusion are part of the path. Choosing an untrustworthy teacher is painful, but it is also part of your learning.

Clarity of intention is of supreme importance here. If you relax and allow a clear intention to form of what you seek, you will find it. It may have been sitting just down the road from you for ages, but you had bypassed it thinking you sought something different. If what you have found has proven unwholesome in some way, please consider why you drew that difficult situation to yourself.

When clarity about what you seek is established, and then you come to a teacher or path that resonates for you, stop and be present with as much wakefulness as is possible. Do not ask that the relationship be free of any difficulty, at least not if you wish to learn. Ask that you be treated with respect, and watch to see if the teacher treats others with respect, even when views differ. Is the teacher settled and stable in his or her own life and practice? Is he able to reveal and express Ground of Being in his actions or words? Does she reveal a balance of wisdom and compassion in her dealings with people? What is this person like in stressful situations? Take a good look at this person's senior students. Do they reveal qualities that you wish to express in the self? Is the teacher able to make time for you? Of equal importance, can the teacher say no when appropriate? A lot depends on your expectations. Ask that this teacher be a guide who can show you the way with which he or she is familiar. Do not ask that the teacher know all paths. It is not the teacher's work to walk the path for you or protect you when you stray off the path a bit, only to watch and note, "Come back, come back." This is an invitation, not a command.

If you are satisfied that the teacher genuinely understands that which you seek to learn and has the qualities that lead to a respectful and caring relationship, then begin to work with this teacher with the awareness that this is a human—he or she is not perfect. I dare say that the Buddha and Jesus belched or passed gas on occasion, as irreverent as that thought may be. If you expect the teacher to be perfect, you will be disappointed.

What of the abusive teacher? People get themselves into an abusive relationship with a teacher for the same reasons they enter into any abusive relationship. You tell me you have entered abusive relationships, relationships of unwholesome co-dependence, and you seek a teacher who will teach you how to avoid such unwholesome choices. Unless you have done your work to the point that you fully realize the suffering such unwholesome relationships create and truly wish to grow past that negativity, you will simply delude yourself and again choose a teacher with whom you co-create an unwholesome relationship.

"Well, how do I get there if I am stuck here and keep choosing the teacher who keeps me stuck here?" No teacher can keep you stuck. It is your choices that keep you stuck. What is necessary, my friend, is to know that you are stuck and to offer the heartfelt intention to move past this stuck place for the good of all beings. You do not need to know yet exactly how you are stuck. The teacher will help you to discover that. But the willingness for honesty, and therefore the willingness to experience discomfort, uncertainty, and confusion, must be present. If you are seeking only security and comfort, you will never find a true teacher.

Those who have been abused by a teacher have felt trust betrayed and are afraid to trust again. Please consider the possibility that you were drawn to abusive teachers, and indeed to other abusive relationships, because you wished to have a good reason to allow yourself to close off your energy field. You come to an edge of known experience, and learning means taking risks and stepping into the unknown. Those who are very frightened of such a step and yet who seriously feel they should take such a step may find subtle ways to close off the way. As a result they can say, "I tried. In fact I tried three times, and each was an utter failure." Then they think they can stay in that safe place.

If you have experienced an abusive teacher or other abusive situations in your life, look to see if you are using that history as a hiding place. It is your decision. Know that you can move past this place of fear. How do you trust? You begin with yourself. Know your own highest intention and trust the innate goodness of your heart. When you trust your own intention, to allow that one step into the unknown, into growth, then you will trust the teacher who comes before you and can help to guide your way. If the heart trembles, that is okay. Always in entering unknown territory, there will be some discomfort. It is not a problem. Don't make it into one.

In your work with any teacher, always know that your own deepest truth is the highest authority. Some spiritual paths depend on surrender. This is not a surrender to the personality self of the teacher. Rather when the ego is surrendered, your own highest self, highest wisdom and love, come forth. This is the Buddha Nature or Christ Consciousness, the pure mind. Here you and the teacher are one. The loving wisdom and compassion of the pure mind are the authority.

Meditation

Q: You often talk about meditation. What does meditation mean to you? Why do you advise us to meditate? Is there another way to learn those things meditation teaches?

You have several questions here. Let us take them one at a time. Is there any other way to learn? Bluntly, no. That is not as limited as it may seem, since meditation takes many forms. Your personality and where you are on your journey determine the best form of meditation for you. Rarely is only one form of meditation adhered to throughout life. As you grow and change, a new method may become appropriate. Try it on like a suit of clothes and, if it fits you, wear it for a time. Allow it to become comfortable and familiar until it becomes like a second skin. Then you are no longer performing an action when you meditate, but simply experiencing, or being, meditation. By that phrase I mean resting in the meditative mind, resting in pure Being, rather than performing an action as planned by the discursive mind.

What is meditation? Meditation is your way home. It is the means to know yourself at deeper levels, and this knowledge allows you to be in harmony with the universe. It is the path out of the illusion of separation in which your human form and feelings bind you. Meditation frees your awareness from such personal identification. It is the way to know your oneness with each other, with all living things, and with God.

The discursive mind seeks to establish a self-identity. Sometimes prayer can enhance that identity, if prayer comes from the place of thought, of personality. Meditation dissolves self-identity. It is the way to let go of mind and of self and to return to pure Being. This is not a statement against prayer, but a caution that some forms of prayer can deepen the dualistic notions. Here I mean those forms of worship that set up a duality, the self speaking to God, wherein the discursive mind asks for what it believes it needs. Such statement can be useful and important, but after the thought is offered, it must be released and the practitioner return to the nondual awareness to which meditation leads. There are also forms of devotional meditation where self and object, self and God, merge. When I use the word *prayer* as above, it is with the specific idea of a self in relation to another.

I have experienced many forms of meditation in my lifetimes. I have been a Christian priest and practiced devotional meditation, living in solitude in a monastery and teaching there. I have been a Buddhist priest and practiced vipassana meditation, devotion, and solitude in a forest monastery in Thailand. I have chanted mantras, practiced martial arts, done Sufi dancing, lived in luxury and prayed in great temples, and lived in poverty and meditated in hovels.

Looking back on all that, I know now what I did not know in each of those lives, that no one method is right. They can all be right. The rightness is not in the method but in your heart. It is true that when the student is ready, the teacher appears, and that teacher will help you to open the doors you need to open. If a certain practice is right for you, you will be led to it when you need it. Open your hearts and trust your inner wisdom, and it shall be so.

You ask if there is one method of meditation I'd teach above the rest. I am hesitant to commit myself here because what is right for one of you at one stage on the path is not what another needs at another stage. I do not contradict myself when I advise one to do this and another to do that. I merely try to direct each back to the center of his chosen path. I also know now that the practice itself is less important than how the practice is approached. If there is intention to use the practice as escape from everyday reality or to use the practice to enhance the ego, then whatever the practice, you will move further into confusion. If there is intention to move toward greater clarity and compassion, most practices will take you there. Some take a more direct route.

As you approach the stage in your journey where you begin to understand your true spiritual nature and aspire to come to an end of all duality and separateness, at that point I would recommend a combination of vipassana, various practices that support the opening of the heart, and devotional meditation.

The vipassana is hard work and requires courage and perseverance. It is the learning of pure presence. With vipassana practice, a wisdom develops that sees how all objects arise when conditions are present for them to arise and then pass away as those conditions cease. When such insight develops, it is hard to hold on to the notion of a permanent self. When self dissolves, pure Being is more easily understood. Vipassana teaches you your true nature and shows you that you have never been separate from that holiness.

Devotional meditation is to remind you constantly to hold in your hearts the reason for this work, which is your love of God and the fact that God is love. Devotional meditation helps you see what remains at the end of the path, when the conditioned realm has all dissolved. It helps you to avoid nihilism.

Practices that support the opening of the heart help you to find balance and to integrate what you learn. It can be very frightening to see the whole conditioned realm collapse. As wisdom dawns about the nature of conditioned reality, compassion and loving-kindness help us hold the human moving through those experiences in a loving way. This balance of wisdom and compassion allows us to integrate what is learned, to know that while all conditioned things are impermanent, we must still attend to pain and trauma. We cannot just shrug them off as impermanent.

Devotional meditation takes many forms. Hold God in your heart and speak to this divinity. Your message may be in the form of words, song, dance, work, or service. You may seek out the great master of your choice and, revering him, ask his help to lead you to God. Your love for this master reminds you of the holiness of your own self, for the spark of God is in all of us. Through the Beloved you come to know the perfection of your own true being and, finally, your oneness with God.

What of those who do not believe in God? Can they go no farther on their paths? If they love enough and serve others through their love, that is their God. They will know God when they are ready. Until then, their love and service is given no less in service to God, just because they do not acknowledge that Ground of Being. Indeed their faith may be greater, as they serve that which they do not know with love and dedication. For those who have been graced by a direct experience of divinity, the path is easier. The experience enhances faith.

I will speak more of vipassana. It is the path to your recognition of your wholeness. It is a meditation of reality, of compassion, of forgiveness. It is a meditation that takes you beyond your fears, deeper into the heart of love where you find your oneness with All that Is.

You have fragmented yourselves into self and other and divided that perceived self into that which is acceptable and that which you must hide. That hidden matter smolders under the surface. It separates you from yourself. You spend your days fleeing from this fire, busy trying to escape it, to outthink it and stay one step ahead. You never pause to see what's burning.

Vipassana meditation provides a firebreak, a still space where you may stop and look. There is no judgment and no blame, there is just reality. Some of that reality is not pretty, but we are not in a beauty contest here. Slowly, you learn to open the burning space, to let in air and light, to allow what is hidden to surface. You have been looking through the filters of what you wished to see, so that what was really there was unknowable. Always, the unknown is more dreaded than the reality. Slowly you pierce the layers of illusion and begin to see with clear vision. The subsurface fires, exposed to air and light, burn out and die away. There is no more fuel to feed them, as each smoldering twig is brought into the light.

This process takes courage, perseverance, faith, and love. As you permit it to happen, you begin to find an undreamed-of wholeness. There is no longer a wall between your conscious mind and your heart, no longer a separation in yourself. There are no longer places that must be hidden. You learn to open to yourself and trust what you find there. What you once buried becomes the fertile ground for exploration. The burned out material from that old subsurface fire becomes the compost heap that provides the rich soil for growth. Always there is growing compassion, forgiveness, and love.

In the practice of vipassana, once you allow yourself to know yourself, you come to understand the nature of conditioned reality. You begin to see the aggregates of form, or body—of feelings, thoughts, impulse, and consciousness—and realize that these are truly not who you are but are merely outer expressions, like the clothes you wear. That with which you have identified as self is only a reflection of true Being. Then comes the question, "If not this, what? If I am not my body, my thoughts, even my highest dreams and aspirations, what am I?" At this point, letting go of the small self, we finally go beyond and see the Ground itself and know, "I am That."

When the heart opens, the wall between self and others may come down. It simply dissolves. You cannot love another until you love yourself, for the other is the self. Once you love yourself, then you know God's love and know that it is an impersonal love that loves all of creation. Truly, God is love.

Choose the method of meditation that best fits you. Listen to your heart or let a trusted teacher guide you. Choose one and stay with it for a long while. Practice daily, if you are serious about your commitment to growth. Use support practices to deepen compassion, to deepen concentration, forgiveness, or letting go, as is appropriate. Whatever your practice, you must approach it with a willingness to be with what's there, with what's real, not just to practice when you are feeling "spiritual." Open to truth. Let awareness blossom. Your love, trust, and work will bring you home.

Within this section of the book are several guided meditations. In the appendix you will find vipassana meditation instructions. Please experiment with these meditations and practice with the forms that feel helpful to you.

A G u i d e d M e d i t a t i o n

Oneness

To be read to yourself or shared aloud with a friend.
Please pause at each space between lines.

Relax your body. The position in which you sit during meditation has different degrees of importance depending on the kind of meditation. Sitting here now, simply find a comfortable position with the back erect. Close your eyes. Breathe deeply several times: deep, cleansing breaths.

Bring your attention to the third eye, the space between and above the eyes. See the inside of your forehead as a blank screen.

Return your attention to your breath. Notice the inhalation and the exhalation. As you breath out, release all the holdings of the past, all the pain, all the attachments. Feel the freshness in each new breath and how it brings your attention to the present. Be here, and now.

Begin to notice that moment between the inhalation and the exhalation. This is the now.

Slightly extend this pause between breaths and concentrate your attention here. As you do, see if you can feel your heartbeat. Simultaneously bring your attention to this now and into the heart center, that center of energy that lies close beside the organic heart. Feel the pulse of life within yourself. The essence of your being lies in the heart.

Reach into your heart. Look for spirit there.

Relax. Be at ease in the heart.

Find your highest self there, that beautiful and perfect spirit and mental body that has existed through all your lifetimes.

Allow yourself to expand. Realize the grandness and perfection that you are, the beauty and wonder of you.

Each of you is a being of perfect light. In your essence you are all perfect. Breathe in spaciousness; breathe out limitation.

Note that this essence of yourself goes far beyond the human sitting here tonight.

This highest self has lived so many lives and been so many people.

You have loved, and you have hated. You have known great joy, and you have known fear and pain. You have been of every race and lived on every continent.

While the human that you are sits here bound in its fears and limitations, your essence knows no limitations.

It is boundless,

it is limitless,

it is perfect.

Feel that essence within your heart. Feel the limitlessness of that aspect of being.

It is your own spirit, but it is not separate.

There are no edges to it, no defined boundaries, because you are part of God. The divine heart is your heart, the heart we all share. Through the heart of God you are part of each other.

Reach out with your hearts to all other beings. Feel your oneness with each other. Reach out in love.

Let go of fear. In the one heart there is no need for fear.

When you love and trust there is no need for fear.

Fear is an armor to protect the self that feels vulnerable.

Fear is small ego self's shout to preserve itself solidly in a universe that ego cannot comprehend.

Fear would wall out the universe and wall in the self.

Fear is the cry of the self that judges itself and sees itself flawed in body and emotion.

Fear is demanding, intolerant, and closed.

Choose love and release fear.

None of you is perfect, and all of you are perfect. In your human form, you are not meant to be perfect, and in your essence you are always perfect. It can be no other way.

Let go of this fear. Trust, and allow yourself to love and be loved. Let your heart expand with love for yourself, your beautiful and perfect self, and for all the others in the world who are also beautiful and perfect.

Feel the edges dissolve; feel the oneness; allow your love to carry you past the cage of fear.

Breathe out fear and armoring.

Breathe in the vast energy and love of the universe.

Rest in that space between inhale and exhale, the infinite now.

Breathe out fear and armoring. Let self go.

Breathe in spaciousness and love.

Rest, opening to this wonderful now.

Breathe out boundaries.

Breathe in the infinite.

You are the infinite. Rest there.

Please continue silently for as long as feels appropriate.

(Longer pause)

Take a deep breath now, and return your attention to yourself. See if you can just return to center and not build up the armor again.

A G u i d e d M e d i t a t i o n

Sympathetic Joy (Mudita)

To be read to yourself or shared aloud with a friend.
Please pause at each space between lines.

Envision yourself walking in a park in a large city such as Paris, beside the Seine River. Some people walk or sit in silence; some talk with friends; some doze on the grass; one is painting; others throw a ball. There are small children playing.

You carry a bag of food that you lovingly purchased that morning in the little market outside your dwelling. You have a brilliant red apple, a loaf of bread, some cheese, a flaky pastry, and a bottle of sweet juice.

You have walked for many hours through the city, seeing many wonderful sights. You stopped in a museum, browsed at little bookstalls, watched the people and the boats on the river. You are feeling very relaxed and open, also tired and hungry. Sit yourself down on the grass. *(pause)* You've brought a small blanket to spread out. You pull the first items out of your bag, a little knife and your loaf of bread and cheese, while thinking, "Ahh! This is perfect." There is fresh breeze, warm sun, lovely sights, a big cathedral on one side, and the river on the other. Perfect.

You have just cut the bread in two and cut off a chunk of cheese. As you bite into it, you notice a very skinny child not more than seven or eight years old approaching you, looking at your food. He comes up within a few feet of you and just stands there. His clothes are quite ragged. He's gaunt, with big eyes.

You take another mouthful and feel him watching you. The thought arises, "I should give this to him," and you feel tension, because it is your lunch and there is hunger in your own belly. There may be judgment of the self or the child or even of his family. If these thoughts are there, there's no need to push them away; just note them and let them sit there with you. "Here is tension; here is shame. Here is judgment."

Invite compassion for the self in whom these arise. They arise out of the thought, "Will I be safe? Will my needs be met?"

You take another bite; it's so good, just delicious, perfect. He's watching you chew. Anger might arise, "Why doesn't he go away?" Make space for that too, with kindness. Continue to extend compassion for yourself with whatever thoughts and feelings arise.

Keep looking at this child as you chew until the spontaneous generosity arises in you that leads you to hand him the other half of the loaf and a piece of cheese. Notice you're not handing him a whole loaf. That's not necessary. You are also hungry. You honor yourself and your hunger as well as him and his hunger.

Watch him bite into this food; watch his need; watch the release of need. Can you feel the sense of joy? Really experience his relief. He hasn't eaten all day, perhaps not even dinner last night. Feel his release of tension. Feel your own joy resonate with his opening energy.

Giver and receiver evaporate. There is just the meal, kindness giving itself, both of you partaking. Chewing together, swallowing together. One hungry belly to feed.

It is important to observe that you did not need to chase away the fear or anger, but simply to have compassion for it.

He finishes his bread and cheese and thanks you in his own way, smiles, and is gone. The little thought arises, "I still have all my pastry. I still have my whole apple." And then you see the three other children watching, all of them as gaunt as the first. Their big eyes stare at the food, drawn by their comrade's success in being fed.

Use no force here; just sit with it for a minute. Allow yourself to share what feels good to share. Allow yourself to enjoy what you do not share.

Let there be joy in giving, joy in receiving.

I'll be quiet for a few minutes while you enter this experience.

(Longer pause)

May all beings everywhere be fed in body and in spirit.

(Bell)

May all beings come to know the openhearted joy in giving and in receiving.

(Bell)

Knowing our own innate radiance and dwelling in compassion, may our open heart lead us to perfect peace.

(Bell)

Compassion (Karuna)

To be read to yourself or shared aloud with a friend.
Please pause at each space between lines.

Traditionally loving-kindness meditation begins with the self. I find
that in your culture it is very difficult for many people to offer loving
wishes to themselves, and so we begin with one to whom it is easier
to offer such thoughts and then come around to the self later. In the
traditional practice, one also offers loving wishes to a neutral person
before the difficult one. Here I have left out this step to make the
practice shorter. Please include it if you wish.

Compassion is not forgiveness, which is a further step, but only the
opening of your heart to the pain of all beings and wishing them well.
There is no wrong or right way to do this practice. If resistance arises,
simply note it and reenter the meditation in whatever way you are
able. You are not requested to dive all the way in but only to enter as
deeply as is comfortable.

As you work with this practice, please modify it and make it your own.

Find a comfortable position, body relaxed, back erect, eyes closed softly.
Bring to the heart and mind the image of one for whom there is loving
respect. This person may be a dear friend, parent, teacher, or any being with
whom the primary relationship is one in which you have been nurtured.

We often take such a person for granted, see what is offered to us but fail to see deeply into that being's situation. Look deeply at that being, deeper than you ever have before, and see that he or she has suffered. He has felt pain of the body or the heart. She has known grief, loss, and fear. He has felt loneliness and disconnection. She has been lost and confused. Along with the joy, see the ways this dear one has suffered.

Speaking silently from the heart, note this one's pain, offering first the person's name.

> You have suffered. You have felt alone or afraid. You have known pain in your body and your mind. You have known grief and loss. You have felt alienation, and the constriction of the closed heart. Your life has not always brought you what you might have wished. You have not been able to hold on to what you loved or to be free of what brought pain. You have suffered.

What loving thoughts can you offer to this dear one? Let the thoughts come with the breath, arising and moving out.

> May you be free of suffering.
> May you find the healing that you seek.
> May you love and be loved.
> May your heart open and flower.
> May you know your true nature.
> May you be happy.
> May you find peace.

Please continue silently, repeating these or alternate phrases for several minutes. Go slowly. Allow your heart to connect with this dear one, to open to his or her pain and offer these wishes, prompted by the loving heart. I will be quiet.

(*Longer pause*)

Now, let this loved one move aside and in his or her place invite in your own self. It is sometimes hard to open our hearts to ourselves. What blocks this love? Just for the sake of experiment, please try to follow the practice and see how it feels, even if it is difficult—but always without force.

Look deeply at the self and observe that, just as with the loved one, you have suffered. Speaking to yourself, say:

I have suffered. I have felt pain of the body and the mind. I have known grief, loss, and fear. I have felt loneliness and disconnection, felt lost and confused. I have not been able to hold on to what I loved, nor to keep myself safe from that which threatened me. I have suffered.

See the ways you have suffered. Without engaging in self-pity, simply observe the wounds you have borne.

Speaking silently from the heart, this time to your own self, say your name.

What do you wish for yourself?

May I be free of suffering.
May I find the healing that I seek.
May I love and be loved.
May my heart open and flower.
May I know my deepest connection with All that Is.
May I be happy.
May I find peace.

Please continue silently, repeating these or alternate phrases for several minutes. Go slowly. Allow your heart to connect with your deepest self, to open to your pain and longing, and to offer wishes prompted by the loving heart. I will be quiet.

(*Longer pause*)

Now let the self move aside, and in its place invite in one with whom there has been hard feeling.[28] It is best not to choose the heaviest relationship at first, but allow yourself to practice with a less difficult relationship and then move slowly to those relationships that bring up heavier emotions.

It is so painful to maintain separation. A wise teacher[29] said, "Never put anyone out of your heart." What blocks opening?

Letting go, we invite the open heart.

If it is difficult, use no force. Note resistance.

For the sake of experiment, you might follow the practice just to see how it

---

[28] You may wish to work with the neutral person first, using the same words.

[29] Neem Karoli Baba.

feels. Please express your own pain too, as you speak to this one. Can you feel the space where your pain and that person's pain are one?

Say this one's name. Speak from your heart.

> You have hurt me, through your words, your acts, even your thoughts.
>
> Through what came from you I have experienced pain.
>
> When I look deeply, I see that you have suffered. You have felt alone and afraid. You have known pain in your body and your mind. You have felt loss and grief, have felt alienated, felt your heart closed. Your life has not always brought you what you might have wished.
>
> May you be free of suffering.
> May you find the healing that you seek.
> May your heart open and flower.
> May you love and be loved.
> May you come to know your true nature.
> May you be happy.
> May you find peace.

Please continue silently, repeating these or alternate phrases for several minutes. Go slowly. Allow your heart to connect with this person, to open to his or her pain, and to offer wishes prompted by the loving heart. I will be quiet.

(Longer pause)

Throughout the world, beings suffer. Not only humans but plants, insects, animals, even the earth herself.

> May all beings everywhere be free of suffering.
> May all beings be happy.
>
> *(Bell)*
>
> May all love and be loved.
> May all find the healing that they seek.
>
> *(Bell)*
>
> May all beings everywhere find perfect peace.
>
> *(Bell)*

A   G u i d e d   M e d i t a t i o n

At Home in the Universe

To be read to yourself or shared aloud with a friend.
Please pause at each space between lines.

This is a meditation to guide you into an experience of the essence of your being, beyond the conceptual images of self as form, personality, or consciousness.

We will work with the assistance of a plant, a photograph of a beloved teacher or revered high being, an object such as a shell or flower, a sleeping pet or child, or even the open sky out of your window. Choose one object with which you will remain throughout this one meditation. At another time you may use a different object. Please seat yourself so the selected object rests before you. If it is small, such as a shell, let it rest elevated to eye level on a table.

Please begin by moving into a comfortable position that you can maintain for some time. Allow the back to be as erect as is possible.

> Body soft, relaxed;
> shoulders soft, loose;
> abdomen soft, open;
> eyes open, soft, unfocused.
> Seeing through and beyond;
> not fixed on anything.

Let the jaw hang slightly open, tongue resting loosely in space, not touching the teeth or the roof of the mouth but floating.

The breath releases with a soft, whispered "ahhhh." Let it flow out from the core of you.

Eyes resting unfocused, seeing through and beyond.

Let the breath flow out, into and around the object. Edges dissolving as the breath moves.

Draw in the in-breath, noting how it enters the body.

Out, offering this object your very life breath,

and in, drawing in its most vital energy.

Out. Let awareness follow the breath,
pausing at whatever resists its full release,
touching resistance with gentle awareness.

In. Noting any defenses against receiving completely,
touching resistance with gentle awareness.

Out. With a whispered "ahhhh." Mouth open, tongue floating; all resistance dissolving.

In. Differentiation between self and object dissolving in the spacious breath.

Out. Boundaries falling away. No edge to your breath, nor to your being.

In. Receiving completely that which has been present since the very beginning.

Out. Releasing completely that which was labeled.

In. No one receiving; nothing received.

Resting in the natural state of spacious awareness.

Please continue for a few minutes in silence.

(Longer pause)

Does the out-breath stop at the object? Let it move out still farther now. How far does it go when offered freely?

Nothing to stop it.

Touching the ends of the universe.

Drawing in from the same infinite space,

> Infinite breath,
>> Infinite being.

Out. Make yourself at home in the universe.

Breath and pure awareness touching everything and everywhere.

No self: No object.

Floating there in luminous pure awareness.

In. The same infinite space within, where it all floats.

Luminous.

> Open.

>> Radiant.

>>> Never-ending.

Rest there.

Expanded outward and within, we find the same essence.

Rest there.

If sensation arises, know it without contracting around it. It arose and will pass, not separate, not other than the spaciousness. Everything is flow; don't create separate objects.

If thought arises, know it without contracting around it. It arose and will pass, not separate, not other than the spaciousness. Everything is flow; don't create separate objects. The breath holds it all.

Let the breath breathe itself.

Rest. Nowhere to go. You are home. Rest.

Everything dissolving into pure being.

(Longer pause)

And now we return to the relative consciousness.

Blink your eyes. Again.

In. Take a deep in-breath and note the relative experience, seeing it from great spaciousness.

Out. Allow the return of self, noting that it is just a convenient concept.

In. That self returning to the notion of receiver.

Let edges reappear, but note that they are concept only, a handy tool for dwelling in the relative condition.

Out. Let the edges dissolve again.

In. With the notion of boundary.

Out. Releasing the notion of boundary.

Play with this for a few moments.

(Longer pause)

You are the relative human with concepts of boundary, of self.

You are the absolute, pure awareness resting free of time, of space, of illusion.

Be both. It takes courage, love, and awareness, but you can do it.

Train yourself to rest in this vast spaciousness of all being, and still to hear the human laugh and cry with a heart of compassion.

This is the beginning and the end of all your practice.

Practice until there is nowhere to go, nothing to do, and then rest there
    resting in the infinite heart,
        at home in the universe.

May all beings come to rest in the pure heart-mind.

(Bell)

May all beings know the perfect joy of their true being.

(Bell)

May all beings find perfect peace.

(Bell)

The Fruit of Practice – A Halloween Story

Since I am officially a ghost, I feel qualified to tell ghost stories. I want to tell you of an experience in a long-distant lifetime. I'm going to tell this story in the first person. When I say "I," you recognize that this is not me, Aaron, but a past incarnation, one small aspect of myself, a being that was a priest, a Christian monastic. I spent much time walking from village to village, seeking shelter at night in whatever farm or village home was available. Sometimes I slept in hovels or even in the field, at other times in what would seem to be a castle or other stately building.

It was late fall, around the time of your Halloween. While Halloween is a secular holiday in your culture, in which children dress up in fancy costumes and seek candy, it has much deeper spiritual roots. This is a time of year when more earthbound spirits seem to be abroad. Perhaps it has to do with the changes of the moon and of the seasons. For whatever reason, that which in many cultures is known as the Day of the Dead is a day in which many earthbound spirits[30] come out. I've often wondered why in your culture you allow little children to run around on such a night.

I suppose in good storytelling form, I should say, "It was a dark and stormy night …" but actually it was a rather fair evening for that time of year. But it was growing dark, and I had passed through fields and woods and had not seen a dwelling. Three miles back I had gone through a village and was told that I would come to a rather large manor house inhabited by an elderly man. Perhaps I could find shelter there.

Just as dusk approached, I saw a very grand house in the distance, much

---

[30] Earthbound spirits: beings that have not completed their transition after leaving the body; they cling to the prior incarnation.

larger than I'd expected. I knocked on the door, seeking really only some bedding in the barn, a place in the straw with the animals. But the servant who opened the door said, "Yes, come in! My master will be happy to have you as his guest." The master was very gracious to me, gave me food and water, and then led me up a long circular staircase to what seemed to be a room in a high tower. I carried a candle and he also carried a candle. When we came into the room, there were several unlit candles there and he lit them so that the room had a warm and comfortable glow.

He nodded, asked if my needs were met, and I said yes. So he said good night and closed the door behind him. He had told me that this was the first room of a suite, and I could see there was a door off of it. He said I would find a bed in the next room, where I could make myself comfortable.

When the door clicked shut behind him, I heard what sounded like a key in the lock. At first it alarmed me, and I immediately went and tested the door. I heard his voice on the other side saying, "I will open it in the morning. It doesn't lock from your side. I have the key—this is for your protection."

It seemed a bit strange to me, but I resigned myself and would not argue with him. Exhausted as I was from the day's walk, I washed at the basin that had been left for me and then opened the door and walked down a long passageway to what I presumed was the bedroom, holding my candle. The scene still reverberates with horror in my memory. In that room were no fewer than four dead bodies in different stages of decay. One was merely a skeleton; its ragged clothes hanging around it. Another two had shreds of flesh left, and the fourth looked like a body of one who had just died in that fortnight. The air in the room had a foul smell. The thick walls and heavy door had prevented the spread of that odor to the outer chamber.

I went back out to the first room, and as I looked closely at my surroundings, I could see the attempts on the door to pick the lock or pry it open at the hinges, and I realized that this—I can only call him sick—man took some strange delight in imprisoning his victims and condemning them to lingering death in this way.

I knew he would not open the door in the morning.

My first reaction was rage and fear. I looked at the window but the room was far too high up to descend safely, even if there had been anything to climb down on. I went to the door and pounded on it. The man's coarse laughter on the other side told me that he had not walked away but was waiting for just that reaction from me, that it fed him, that he drew his energy off my fear. I determined not to give him that gift of my fear, and so I sat and began to pray.

Through the early hours of the night I simply sat and meditated with my fear of death, with my outrage, with my dread of this fate, until my mind quieted enough that I began to find some compassion for him, who was so clearly sick in this distortion that he held. I did not believe in evil then any more than I believe in it now, but as you have heard me say, there are those who offer very great distortion and do very great harm in their negativity. I began to reflect on how immense his pain must be that he needed to do this to another.

Slowly my anger quieted, and I found forgiveness for him and for myself, for that which was also negative in myself. And then in a deeper meditation I asked, "Is there any way out, or must I die?"

I began to have a vision: a stone shaped like a wedge—a keystone. It came to me so strongly that after an hour of meditation upon that stone, I got up and searched the room. There was one wall, the outer wall, that was rock. But there was no stone of that shape, and even if there had been, even if it had opened, it simply would have taken me to an immense precipice.

I cannot tell you how much I did not want to walk into that bedroom, to face those corpses. I had been sitting in the front room with all three candles lit, and I realized that they were burning down and soon I would be left in darkness. I blew out two of them, leaving myself just one.

Gathering my courage, I walked back into the bedroom and searched and searched. No keystone. I went back to the living room and sat. But the stone stayed firmly in my mind, and a small voice said, "Behind, behind." Behind meant back into the bedroom.

There was one nook with a drapery across it. I confess I had not looked there, certain that I would find another corpse. Instead I found that it was a closet with a few articles of clothing in it. And on the back wall was the keystone.

My heart stopped. This was a stone wall, and yet it was an inner wall. I looked for a door there, some mechanism, but none was apparent. Finally by the flickering light of the candle, I touched that stone, pressed my hand against it. Then there was an almost silent hum, and a bit of creaking, and the wall literally began to open itself. The doorway was so perfectly hidden that even one who knew it existed would have had trouble finding it. It was not linear but followed the outline of the stones.

I pushed it closed and saw the outline of it disappear into the mortar between the stones. I pushed the keystone again, and the door opened just a crack, enough for me to take my fingers and pull it toward me a bit. And there beyond was a staircase, very dark, very steep.

There were some windows in the room, and the moon was full outside, so even though my candle was dim I had had some light. Now ahead of me was only blackness. I would like to be able to say to you that I simply trusted God, trusted Jesus, took Jesus' hand, and descended the stairs. But there was very little trust or faith in my movements. Rather, there was a sense of dread in this room surrounded by corpses, of which I was soon to become one unless I freed myself. That blackness seemed the only hope, so I took my candle and stepped into it.

I removed my boots and carried them lest the noise betray me. I went down and down, tiptoeing on stocking feet. I went down what seemed much farther than the ground level. As I descended, I began to hear running water. I will not describe in detail the cobwebs, nor the sounds of rats and the touch of them as they rushed past me.

I reached the bottom step and held up my dying candle. In the flickering last light, I could see a rushing stream about five feet below me. And then my candle went out.

It was clear to me there was no other way out. It was clear from the man's maniacal laughter and the corpses of guests before me that he did not intend simply to frighten me and then let me loose in the morning but would take delight in my continued fear and suffering. I had been born on a seacoast, the son of a fisherman, and I was a very good swimmer. I decided that the water must be going somewhere and to trust myself to it, rather than returning up the stairs to the corpses, the fear within that room, and likelihood of death. And so, I tied my boots to my belt and stepped in.

The current was not as fierce as I had thought it would be. In fact, it was rather mild. I decided to swim with the current, face on the surface, holding my hands ahead of me. This was fine for a while until I came up against a wall, which reached below the surface. The current pulled down and under the wall. I realized I had to dive underwater and pray that I would come up soon.

Treading water there in the blackness, a wall in front of me, my feet touching an opening into which the water ran, four or five feet down, suddenly I felt myself very comforted. I realized that I wanted to escape, but I did not hate the one who had imprisoned me. I realized in that moment that, if I escaped, I would not come back to seek revenge on him but would hope in some way to heal him and bring him into the light. And so that became my prayer just before I dived in: not for revenge, but for the good of all beings, may I survive this. And then I dived.

And I swam until I felt my lungs would burst, feeling the rocky roof of my submerged passage until suddenly it opened out. There I was in the river under the night sky.

I was out, and I suppose you might think that was the end of the story. It was still only the middle of the night. I sat on a rock just at the opening of this underground stream, the manor house looming above me, and offered thanks for my deliverance. Then I thought of this man, lord of his castle and diminished to a sorrowful state by his fear and confusion. I asked myself and asked God, is there any way that this man can be saved from his negativity? Is there any way that I can help him come into the light?

The first images that crossed my mind were to find some fellow priests or villagers, bring them back with me into the castle, and bring him up to that room, to accuse him. But I knew that would only drive him farther into darkness, and while he might suffer, might be imprisoned, his heart would not open.

And then I had a wonderful and terrible idea. So terrible did it seem, in fact, that at first I could not bring myself to consider it. But finally it seemed that the idea truly was of divine origin, and that, if I attempted it with love, I would succeed.

And so, leaving my boots, I jumped into the water, filling my lungs as full as I could with air, for this time I had to swim upstream. I dived into the tunnel and surfaced on the other side to swim, grabbing at the rock walls to pull myself along until I finally touched at the foot of that stairway.

I climbed the stairs in the blackness and emerged in the bedroom. I knew that he could not know about this secret doorway, nor of course had any of those who had died. One by one, carrying each corpse carefully so as to be noiseless on the stairs, I brought each terrible burden down to the bottom and laid them on the ledge by the water. Then I went back up and cleaned up that room as well as I could, made it look inviting and comfortable. And finally I stepped into the stairway again, and this time I pulled the wall closed behind me until it clicked and went down the stairs, past the bodies and into the water. I dived underneath the wall and came out, once again free in the night. I pulled on my boots and walked for an hour, until I came to a barn where I rested.

Early the next morning I begged breakfast and dry clothes, and hung my monk's robe out to dry in the sun and breeze. When the sun was fully up, I walked back and knocked on the door of the manor.

If the servant was surprised to see me, he gave no sign. I do not believe he had any idea of what his master was doing but supposed that those who had been guests had gone on the next day.

I said that his master had unlocked the door early as I had requested, but I had wanted to come back and thank him. Was he there?

The servant brought me in to where the master breakfasted. He looked at me as if he were seeing a ghost. Never have I seen a man so surprised, so alarmed. "What are you doing here?" he stuttered.

"Well, I came back to thank you. I had a most comfortable night."

"You …you what?"

"Ah yes, I was so tired, and it was such a comfortable room. And then this morning, when you unlocked the door so graciously at the predawn hour that I had requested, I was afraid I had not thanked you properly. So I have come back to thank you."

He said, "It was a comfortable room?"

"Oh yes. It's a wonderful bed." And I invited him to come back up with me. I asked him, "Have you ever lain on that bed?"

He didn't want to come. His confusion finally drew him along as did his curiosity, and so we went upstairs, through that outer room and into that now comfortable and cleaned bedroom. No corpses to be seen.

I said, "Lie down on it; it's such a wonderful bed. I had such a good night here. What a good man you are. You must be blessed by God to offer such hospitality. May God continue to bless you for your hospitality and your love of others."

"But I am a bad man." He blinked and shook his head as if his whole murderous assault on so many was but a nightmare.

"No, you are a kind man," I replied. By what evil vision do you believe yourself to be bad? You are generous and kind. But if you see wickedness in yourself, as there is in all of us, ask his forgiveness and vow to abandon such negativity."

"Yes, he said, "Thank you." And then he asked me, "Will you have breakfast with me?" And we ate together. I asked him if I might come back and perhaps bring a fellow monk with me. I thought I'd be walking back that way later in the month.

When I returned, I made sure to choose a fellow monk who was also a good swimmer, just in case. We were again treated to dinner and shown to those rooms. No corpses this time.

Once again he left me with a candle and closed the door. I asked him, "Aren't you going to lock it, so I'll be safe?" He said, "No, I don't think I need to do that." And then I heard his footsteps descend the stairs. I will confess that I did not go to sleep. I was not sure that he would not come back and attack us sometime during the night. I did not know how complete his conversion had been, or whether he was shamming. But when we arose in the morning, he invited us to come and breakfast with him. He told me then that he felt like one awakening from a nightmare and asked me to send other monks or any other guests his way, that he would always welcome them.

I suppose a moral might be offered, but I think that would spoil a good story. So I will choose to leave this one where it is, and leave you to your own thinking about it.

Namaste

I wish to say just a few words in parting. First, I thank you for permitting me to share my thoughts with you, and for the time and effort you have given to reading my words.

Remember that you are also spirit. There is nothing I have said that you don't already know in the deepest wisdom of your being. The only difference is that I have more conscious access to that wisdom.

Please do not take my word for any of what is written here. Practice, learn, and understand for yourselves. Your own guides are readily available to you, but they cannot shout at you through closed doors. As you open your hearts, you open the doors between our planes and facilitate communication.

Remember that, whatever guidance and help we can give to you, we cannot walk the path for you. You must take the steps to maturity for yourselves, knowing that there is always a hand offered in loving support. You are never alone, yet you must do your own learning.

Above all, enjoy the incarnation and each other. Your joy brings so much light, my dear ones. Your joy is a manifestation of your love. It brings light to where there has been only darkness, love to where there has been only hatred. And that is why you are here.

When you learn to live in the eternal now with an open heart, fear will be seen for the delusion that it is, and love will be the only reality.

At that time, there will be no more separation in the universe. It is a day we will all experience. Meanwhile, each step taken with loving awareness leads us closer to experiencing the fullness of light that is the birthright of each being.

May each of you feel my love and that constant love which surrounds you as you find your way home.

There is a beautiful word of greeting and parting in eastern countries, *namaste:* the light and inner wisdom within me bows in respect to the light and inner wisdom within you.

So to each of you, Namaste.

Aaron

Appendix A:
The Universe According to Aaron

There are three general areas of frequently asked questions. The first two are of the who are we? and why are we here? genres. The third and larger question covers the area, how may we do the work we came to do? I'd like to address the who are we? and why are we here? questions as fully and clearly as possible here. You are energy and light. As you sit here in your human form, know that this body is just one aspect of yourself. You each have a higher self, that beautiful and perfect part of you that has experienced all your lifetimes and is intimately familiar with the home for which you yearn. You began as a spark of God and walk the human path to maturity, so that the expressed parts of you may grow increasingly compatible with divinity, that is, so the illusion of distortions may be purified, and that you may find your way home. Your incarnations are the schoolroom for this higher self, which is already perfect in its essence yet grows in wisdom through the learnings of each lifetime. Here is given the opportunity for that small spark to evolve, to learn and grow and blossom into a brilliant sun.

Let us start at the beginning. First there was awareness, awake but undifferentiated into a self and other. With the first moment of self-awareness of each spark of the divine came the first delusion of separation from All that Is; the expression of the infinite perceived itself but with distortion. That minute bit of energy, experiencing itself as separate from God and the universe, then began the long journey back to full understanding of nonseparation. In the course of the journey, it will come to know its true nature as part of all things and to realize that it is both a spark of the whole and a brilliant sun in its own right. It will not become these things; it will learn that it has always been so. It is a voyage of discovery of the truth, not creation of truth.

This bit of energy has many potential pathways to evolution. One possibility is to move to material form on a place such as earth. There are other paths to evolution beside the one of material form and other ways to experience material form, but you are here on earth so we will speak now of this particular path.

This aware energy, evolving through material form, first materializes as gas, as mineral, as what you consider nonorganic matter. Then it moves to plant life of one type or another, from simple to more complex. Next it experiences itself as animal, and finally as human. In some cases, the energy evolves first through other material or nonmaterial planes and then comes to earth when ready to express as human.

In each of these manifestations the materialization has a certain proportion of shadow to light and a certain density to its energy. I do not use density as related to the physical body, in the sense that you consider a rock to be physically denser than spun cotton, but use the term as descriptive of the density of the light body. For those of lower density, the light body contains more obscuration. Thus, the intensity of the light itself is less. The lower the density of the light body and the more obscuration therein, the lower is the frequency of the energy vibration of that life form; thus, it resonates to, and emits, a lower vibrational frequency. That does not mean it is inferior, only that the vibration differs. The frequency is that which is appropriate to the form into which the energy manifests.

In your manifestations you follow the law of karma, which draws you back to form again and again, until this karmic stream expresses itself with enough clarity that it is not drawn back to the schoolroom that is earth. When the habitual tendencies that draw you back into form are resolved, the being will move on to the next step on its path, learning beyond the earth plane.

It is important to note that karma is never punishment. Rather, it is the opportunity to repeat the needed lessons until you learn what you need to learn. In this most perfect schoolroom everyone eventually passes. There is no failure, just the need to review lessons until they are mastered. The courses are ungraded, and you may take each class as many times as you wish. When you think it's understood, the universe offers a quiz so that you may verify the depth of that understanding. At times the final exams may seem rather tough, but ultimately, the material will be perfectly clear, and the hardest exam will be passed with flying colors. After a brief rest, you resume classes. What is the next thing to be learned?

The word *karma* relates to action. All intentional actions, words, and thoughts are karmic and lead to results. Some of them are wholesome, and some are unwholesome. The difference lies in both the act itself and the intention behind the act. Karma may be thought of as the planting of a seed. Simply put, if you want sweet fruit, you must plant the seed for sweet fruit. If you plant the seed for sour fruit, all the nurturing and wishing you can give it will not induce that tree to produce sweet fruit. Only sour fruit will grow.

If you wish peace, harmony, joy, and love, those are the seeds you must plant. When you plant hatred, fear, and discord, those are what you reap. Essentially, your incarnations offer the opportunity to learn how to plant the seeds of compassion, acceptance and loving-kindness, so that you reap those fruits.

It's not easy because even when there is a desire to plant a seed of generosity, fear may arise and distort that intention so that greed is planted along with generosity. That is also not bad but just a sign that fear has not yet been resolved. Whatever is present and not resolved will express itself if there is not full awareness of it. Thus, your incarnations are a time to learn awareness of what is present, to learn to live with increasing skill, to learn to offer love rather than anger or greed as a response to the stimulus of fear. The learning comes slowly and painfully at times. Remember that you are not expected to be perfect. If these distortions were already resolved, you'd have no need to be incarnate in a body and learning on the earth plane. Your mistakes are part of the lessons. Allow them to teach you kindness and compassion for the being that errs, rather than contempt for that human.

Those of you who are evolving fully through the earth plane have taken rebirth over and over, in one form or another. Your first lives on the earth plane were first density, in the form of mineral, which includes water. The lesson at that level of density is awareness. The spark moved into awareness at the moment of experiencing the illusion of separation. With this first move into personal expression, there is the beginning of the experience of a pull to the light, not yet with self-awareness, but always reaching for the light.

When the lessons of first density are sufficiently mastered, the being moves into second density. The forms that density takes on earth are plant and then animal. Yes, all of you who are evolving fully through the earth plane have been mineral, plant, and animal in some of your many past lives. The main lesson of second density is growth into self-awareness. The rock begins to have awareness and then is ready to move into the simplest forms of plant life. Increasingly aware through many incarnations, the being first experiences group self-awareness and finally individual self-awareness. The ant or bee is aware on a group level. The pet dog or cat moves into personal self-awareness. Those animals that are your pets are often in the final stages of second density.

The third density is human. Your primary lessons on this plane are faith and love. These are not the only lessons, but the primary ones.

When you move beyond the need to incarnate in human form, you are still learning. There is simply no longer any need for materialization as an aid to that learning. The karma that pulls you into the heavier vibration of materiality has been resolved. The primary fourth-density lesson is compassion, and the fifth is wisdom. Again, this does not mean you learn no wisdom and compassion as a human, but in higher densities you further develop those qualities.

There is an overlap between the lessons of wisdom and compassion. One cannot be learned entirely without the other. To aid this learning, fourth-density beings dwell in groups where sharing is at a more intimate level, and then move from there into fifth density to find deeper wisdom.

When you enter fourth density, you find yourself capable of full telepathic sharing and are beyond the dictates of the emotional body that would lead you to feel shame or pride. Thus, all sharing is honest, and you no longer need to experience something yourself to understand and learn fully. As you share in this way with your peers, your beloved companions, you enter loosely into a group energy, where beings are free to come and go as feels appropriate. You always have free will. When the time is right, a being will begin to move away from that group to better understand and find deep wisdom in its own being. When it is useful for its own learning or to teach others, the being will return to a group, moving back and forth.

The sixth density …I find it hard to put a label on this. A friend, Ra, [31] describes it as learning of love and light. I understand what Ra means, but you may benefit by further explanation. Unfortunately, I lack the words to define it more accurately. Essentially, the end of sixth density is a movement to total knowledge and acceptance that you have never been separate, a movement back into such total unity with the One that, by the end of sixth density, you are ready to allow the dissolution of all memory and individual identity. This does not mean that you cannot put on a cloak of consciousness, cannot regrasp those memories if needed. That is what I do. In order to teach, I need personality and memory, so I resume these past attributes. The difference is that there is no attachment to them, nor any delusion that this "Aaron" is who I am.

---

[31] The group entity or "social-memory complex" Ra, in *The Ra Material*, channeled by Elkins, McCarty, and Rueckert.

The seventh density has been described as a gateway. It is beyond my experience. I assume the experience of the seventh density gateway to be similar to the gateway of enlightenment experience in third density, of realization of the true self and release of self-identity with the body and ego, but in a far more profound way. To move into seventh density is to release individuation fully, not just to release self-identification and attachment to individuality, but to release individuated experience totally. Many beings hold themselves at high sixth density, not crossing that gateway, in order to continue to have access to individuated thought and expression so as to allow teaching. Please remember that seventh-density beings do not cease to exist. They only cease to maintain individuation. The energy continues and serves all beings as it enhances love and light. It is the Ground out of which all expresses. Seventh density is a gateway to the eighth density, and that I cannot describe to you at all. It is the drop of water fully returned to the sea. Let us simply label it as mystery. It is God.

There is a wide range within each density. They do not have fixed borders; movement from one to another is a process of gradual transition. It is also important to remember that you are not forced into these densities. This is an open-classroom school. But as the third grader will feel a bit bewildered when he sits down and listens to the teaching in a sixth-grade classroom and will eventually choose to return to a more appropriate class, so you tend to stay in the appropriate class because that is where learning occurs. Remember that there is no competition to move faster than another or to outdo another. You are most content to be where you learn.

Some of you disagree with that statement, feeling a pull to graduate from this density. Yes, and that is appropriate for your present level of learning. Does the able student about to finish her grade in the spring not look forward eagerly to the next grade? Does the spring bulb not send out shoots that seek the sun? You know that movement beyond the veil of third density will give you fuller exposure to the light for which you so yearn.

You move around a bit, then, and may even move to a lower density for some reason. We spoke of this once when watching a caterpillar. One of you asked me, and I said a small bit of the spirit energy could choose to incarnate as a caterpillar, if it felt that was the best way of learning. Yes. For example, you might incarnate as a tree. If patience were an issue that you were having trouble resolving in third density, karma might lead you to this form of experience and learning.

You would not then be a self-aware tree or caterpillar. That bit of light and energy accepts the density into which it moves. The full energy does not move into the specified form, only that amount of the full energy that the particular form can contain. Thus, the highly evolved being you call Jesus, accepting incarnation into human form, became a third-density being for the time of that incarnation. The sixth-density form did not cease to exist though.

There is no formal graduation from one plane to the next, with examinations to be passed. Rather, graduation must be seen as a readiness to enter into the lessons of the next level, so that one knows that is where one wants and needs to be. One chooses the ideal spot to learn the lessons that one must learn, without concern for density.

I believe that is enough background information about densities. I call some of this material "the furniture of heaven." There is a curiosity and an interest in having some understanding of the whole plan of which you are a part. But you are in third density now. You don't need to know the furniture arrangement in heaven; you are not there. There is a story told about the Buddha; he was asked if he taught all that he knew. The Buddha pointed to the surrounding forest, held out a handful of leaves, and said, "What I know is as the leaves of the forest; what I teach is only as this handful of leaves, but this is all you need to know to find liberation." He wasn't being contrary or untrusting. He preferred to focus and address the primary issues of human suffering and where freedom might be found, a deeply compassionate reply. In another scripture, the Buddha points out that, if you are struck by an arrow, you don't ask the doctor to find out who shot it and of what wood it was made before he pulls it out. By the time such information would be gathered, you'd be dead. All you need to know is about this life and this density. So let us concentrate our inquiry there.

As a third-density human you are made up of four bodies: the physical, emotional, mental, and spirit bodies. The physical is obviously the present manifestation. When you are no longer in this body, what remains are the other three, together in what we call the astral body. You continue to move in and out of material form, all the while working to clarify the shadow in the heavier bodies.

You are not working to end thought and emotion. You can never be entirely free of thought or emotion for any sustained period while in human form or within third density. Rather, you are working toward what we would call equanimity with emotions, where the rising of an emotion no longer leads to reactivity and contraction.

I've just talked briefly about group entities and the totally honest and unselfconscious sharing of such entities. On the astral plane between lifetimes, you communicate telepathically, yet you still broadcast emotion. Thus, third-density beings feel some discomfort in the company of higher density beings because they are aware that the broadcast emotions create some discomfort. You are like the young child who is aware that the elders smile at his antics in loving tolerance; he soon returns to his friends where he can more fully be himself. He will have the opportunity to be an adult in later years; there is no need for him to perfect adult skills as a child.

So you keep returning to the physical plane, practicing kindness, faith, and love, learning to move beyond reactivity to the emotional body. In third density, the emotional body is still experienced strongly in the conscious self and is often in control. As the conscious mind relaxes the need to control, it may learn to communicate with the superconscious, or higher self. When you do so, you have access to a far higher inner wisdom that the conscious, rational aspect of self often shuts out. When you accept the arising of emotions nonjudgmentally, or make friends with yourself, to phrase it another way, then and only then are you ready to learn the lessons of nonjudgment to others. This readiness is the gateway to fourth density.

Let us speak briefly of what lies beyond that gateway. The fourth-density being still has an emotional body but has no need to broadcast it. Through fourth and fifth densities the emotional body dissolves completely, as the lessons of compassion and wisdom are mastered. The energy ready to enter sixth density is composed only of mental and spirit bodies. This is often referred to as the higher self.

Yes, you all have this aspect as part of you now, as you exist in material form. Time is simultaneous, not linear. You are always all that you are; you are not becoming something new, only learning to know the fullness of what you are.

The mental body is retained through sixth density. Within the mental body is the function of memory, and for a time there is still some level of identification of memories as belonging to a self. Just as at the threshold of fourth density there is a readiness to let go of the emotional body enough so that it no longer dictates action or thought, so at the threshold of seventh density is there is readiness to release the mental body.

As one moves into seventh density, the mental body begins to dissolve. What remains then is the spirit body. This is pure Beingness, moving back to awareness of total nonseparation with All that Is. It is that aspect of you that is the original spark of God, that bit of perfect energy and light. There is no self there, indeed no mental body capable of generating the concept of self. There is only that pure energy of love, shining on for eternity.

Please note that nothing is ever gained or lost. The pure spring becomes a stream and then a mighty river, yet the spring water is still there. When you look at the water a hundred miles downstream, the pure spring is there. Where else would it go? There, also, is the river. Both are present. In the same way, when we see the human, the higher self and pure spirit body are there always. Where else would they go?

So here you are, in this beautiful body and this perfect classroom. How do you learn? Where do you go from here? On the spirit plane between lifetimes, all I have shared above is clearly known. With each incarnation you agree to a forgetting. It is as if a veil dropped into place, separating you from the spirit plane. You frequently ask me why. My dear ones, you are here in some part to learn faith. How could you learn that if all were clearly seen? Your growth would be a matter of will power and determination, like a mountain climber with an altimeter that measures how many feet yet to climb. You are not here to practice will power, but love and faith. The veil gives you the constant opportunity for such practice.

At times you have glimpses through the veil. A momentary, deep clarity is given as you peer through this fabric that has thinned in places. That glimpse is enough for experience to confirm belief, so that your faith is not blind faith but is built on a foundation of inner knowing.

Beings at all levels of evolution are on earth. None is better than another. Is the wise adult better than the child or only more mature and experienced? The lessons being learned are varied. Some are learning about materialism, about grasping and generosity. Their concerns may be largely physical. Some of you are older spirits and are moving to the lessons of nonjudgment, of acceptance of all within the human experience. By acceptance, I do not mean condoning reactivity and the suffering it may cause, but acceptance that within the human there is both love and fear. These are not opposites but a part of each other. Unconditional love accepts all of that without need to deny anything in the realm of human experience.

Those of you who are drawn to read this have reached a level in your growth where the veil is thinning and you are more aware of the spirit plane. Your increasing experience with spirit helps provide a foundation of deeper trust from which you may do your work.

I say that none is better than another. Then what of good and evil, as you phrase them? These terms are laden with emotional connotations. Let us instead use *light* and *absence of light*. Yes, there are those who act in ways that harm others, who make that choice with free will. These beings are responsible for their choices, derived from fear and deep misunderstanding.

Their words, acts, or thoughts may result in much suffering for themselves, other beings, and the earth itself. Nevertheless, the essence of such beings is not evil. All spirit bodies are pure and brilliant light. But the spirit body of such a being is connected to emotional and mental bodies that are mired in misunderstanding. It may be young or very old. Regardless, it has far to go in learning the lessons of love for which it took birth.

It is not necessary to condone the acts and thoughts of such a being in order to move into compassion for it and for the suffering in which it dwells. You cannot learn for another. You cannot truly teach another, except through the example of your own love. Your challenge is to move past your fear and judgment and allow the heart of compassion to open. You might even wish to thank that being, for its misunderstandings provide a catalyst for your practice. How could you learn nonjudgment and compassion if there were nothing that you might tend to judge?

The same is true of the situations in your life. Everything is meant to teach you. You are always exactly where you need to be to learn what you came to learn. At times that learning is painful, yet learning does not need to be painful. It is not pain that teaches you, but awareness. Your pain screams "Pay attention!" and that attention teaches. As you become increasingly attentive, as you open the heart's door without judgment to all that moves through and past you, you will find that you learn with less pain. There will always be some pain, yet that truth does not mean there will always be suffering.

Pain and suffering are not synonymous. Pain is pain, unpleasant to be sure. Suffering grows out of resistance to what is, from wanting things to be different from what they are. As you come to understand this, you will find the infinite space in your heart that allows the experience of pain without so much fear of it. Pain will cease to be experienced as your pain or my pain but becomes simply pain, the world's pain. It can be experienced with an open heart, without hatred and resistance. Pain flows through you; joy flows through you. As you move beyond attachment and aversion and to what we call choiceless awareness, you will find that suffering does end.

We have moved through the questions, who are we? and why are we here? As for the third question, how do we do the work we came to do, it is the heart of this book. Just remember and trust that you are here to heal that which cries to be healed, within yourselves and within the whole earth. Trust this gift of incarnation, this experience. Work with love, courage, and faith. Practice awareness and mercy, for yourselves and all beings. Be gentle to all things, including yourselves. Know that you are loved beyond your capacity to comprehend that word. There is nothing more precious in the universe than each spark of the eternal.

Appendix B
Vipassana Instructions[32]

Beginning

It is helpful to establish mindfulness of body at the beginning of practice. We tend to be less in our bodies and more in our minds and the content of thoughts. When we do formal practice such as sitting, standing, and walking meditation, we first need to learn to be in the body. Awareness of posture is helpful here, as is awareness of breath and of physical sensations. Then we expand our awareness beyond body sensations to awareness of emotions and other aspects of mind.

If you sit on the floor, you may be most comfortable with a *zabuton*[33] or a cushion or blanket that you can place beneath your ankles and feet and knees, so that they are cushioned from the hardness of the floor. A *zafu*[34] or other cushioning underneath your buttocks will lift your spine. Position the cushion so that you're not sitting on the flat surface and rolling backward, but rather sitting on the forward edge of the cushion so that your pelvis tips under and the spine is naturally lengthening upwards. You may also sit on a chair. It should have a flat surface or even tilt forward slightly. Place the feet slightly apart. Sit with the back erect. Try to sit without leaning back. Whether you sit on a cushion or chair, let the hands rest comfortably on the lap or be cupped one hand inside the other.

At the beginning of the sitting, it may be helpful to take a few deep, long breaths, inhaling, and then slowly exhaling. As you exhale, allow your body

---

[32] From Barbara Brodsky and John Orr.

[33] Zabuton: a flat cushion that goes under the body and feet.

[34] Zafu: a round support cushion.

to release tension in those areas where you habitually hold it—perhaps the shoulders, chest, stomach, or the back. With each exhalation, feel your body soften and relax.

To bring awareness to you posture, start with the base of the body, noticing the position of the buttocks and knees as a tripod. Bring your attention to this foundation. Notice the position of the legs and the pelvis.

You are not lifting the spine from the top or the bottom. Rather, bring awareness to the erector muscles on either side of the spine; these lengthen the spine gently upward toward the shoulder blades. You may feel as if gentle hands supported erectness by lifting under the edges of the rib cage. Feel a little bit of lifting under the shoulder blades too, lifting without tensing the lower back. Allow the lower back muscles to relax.

As you experience this gentle lifting beneath the rib cage, beneath the shoulder blades, see that there's some space created between the bottom of your rib cage and your pelvis. Feel it lengthen..

Roll the shoulders back; let the tops of the shoulders fall away from the ears. The tops of the shoulders are relaxed. Notice some roundness and curvature where the upper arm meets the shoulder socket. You can have your hands cupped one inside the other on your lap, perhaps the thumbs touching together, or rest them on your thighs if that is more comfortable. Each position has its own benefits. See what fits you. There are no fixed rules.

Tuck in the chin slightly while the throat remains soft and relaxed; gently push backward on the upper lip. The throat and the neck remain relaxed, untensed, as are all the facial muscles. Feel a sense of gentle hands lifting the head, just below and behind the ears, skull softly lifted to erectness.

Relax the skin of the forehead down toward your eyes. Let the eyes be soft, the eyelids gently covering your eyes, unless you're used to meditating with your eyes open. If you are accustomed to practice with the eyes open and are comfortable like that, that's fine. The area behind the eyes is relaxed; the corners of the eyes are smiling.

You may wish to focus the closed eyes on the inner wall of the forehead, the third eye. See it as a blank screen upon which the inner gaze rests.

Invite the facial muscles to soften, relaxing from the inside out. Any tightness in the face, any holding, can release. As you smile and relax into your body, tension can let go.

Let the lower jaw hang open so that the lips separate a bit and any tension in the joints of the jaw can release. Invite a slight smile in the corners of the mouth, the inner smile, Buddha smile, a feeling of lightness in the corners of the mouth.

Smile into the moment and into your body. Be aware of any sensations as you smile into your body. Perhaps sensations are apparent, perhaps not; either way, it's okay.

Bring gentle awareness to the throat, smiling into the mid-area of the throat, the Adam's apple area. Move awareness down into the base of the throat, your jugular notch.

Smile down into the chest, left side of the chest, left lung, right side of the chest, right lung. Smile into the body. Experience it. Establish mindfulness in the present moment, mindfulness of body.

Smile into the heart center, in the area of the physical heart. Touch the heart with awareness.

Smile into the abdomen. Take a deep breath into the chest or the abdomen. Take a deep breath, hold it momentarily, and then slowly exhale. As you do, feel the chest and stomach relax. Do that two or three times: silent deep breaths, each exhale offered with awareness. Relax into your body.

As you smile into the abdomen, let it be soft. Soft belly, Buddha belly. No holding of any tension in the stomach. Let go of fear. Relax the abdomen.

As you breath, you may notice a slight lifting in your sternum, as though there were a string tied to your sternum and it were being lifted up on an angle.

Right now, you are breathing, a natural function of your body. With mindfulness of breathing, you simply turn attention to this process that is happening already. Your body is breathing in, and it's breathing out. *Anapanasati* translates as mindfulness of breathing—simply be aware when you're breathing in, aware when you're breathing out. It's taking one breath at a time. Know when you're breathing in, and know when you're breathing out. Breathing in, be aware of the whole body. Breathing out, be aware of the whole body.

(Some time of practice)

Breathing

Allow a smile in the corners of your eyes and mouth, an inner smile, just an inner feeling of lightness in the corners of your eyes and mouth. Call it Buddha smile. It's a radiance, a lightness.

Focus on the breath as the primary object. Be aware of the breath at the nostrils or wherever it's clearest to you. If your normal breathing is through the mouth, be aware of the breath coming and going through the mouth.

Notice the physical sensation of the breath touching at mouth or nostrils, the coolness of the in-breath, the warm softness of the out-breath.

Know when you're breathing in; know when you're breathing out. Allow the breath to find its own rhythm and flow. You are not controlling it, just observing it, trusting in the body and the breath. Knowing when you're breathing in, and knowing when you're breathing out, your breath becomes the primary object.

Know when you are breathing in. Know when you are breathing out. Know when you are breathing in a long breath. Know when you are breathing out a long breath. Know when you are breathing in a short breath. Know when you are breathing out a short breath.

Sometimes it can be helpful to extend and lengthen the breath at the beginning of a sitting, so that you begin to focus on the entirety of the inhalation and the exhalation, and on the pauses or apertures between the inhalation and the exhalation and between the exhalation and the inhalation.

This pause between the breath is the *now*, just this very moment. Noticing this aperture helps to bring you more deeply into the present moment and concentrates the mind; awareness also brings us deep into the heart center.

Experience your breath as a circle. There is a beginning portion of the inhalation, a middle of the inhalation, and then the later part of the inhalation, a slight pause in the breath, and then the beginning of the exhalation, the middle portion of the exhalation, and the end of the exhalation. A slight pause, and, again, the beginning of the inhalation, and the whole cycle begins once again.

As you allow the breath to become more subtle and natural, you may not sense the entire length of the inhalation or the exhalation. That's okay. Become aware of as much of the breath as possible.

Know when you're breathing in and know when you're breathing out, when you're breathing in a long breath and when you're breathing in a short breath. Breathing in, allow the whole body to be calm and at peace. Breathing out, allow the whole body to be calm and at peace.

As the mind begins to slow down, and becomes more calm and focused, awareness penetrates more deeply. The full length and duration of the breath and the pauses between the exhalation and the inhalation become more noticeable.

(Some time of practice)

Natural Concentration

The breath is the primary object, but concentration is not held here with force. With natural concentration, you focus attention on what is dominant in your experience. If a physical sensation, thought, image, or emotion pulls attention away from the breath, know that your attention has moved from the breath. Know when your attention has moved to physical sensation, thinking, image, or emotion.

People sometimes think, because a strong sensation, thought, image, or emotion draws their attention and they're not with the breath, that they're not meditating, that they're being distracted, or that they're not concentrating. Actually, focusing upon that strong sensation develops deeper concentration, because the mind is holding to an object. That's a very powerful focus. It's a fine opportunity to develop concentration and mindfulness.

Remember, it's not better to be with one object than another, not better to be with the breath than with a physical sensation, image, thought, or emotion. Be with whatever is the predominant experience in the moment.

If you find that an intense sensation keeps pulling your attention away from the breath towards that sensation, turn your attention to it. Lightly note it, creating some space for the experience, placing awareness on the sensation.

If the sensation is unpleasant, watch the tendency to want to push the sensation away, to not want it. Without judgment of the aversion, just notice what arises. Move deeply into the sensation and see how it may change, how it may not be one block of pain, one strong sensation, but little sensations that are arising, changing, and ceasing with varying levels of intensity.

If the sensation is pleasant, watch the tendency to want to hold on to it. Let there be no judgment of the attachment, just notice it arise. How does sensation change as you touch it with merciful, nonjudgmental awareness? What about the attachment to that pleasant sensation?

Are some sensations neutral, calling up neither like nor dislike?

As you create room for a physical sensation, you may find that it moves to another part of the body, from the shoulders down to the back, to a different part of the back, or to the legs. Stay with the experience as long as you are able without doing violence to your body or to yourself. Learn how to work skillfully with meditation and strong bodily sensations.

If tightness in the legs or back or itching, tingling, pain, any physical sensation becomes predominant, turn your attention to the sensation and note it three times: "sensation, sensation, sensation." If you prefer, note it more specifically as, "tingling, tingling, tingling," "tightness, tightness, tightness," or "itching, itching, itching." Don't note it as, "I have pain in my right knee," which snares you into the story of the pain and a self who owns that discomfort. Just observe the sensation and note it in any appropriate way.

As you turn your awareness to the sensation, notice what happens to it. Does it disappear immediately? Does it fade gradually? Does it intensify? Lessen in intensity? Move about? Change into another sensation?

When you find a sensation changing in any way, bring you attention back to the breath as the primary object. Know you have returned to the breath. Know when you're breathing in; know when you're breathing out.

As you're aware of your breathing, thoughts may arise. They may be memories or planning thoughts, judging thoughts, or fantasies. If the thoughts become predominant, if you find yourself more with the thoughts than with the breath, bring your attention to the thought.

Note a thought of the past as, "remembering, remembering, remembering." Watch what happens as you note it. Does it disappear immediately? Does it fade gradually? Does it persist or turn into another thought? What's the nature of it?

Is there a planning thought, a future-oriented thought? Note it as, "planning, planning, planning," or as, "fantasizing, fantasizing, fantasizing." Watch and see how it changes as you watch it.

When the thought is no longer predominant or changes in some way, gently bring the attention back to the breath as the primary object. Know when you're breathing in; know when you're breathing out.

You may have an image that arises in your mind. Some people experience their minds more in images than in thoughts. Treat the image the same way as the thought. If, for example, an image arises of you seeing and talking to someone, and if that experience is strong enough to bring attention away from the breath, turn your attention to that image. Note it as, "seeing, seeing, seeing."

What happens to the image when you touch it with awareness? What is the nature of this object? Does it change when you focus your attention upon it? When the image no longer predominates, bring your attention back to the breath as the primary object.

If emotion arises and predominates, know that you are experiencing that emotion. Note it as, "anger, anger, anger," or perhaps as, "fear, fear, fear," or bliss, joy, jealousy, restlessness, boredom—whatever it may be. Again, note, "anger, anger, anger," not, "I'm feeling angry about what he said," so as not to become entangled in the story, only to know that this mind-body is experiencing anger.

What happens as you note it? Does it strengthen? Fade? Change? Dissolve? When it is no longer predominant, move awareness back to the breath.

Know when you are breathing in. Know when you are breathing out. Know when you are breathing in a long breath. Know when you are breathing out a long breath. Know when you are breathing in a short breath. Know when you are breathing out a short breath. Breathing in and breathing out, be aware of the whole body and mind.

(some time of practice)

Deepening
If the physical sensation, thought, image, or emotion returns and is predominant, again move awareness to it—gentle, nonjudgmental awareness. Let it be choiceless awareness that moves to whatever is predominant in the mind and body.

If the sensation, thought, or emotion has returned and called awareness to it, there is something there that needs to be investigated, not by probing and theorizing but by observing, by being fully present with that sensation, thought, or feeling and allowing it to be present within the mind-body.

Choiceless awareness. No preference of the breath, the thought, the sensation. Being fully with whatever is. No judgment. Observing.

When sensation, thought, or emotion changes or is no longer predominant, invite awareness back to the breath.

Know when you are breathing in. Know when you are breathing out. Know when you are breathing in a long breath. Know when you are breathing out a long breath. Know when you are breathing in a short breath. Know when you are breathing out a short breath.

See how you relate to sensation, thought, or emotion when it arises. Is there a desire to push it away, not to want it because it's unpleasant? Is there a desire to hold onto it when it is pleasant?

Mindfulness of physical sensations can teach us a lot about our relationship with our body and about our patterns of attachment and aversion. If a pleasant sensation like tingling, moving of energy, or a feeling of lightness in the body becomes predominant, turn your attention to it and note it as, "tingling, tingling, tingling," or "lightness, lightness, lightness." What happens to it as you touch it with awareness? Does it disappear immediately? Does it fade gradually? Does it intensify? Does it change into another sensation?

How do you relate to the situation? Is there a tendency to want to hold onto the sensation because it's pleasant? Is there attachment to the continuation of the sensation in the body? Can you experience the bodily sensation with equanimity, noting it, seeing what happens to it?

What if it is an unpleasant sensation, like pain, tightness, or burning? What happens to it when you touch it with awareness? Does it fade, move, intensify, change? Is there a desire to push it away, to get rid of it? Can you just experience the unpleasant sensation with equanimity, noting it and watching to see what happens to it?

Notice how the primary object changes. First the sensation may be predominant. If it is an unpleasant sensation, aversion may arise, followed by a strong desire to be free of that sensation. There is a shift in experience. The sensation is no longer predominant. The desire energy now holds the attention. See this shift in object and return to the breath. If the aversion or desire comes back, note it as, "wanting, wanting, wanting," and be with it until it changes or dissolves.

Notice the same process with the arising of thought, image, or emotion. Is there a desire to hold onto the pleasant, to get rid of the unpleasant? Can you watch that liking, followed by the next primary object, desire, or attachment—wanting to hold on to? Can you watch aversion, followed by wanting to get rid of? What happens to the attachment or aversion when you watch it? Remember that the sensation or emotion is no longer primary. Let it go gently and be with the mood of mind that has arisen with the object.

If fear arises about what is observed, and if the fear becomes predominant, allow that to become the focus. "Fear, fear, fear." What happens to the fear as it is watched? Can awareness watch fear without fear? Can there be equanimity even with fear? What is the texture of fear? How does it feel in the body? When it changes or loses its intensity, return again to the breath as primary object.

Know when you are breathing in. Know when you are breathing out. Know when you are breathing in a long breath. Know when you are breathing out a long breath. Know when you are breathing in a short breath. Know when you are breathing out a short breath. Breathing in, be aware of the activities of the mind. Breathing out, be aware of the activities of the mind.

Can there be no judgment of what you're experiencing? If judgment arises, note, "judgment, judgment, judgment." Judgment is just a mental formation, a specific kind of thought that also carries a body tension. As you note it, see what happens to it; see its impermanence, its emptiness. Can we watch with equanimity as judgment arises, without judgment of that experience? When judgment is no longer predominant, bring the attention back to the breath as the primary object. Breathing in; breathing out. Breathing in and breathing out.

If the primary object is a physical sensation and is so strong and accompanied by such strong aversion that it no longer feels possible to stay with it, you can move.

Before you move, see the intention to move. The body doesn't move automatically. The mind must give the impulse for the body to move. If pain leads to intention to move the position of the legs, for instance, be aware of that intention, and then mindfully shift position to ease the discomfort. Be aware of the sensations, aware of the intention, aware of the movement.

Meditation continues; there's no break in the continuity of the awareness. Note the ease also, then return to the breath, breathing in and breathing out, breathing in, pause, breathing out.

As thoughts arise, if they're strong enough to draw attention away from the breath, treat them the same way as bodily sensations. Sometimes emotion feels intense. You cannot shift positions to escape the pain of thoughts or emotions. Can you watch them and make space for them? What happens to the emotion or thought as you note it? Does it disappear, fade, intensify, lessen in intensity, or turn into another memory or thought pattern? See its impermanent, empty nature. It changes or dissolves in time. When you see a change in some way, and the specific thought or emotion is no longer predominant, bring your attention back to the breath as the primary object.

Remember, that which is aware of a painful emotion like fear or anger is not afraid or angry. Learn to rest in that awareness, not as a way to escape the painful experience, but as a way to create more space with it. When awareness watches fear, see the simultaneous possibility of fear and non-fear. It is not necessary to destroy fear to find the fearless. It is not necessary to destroy anger to find loving-kindness. Both exist together.

It may be helpful to feel the sensation the emotion brings to the body, such as tightness in the belly with anger, and focus there. Soften around that tension, with a kind presence. What happens to the anger when the belly softens?

Know when you are breathing in. Know when you are breathing out. Know when you are breathing in a long breath. Know when you are breathing out a long breath. Know when you are breathing in a short breath. Know when you are breathing out a short breath. Breathing in and out, be aware of the activities of mind.

(some time of practice)

Insight

In insight meditation, we want to see the nature of body and mind and of all the five aggregates—form, feeling, perception, mental formation, and consciousness. Watch them arise and pass away. Watch them change. Notice the interrelationships between them, not thinking about these interrelationships, just noticing, observing the constant movement.

You may have a deeper insight into the impermanence of these aggregates and the emptiness of self therein. Observe body and mind, sensations, thoughts, feelings, perception, consciousness.

You may begin to notice that all phenomena, which are empty of a separate self, arise when conditions are present to lead to their arising. When those conditions cease, the phenomena fade.

Let there be no judgment of what is seen, no preference for the place awareness shines. Be fully with what is, observing.

If preference or judgment is seen, notice that—"preferring, preferring, preferring," or "judging, judging, judging." No judgment about the preferring or judging. There is space for it all to float in choiceless awareness.

When sensation, thought, image, or emotion changes or is no longer predominant, move awareness back to the breath.

Objects arising, dissolving, always in motion, impermanent, empty of self.

Consider the lines from the Heart Sutta:

> …All dharmas are empty.
> They are not born nor annihilated.
> They are not defiled nor immaculate.
> They do not increase, nor decrease.
> So in emptiness, no form, no feeling, no perception, no mental formation, no consciousness ….
> No knowledge, no attainment, no realization, For there is nothing to attain….

See the illusion of permanent self dissolve as awareness penetrates and knows the illusion. Moving deeper, beyond the small self, beyond aversion and attachment, beyond ignorance.

Find space for all experience to float in that heart we all share. Rest in the vehicle of choiceless awareness.

Become aware of awareness itself. See objects arise out of spaciousness and dissolve back in to spaciousness. Become aware of the nature of that which sees, that which knows. Gradually, you will rest in the Unconditioned itself, seeing conditioned phenomena come and go like clouds through an empty sky.

Know when you are breathing in. Know when you are breathing out. Know when you are breathing in a long breath. Know when you are breathing out a long breath. Know when you are breathing in a short breath. Know when you are breathing out a short breath. Breathing in and out, observing the impermanent nature of all dharmas. Breathing in and out, observing the fading of all dharmas. Breathing in and out and contemplating letting go.

Grasp at nothing. Cling to nothing. Push away nothing in your experience. Be present. Be mindful. Be aware.

It is a gentle, timeless process. Just watching it all unfold. Choiceless awareness. All experience floating in the open heart.

Deep Spring Center

Deep Spring Center, the organization, is located in Ann Arbor, Michigan. We offer meditation retreats, sponsor meditation classes and conduct workshops in our home community on a variety of topics related to meditation and spiritual inquiry. We publish a newsletter and spiritual manuscripts from Aaron, and also offer a web site that contains many of Aaron's books and transcripts. There are presently 8 books by Aaron available from Deep Spring Center.

Why "Deep Spring Center"? This is Barbara's story:

"Over forty years ago, when I first began to meditate, one day I had a vivid image of accessing a deep spring within myself as I moved into a meditational space. It was a bottomless spring, connected to the Infinite and Eternal. From that spring I drew sustenance and insight, not a personalized source of strength and wisdom but a far deeper one to which my meditation opened me. It was a place of deepest connection, deepest love. I saw that source was in all of us, the center to which we may all come. I came to think of it as a spring. The spring was 'self' but the waters were the pure energy and love of the universe. That spring has been with me all these years. I hope that all beings find that deep source within, and that it may lead us all to joyful connection and to peace."

Barbara and Aaron also lead retreats and workshops worldwide. Their teaching schedule is posted on the web site.

Deep Spring Center
3003 Washtenaw Ave., Suite 2
Ann Arbor, MI 48104
(734) 477-5848
www.deepspring.org
info@deepspring.org